WHAT

KEEPS

LEADERS

UP

AT NIGHT

WHAT KEEPS LEADERS UP AT NIGHT

Recognizing and Resolving Your
Most Troubling Management Issues

NICOLE LIPKIN

HarperCollins
Leadership

An Imprint of HarperCollins

What Keeps Leaders Up at Night

© 2013 Nicole Lipkin

Published by HarperCollins Leadership, an imprint of HarperCollins Focus LLC.

Any internet addresses, phone numbers, or company or product information printed in this book are offered as a resource and are not intended in any way to be or to imply an endorsement by HarperCollins Leadership, nor does HarperCollins Leadership vouch for the existence, content, or services of these sites, phone numbers, companies, or products beyond the life of this book.

Bulk discounts available. For details visit:
www.harpercollinsleadership.com/bulkquotes
Email: customercare@harpercollins.com

ISBN 978-1-4002-5286-2 (paperback)

To all the people who have enriched my life.

Contents

Acknowledgments

SO MANY WONDERFUL PEOPLE made this book possible. Without my support team I would have spent many agonizing days and sleepless nights wrestling with the manuscript, but instead, my friends and colleagues made it a fun, thoughtful, and inspiring adventure.

A few people merit special mention. First, my warmest, most heartfelt thanks go to my literary agent, writing collaborator, and, most important, my friend, Michael Snell. His creative input and editorial contributions helped to shape the book into its final form. Working with him so closely benefited me both professionally and personally, and has made me keenly aware of my propensity for malaphors.

I must give a loud shout-out to my secret editor, idea maker, great friend, personal cheerleader, and personal punching bag, Justin Crump. Thanks, Justin, for putting up with all the craziness and for tirelessly helping me organize my thoughts and ideas, on and off the page. Nothing brightens my day more than a healthy dose of your dry British humor.

Special thanks also go to wordsmith *par excellence* Patricia Snell, who scrutinized every chapter to tighten the writing and polish the storytelling. Dr. Ann Bowers-Evangelista took an eagle eye to the psychological and business content, providing enlightening feedback and challenging me to examine issues from different perspectives. Thanks, Ann. To my confidence booster, confidante, and marketing guru, Betty Rauch, I blow a great big kiss.

I deeply appreciate all the efforts of the folks at AMACOM Books—in particular, my editor Christina Parisi and associate editor Michael Sivilli. Thanks so much for your advice, edits, advocacy, and buoyant sense of humor. And thank you, my copyeditor, Carole Berglie, for putting on the final touches, and you—dear design team, specifically Michael Warrell—for making the book look great.

I would also like to express boundless appreciation to all of my co-workers for lending their support and picking up the slack while I was burning both the daylight and the midnight oil writing this book. And, dear clients, I owe you a big debt of gratitude for giving me the opportunity to keep doing the work I love to do.

I would especially like to offer a big curtsy to my brother and dear friend, Ethan, not only for his help with this book but also for being my number one supporter, perspective giver, and reminder that it's okay to take an hour off from time to time. I also shower special thanks on Till for his enduring encouragement, love, support, and silliness. I can't even count all the terrific friends who made this endeavor possible by standing by my side, cheering me on, and providing a few laughs along the way. You know who you are. But I must single out three phenomenal women (Hilary, Rosa, and Ali) who talked me through some long days and nights. Your unconditional love, fresh perspectives, and impromptu hugs carried me along more than you will ever know. Not quite last (nor least), a big smooch to El Guapo Meatball and Kreplach, my lovely little kitties, who did what kitties do best—sticking by my side (or on my keyboard, on my head, in my lap, across my research papers), day in and day out, over the past nine months. Last but extremely not least, I acknowledge the memory of my parents. Without their grace, humor, love, and strength, I would never have reached this most amazing point in my life.

What Was I Thinking?

I LEFT CORPORATE AMERICA IN 2005 to put my full energy into growing a psychological and consultation services practice. To build the practice I tried to hire only well-balanced mental health clinicians who require minimal management. These self-motivated, down-to-earth, easygoing people have built their own practices under my company's umbrella.

As the company grew and I started building my leadership consulting business, I needed to hire someone to take care of routine functions in the practice. I had composed, in my head, a job description that included handling client referrals, medical billing, accounts payable and receivable, and other general office procedures. I hired a young woman, Hope, who had never actually managed an office but who wanted to become a psychologist. Hope brought to the job what seemed like useful experience in customer relations, recruiting, and marketing. And she seemed like a quick learner, someone who could pick up the other skills she needed in a flash.

From day one, I taught Hope the business side of psychology, a valuable lesson for someone starting a career in the field because you don't learn this in school. In addition to the basic office medical procedures, I tried to coax her gently toward the two important qualities she would need in order to pursue her chosen career: professionalism and poise. Hope was a Millennial and typical of her generation. She possessed both a lot of idealism about her future and a sense of entitlement to the good things in life. Despite my best efforts, she gradually became my worst nightmare. She made careless and costly mistakes in billing and bookkeeping. She treated both patients and clinicians with a supercilious attitude. Unable or unwilling to pay attention to the details of her job, she rarely followed through on important tasks without several reminders. The clinicians constantly complained about her and often just threw up their hands and did the work she should have done.

My patience wore thin. I was spending more time micromanaging Hope than I would have spent doing the work myself. With the practice suffering, thousands of dollars lost in billing mistakes, and office tension growing alarmingly, I sat Hope down for a performance review. Because I still thought I could get her on track, I did not consider firing her. I simply could not accept the idea that I had made a mistake by hiring her in the first place. As I critiqued her work, I told her I could not possibly give her a raise, but would like to work with her to set goals that would improve her performance over the next three months. A crestfallen Hope finally said, "Nicole, I wasn't really expecting a raise. I know I keep making mistakes. But I need you to know how difficult it is to be my age and still rely on my parents to pay for my cellphone, credit cards, and vacations." Huh? When I suggested she do a better job to earn a raise or take on another part-time job, or even find a better paying one, she tearfully responded, "But, Nicole, this is supposed to be my FUN year!"

I should have fired her that day (or three months after she started), but I clung to the hope (no pun intended) that she would change, thereby proving I was a good boss. As you've probably guessed, the situation only got worse. I was drowning in a sea of frustration, stress, and anger. I was mired in the mud of the status quo, unwilling to consider change and cut my losses. My cognitive biases were running amuck, interfering with my beliefs, attitudes, thoughts, behaviors, and decision making. My mounting stress rendered me deaf, dumb, and blind. All I did was complain behind Hope's back and treat her inconsistently. In a weird way, I was paying her to torment me and just couldn't snap out of it. I finally had to admit I was, in fact, a bad boss.

One day, Hope strolled into my office and handed me her two weeks' notice. Her father had offered to pay for a month-long vacation to Europe. After her paid holiday, she told me matter-of-factly, she would come home and find a "real job."

Finally I was "Hope-less," and loving every minute of it. Nevertheless, the experience kept nagging at me and ultimately became the inspiration for this book. How could I—a well-trained psychologist with a doctorate in psychology and an MBA, a "corporate shrink" who coaches others to become better leaders and managers, and the author of a book on managing Generation Y folks—screw up so badly? How could I let my clinicians and company culture down? How could I let our clients down? How could I let myself down? What, in short, was I thinking? If I could unwittingly go from good boss to bad boss in the blink of an eye, couldn't anyone?

I crossed the line from good boss to bad boss because I didn't do what I've spent my career helping others do. I didn't pay attention to what makes our brains tick, to the basic principles of psychology, and to the age-old tenets of human nature.

The philosopher Jean-Paul Sartre famously wrote about the "gooeyness" of human nature. Whether we sit at the top of the corporate pyramid, ensconced in C-suite splendor, or spend our long days delivering goods coast to coast in an eighteen-wheeler, we are all human beings. Being human is a messy, quirky, complicated, frustrating, perplexing, and sometimes frightening experience.

All leaders and managers should invest as much time mastering the soft, human, mental side of business as they do the hard financial side. The more we know about the tiny firings and misfirings of our brain chemistry, the power of environmental conditions, the inner workings of group dynamics, the nature of deeply rooted and firmly fortified psychological defenses and biases, and the function of cognitive processes, the fewer mistakes we will make with our people and the more quickly we will correct the mistakes we do make.

Over the years I've helped clients, business leaders, and would-be leaders solve the challenging problems that nag at them and keep them up at night. In this book we will explore ways to recognize and resolve eight of the most troubling management issues leaders face today: the leadership snafus that make us temporarily go from good to bad, miscommunication, debilitating stress, unhealthy competition, elusive success, scary change, damaging group dynamics, and loss of motivation and engagement.

The solutions, as the saying goes, "are in your head." You may not permanently solve your most perplexing leadership problems, but you can learn to deal with them more effectively. You will screw up, you will regret something you said, you will engage in a bad fight, you will feel unsatisfied with a success, you will fight change, you will do something in a group you would never do on your own, and you will think your company or your people don't give a damn about you. But, and this is a very big *but*, you can gain greater awareness of what causes these recurring problems and find better solutions by recognizing and addressing those causes more quickly and effectively.

The advice I've assembled in this book comes from a lifelong study of human nature, psychology, and neuroscience, both in and out of business. I've learned that two "ups" can make a "down," and when we do screw up, it makes no sense to beat ourselves up. You can't change what's already happened, but you can change what you do next. That became my motto, as I've learned to pause and consider the psychological and physiological reasons I or someone else did what they did. I've learned that the solutions always begin with raising my self-awareness and helping others raise theirs.

In this book, I offer some fresh ways of looking at and thinking about some of the most troublesome people problems that leaders encounter every minute of every day (and night). Such problems have sometimes kept me up at night. I'm willing to bet they've also disturbed your sleep from time to time. Nothing would make me happier than to help you get a good night's sleep for the rest of your life.

WHAT

KEEPS

LEADERS

UP

AT NIGHT

I'm a Good Boss.
So Why Do I Sometimes
Act like a Bad One?

IN 1995, DUTCH MILLIONAIRE Jaap Kroese bought Swan Hunter, a famous but troubled shipbuilding company in the north of England. In 2000, Swan Hunter won the lead contract to design and build two landing ship docks for the Royal Fleet Auxiliary. The contract specifications required Swan Hunter to build the ships for £210 million with delivery scheduled for 2004. However, by July 2006, Swan Hunter had finished only one ship and had exceeded its budget by millions of pounds. Britain's Ministry of Defense, upset by Swan Hunter's poor performance, pulled the contract for the second ship and awarded it to their competitor, BAE System Naval Ships. The loss of this contract, financially devastating, disqualified Swan Hunter from further work for the Ministry of Defense. By November, Jaap Kroese announced that his company, Swan Hunter, would need to sell significant assets to make up for these losses until new business began in 2008. When that new business never materialized, Swan Hunter was forced to sell its iconic riverside cranes to an Indian shipyard.

Simply said, this sad tale reveals a lapse in judgment. The story starts with fifteen-year-old Jaap Kroese working in the maritime shipping industry, and culminates in a successful career in the oil-rig industry. Kroese purchased Swan Hunter with the expectation that he could return this troubled company to world-class status. Immersing himself in the business with unflagging enthusiasm and boundless energy, he made the choice to live at the shipyard, away from his wife, monitoring the company and getting to know his workers. He was known for greeting all of them as they showed up for work. His efforts won him near-legendary status in the media as a no-nonsense, hands-on businessman. That strength became his weakness, though. Diving into the fray and getting his hands dirty making every small decision inspired the loyalty of his troops, but it came at a cost. Working so close to the ground, he was unable to see the big picture. He had a worm's-eye view, not a bird's-eye view. Toiling in the ship's hold with the welders may have inspired loyalty, but it caused him to lose sight of the project's costly management mistakes, budget overruns, and schedule failures. Adding insult to injury, BAE Systems finished both of their ships ahead of Swan Hunter, taking over Swan Hunter's work on the final vessel.

GOOD BOSS GONE BAD SYNDROME

By many measures, Jaap Kroese was a good boss. Those who worked side by side with him liked and respected him. What went wrong? His hard work at the worm's-eye/worker level eventually led to failure at the bird's-eye/strategic level. Good bosses go bad for a lot of reasons.

Even the best boss in the world can have a bad day. No one escapes the occasional bad mood, irrational thought, angry outburst, nasty self-right-eousness, bad decision, or mistrustful reaction; imperfections make us human. Most often we commit these missteps in private. But behave that way just once in the glare of the public spotlight, and you earn a reputation as being "that sort of person." Why? Because presiding over other people can give you celebrity power. In the 2011 Republican presidential debates, Texas Governor Rick Perry, who was elected governor near effortlessly for three terms, could not remember the third federal agency he proposed to abolish. From that moment on, he became the "dunce candidate."

No one deals perfectly with hormonal fluctuations (yes, they afflict men, too) or biological ups and downs. Ultimately, regarding leadership process and procedure, it all boils down to people. Good leadership requires dealing effectively with messy, quirky, unpredictable, confusing, irrational, and clumsy people. That is what makes the business of leadership so insanely difficult and complex.

When you take a close look at why good bosses go bad (temporarily versus the chronically horrible bosses that go bad every minute of the day), you usually find three overarching reasons:

- Too busy to win.

- Too proud to see.

- Too afraid to lose.

Think of these root causes, not as cancers that can kill, but as common colds that anyone can easily and quickly cure with the right medicine. Once you understand why you sometimes display the symptoms of the *good boss gone bad* syndrome, you can use your newfound self-awareness to cure what ails you.

TOO BUSY TO WIN

On a recent business trip, I met a nice guy, Rob, sitting next to me on the plane. After a few minutes, Rob and I started chatting about his work. As my clients often do, he opened up and soon started sharing his unhappiness at work. Recently promoted to a management position, he found himself overwhelmed, falling behind on his assignments, and unable to keep up with the avalanche of emails and phone calls from his direct reports. He would wake up every morning with dread, his stomach in knots. "I feel like a one-armed juggler with ten balls in the air. My boss keeps piling on the work. He has no clue I'm in over my head." When I asked Rob why he didn't assign more work to his people, he said, "I want them to like and respect me. I worry that they will turn against me if I assign them stuff I could easily do myself." Ironically, he realized his people were actually losing respect for him as he became frantic and emotional. No one was hitting his or her numbers, and he felt himself losing ground every day. "I'm stuck," he admitted. "I'm just waiting for my boss to pull the plug and send me back to the trenches."

Like Jaap Kroese, Rob had gotten himself mired in a classic "too busy to win" situation. Every successful manager treads a fine line between productive and unproductive busyness. It's easy to cross the line and become just another good boss gone bad. Thankfully, though, you can take a few sure steps to get back on the right side of the line.

Before we consider those steps, let's dispel one myth right off the bat. Busyness is not necessarily *bad*. It proves that you are an active, productive, engaged, and successful person, assuming that you are not busy for busy's sake. In fact, people who wallow in a state of unbusyness often suffer from the effects of social isolation, depression, withdrawal, and anxiety, to name a few results.

We know that people feel better when they stay busy. In 2010, researchers Christopher Hsee, Adelle Yang, and Liangyan Wang designed an experiment to test that theory. They instructed students to fill out a survey, then choose one of two options: either to stand around and wait for 15 minutes before completing another survey or to walk about 15 minutes to another location where they would drop off the survey before returning to take the next survey. In each case, students received candy as a reward. Still, more students chose to walk, to be active and not be idle.

When the researchers measured the participants' sense of well-being, they found a higher degree of happiness among the walkers. Next, they repeated the experiment but did not give the students a choice. They told some students to walk and the others to stay put. Even when some of the "idlers" were forced to do busywork, the walkers felt happier.

Suppose, however, that the researchers had ordered half of the students to run a mile to the drop-off point while juggling those ten balls that made my seatmate Rob so unhappy. Keeping busy may make you happy, but at some point excessive busyness can overwhelm your coping capabilities. That's when we become too busy to win. Excessive busyness can impair performance and productivity, making you increasingly forgetful, fatigued, and prone to poor decision making and problem solving. Feelings of isolation abound as communication with others breaks down. The resulting frustration, anger, and impatience can lead to physical ailments, job loss, and, in some cases, mental health problems.

It all depends on a person's personal threshold. Some people can naturally take on a heavier workload than others. A higher threshold doesn't make you a better person; it just makes you different. If you ever find yourself succumbing to the too-busy-to-win variation of the *good boss gone bad* syndrome, you should pause to examine the situation and try to gain a little self-awareness. Only then can you consider solving the problem. Start by asking yourself three questions:

1. Have I gotten so lost in the trees that I can no longer see the forest?

2. Have I taken on extra work thinking I can do it better or because I don't want to waste time telling someone else how to do it?

3. Have I resisted delegating work because I want my people to like and respect me?

If you answer yes to any or all of these questions, you may have become too busy to win. Before we consider cures for this syndrome, let's take a look at why it happens.

THE ROOTS

Our investigation starts 10,000 years ago. Our Cro Magnon ancestors competed so strenuously for such scarce resources that they needed to conserve energy whenever possible in order to survive. Today, however, living has gotten a lot easier. Acquiring food, water, and shelter requires effort, but technology has reduced much of that backbreaking effort. Has our brain, born in Cro Magnon times, fully adjusted to this fact? Not quite. Rather than making life a big bowl of cherries, technology has handed us a big pile of pits. Instead of allowing us to relax, it has made us busier. A poignant article by Pico Iyer in the *New York Times* (December 29, 2011) discusses the impact of technology on humans and how much people will willingly risk financially and emotionally to find stillness. He describes the continual interruptions coming through as phone calls, emails, alerts, messages, and so on that seem to inundate our lives. As Iyer states, there are more ways to communicate, "but less and less to say—we're rushing to meet so many deadlines that we hardly register that what we need most are lifelines."

The avalanche of information not only overwhelms our personal lives, it also smothers us at work. Difficult personalities, worrisome downsizing, red-tape entangled bureaucracy, and complicated workplace politics quickly deluge us. It should only come as a surprise if you *don't* get too busy to win. Although you may love to hate this state of affairs, you probably secretly take a certain amount of pride in the fact that you have way too much on your plate, especially if you're the boss. If you don't believe that, ask yourself:

- When I'm busy, do I make that fact known to others?

- When people see how busy I am, do I think I gain more respect?

- When I hear other people complain about being too busy, do I feel superior or, on the other hand, a little jealous?

- When I am idle am I uncomfortable? Do I fill my downtime with a lot of activity?

Positive answers reflect a tendency to get too busy to win. It happens to a lot of people. Many cultures, particularly Anglo-Saxon (think Protestant work ethic), reward busy people and define not-so-busy people as lazy good-for-nothings. We often feel superior to the "lazy" (though secretly envy their idleness). At the same time, we naturally desire the affection and respect of others. We may, therefore, find it hard to get off the busyness bandwagon so we stuff lots of activity, often unproductive, into the idle spaces.

Humans tend to take everything too far. Give us a resource—anything from Godiva chocolates and Jack Daniels, to Twitter and Facebook—and we can easily overdo it until it becomes a problem. The same holds true for busyness. If you overuse your energy, talent, and mental or physical prowess, you can quickly turn an asset into a liability.

These days busyness can easily seduce you. In fact, in today's wired world, people can so easily connect with others that they find it almost impossible to remain "unbusy." While people rely on the Internet, social media, mobile phones, and other instant communication to keep them connected, many feel more emotionally detached. In the workplace, all of your networks can absorb you completely. Soon, keeping on top of all those "friends," "followers," "connections," and "buddies" can become a full-time job in itself.

According to Victor González and Gloria Mark, the average worker today spends no more than three minutes before they are interrupted or before another task is initiated. When your job involves overseeing the performance of other people, you may not enjoy a single uninterrupted second during the workday. No wonder your head starts hurting before noon and you become irritable with the first person who walks in the door. So let's see what's going on in your brain.

THE SATURATION

Quite often we do not even recognize that we have come down with a case of too-busy-to-win. No sane frog would willingly hop into a pot of boiling water. But place it in a pot of cold water on the stove and it doesn't feel the slowly rising temperature until it boils to death. In much the same way, the brain gradually adjusts to increasing busyness until it starts to fry. This explains how you can so easily get caught up in the *good boss gone bad* syndrome.

Our brains and bodies, naturally processing sensory information, use our eyes, ears, and skin to accomplish that task. Millisecond by millisecond, our sensory organs receive information, taking in important signals while filtering out the extraneous noise. Without this mental filter all the input of modern life would completely overload our minds and render us incapable of processing anything. Since busy bosses receive more signals than the typical worker, it should come as no surprise that they fall prey to sensory overload.

How do you know when you have reached a state of super-saturation? Well, it's not so easy because, unlike machines, our bodies and minds can cope with an incredible amount of sensory data, especially during periods of short-term stress. However, we find it almost impossible to function effectively when afflicted with prolonged stress or sensory overload (see Chapter 3 for more on this subject). Imagine a plastic shelf on which you keep piling books. It might support fifty-four books; but when you add the fifty-fifth, it suddenly snaps in two. If you had been paying attention, however, you would have seen it start to sag at book thirty-nine. In much the same way, you can deal with an increasing number of tasks and responsibilities, but at some point, you begin to bend under the pressure. If you're not paying close attention, you do not feel the bend until you snap under the final addition to your workload. Think about your current workload or the last time you felt overloaded, and ask yourself if you:

- Lose your temper more quickly?

- Regularly seem more anxious?

- Get more impatient than usual?

- See and solve new problems more slowly?

- Lose your focus more frequently?

- Suffer more memory lapses?

- Perform meaningless tasks repeatedly?

- Find yourself preoccupied with making to-do lists?

These symptoms signal that you are forcing your brain to operate in too many places at once, and you will almost surely find your productivity slipping. Do you fancy yourself a good multitasker? Recent studies (such as by Harold Pashler in 1994 or Rachel Adler and Raquel Benbunan-Fich in 2012) indicate that effective multitasking is as rare as a truly photographic memory. Those who think they do it well actually perform every task less well than they would if they focused on it. The human brain simply cannot concentrate on more than one, or in rare cases, two, cognitive tasks at once. Sensory overload will cause the brain to focus on one immediate task at the expense of others, or it will prompt it to take on a set of mindless tasks that soothe it the way rocking soothes a cranky baby. That explains why super busy people love making lists.

Bosses who become too busy to win can easily fall into a cycle of self-sabotage. When your workload grows too heavy to bear, you get mired in the little stuff and lose sight of the big stuff. The forest (managing others) disappears as you wander among the trees. Without enough of your skillful management, your people start making more mistakes, adding even more to your workload because you must now devote time to fixing those mistakes. It becomes a vicious cycle. The more you mess up, the more your people mess up, and the more your people mess up, the more you mess up. How in the world do you get out of this downward spiral?

THE CYCLE

Psychologists use what they call the conscious competence model to describe a person's ability to learn. The model includes four stages (Figure 1-1). An old proverb nicely captures these stages:

FIGURE 1-1 The Productivity-Conscious Competence Model

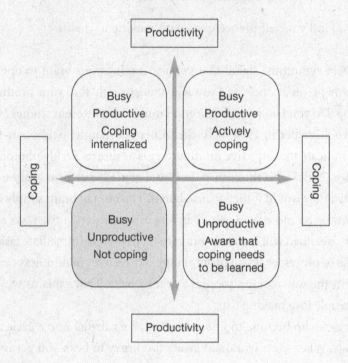

He who knows not, and knows not that he knows not, is a fool—shun him. *[Stage 1]*

He who knows not, and knows that he knows not is ignorant—teach him. *[Stage 2]*

He who knows, and knows not that he knows, is asleep—wake him. *[Stage 3]*

But he who knows, and knows that he knows, is a wise man—follow him. *[Stage 4]*

At Stage 1, Rob (remember him?) languishes as busy as a one-armed juggler, but has no inkling that working this way has adversely affected his decision making, undermined his authority, and decreased his overall productivity. He is busy, unproductive, and not coping.

At Stage 2, Rob realizes that he has taken on more than he can handle effectively, but does not know how to address the problem. He has taken note of the symptoms and has paid attention to complaints from others—perhaps his peers, his boss, or his direct reports—but he sees no way to get himself out of this predicament. He is busy and unproductive but aware that he needs to acquire better coping skills. This is where Rob was as we sat on the plane.

At Stage 3, Rob begins to make some positive changes because he has figured out a way to address the problem and pull himself out of his too-busy-to-win tailspin. Now he is busy, productive, and actively coping.

At Stage 4, Rob learns the coping skills he can use whenever he finds himself slipping back into the too-busy-to-win trap. Now he is busy and productive and has internalized effective coping skills.

Caution! It takes a lot of deliberate effort to move from Stage 1 to Stage 4, but you can easily slide back to Stage 1 without realizing it. You need to keep a wary eye on your workload and the appearance of any too-busy-to-win symptoms. It all boils down to gaining and maintaining self-awareness.

None of us sees ourselves with complete clarity and accuracy. Therefore, you should consider relying on a trusted adviser, colleague, family member, or friend to serve as your too-busy-to-win barometer. Choose someone who will tell you immediately if he or she sees any symptoms of the problem. By the same token, if you sense yourself easing into a state of work overload, invite your confidant to confirm your feelings.

In any case, when the symptoms appear, force yourself to take a break. A colleague of mine, Michael, asked my advice after he had worked four 15-hour days in a row, including the weekend, when his computer crashed while he was conducting stressful interviews with prospective business partners. "I was on the phone six hours a day with Apple and Carbonite techs. My ear felt as if someone had hit it with a hammer. I was listening, typing, and evaluating writing samples at the same time. When I went to play tennis on the fourth day, my body felt like a wet noodle, and I just could not hit the ball over the net." I urged Michael to stop everything for an afternoon, practice deep breathing, take a long walk on the beach, make his favorite food for dinner, and watch a mindless movie. The next morning he felt like a new man. "Amazing. It was so hard to stop working in the middle of all the up- roar, but when I came back, I got more done in three hours than I had in the previous two days. And, by the way, I crushed my opponents on the court."

TOO PROUD TO SEE

Lieutenant Colonel "H" Jones, a highly respected and inspirational com- manding officer of Great Britain's 2nd Battalion Parachute Regiment, led the Battle of Goose Green during the Falklands War in 1982. When a sub- ordinate with a clear view of the action offered him a way to penetrate the Argentine defensive line, Jones barked, "Don't tell me how to run my battle." Preoccupied with the obstacle in front of him, he could not tolerate his sub- ordinate's intrusion into his thoughts. Jones's assault on the enemy's defen- sive line failed and failed again, in the process killing several of Jones's close colleagues. Jones, in a singular act of bravery, chose personally to lead the next charge, a decision that cost him his life. Soon after the debacle, the reg- iment's second in command took charge and, partly heeding the advice of the subordinate Jones had ignored, penetrated the line and won the battle.

Jones died, in part, because he was too proud to see. This variation of the *good boss gone bad* syndrome does not imply a narcissistic or egomani- acal boss; it just means that otherwise competent leaders can get temporarily too caught up in the business at hand that they cannot receive the infor- mation they need to make an informed decision. The troops liked and re- spected Jones and thought him a good leader. He usually commanded with distinction, but during this one critical event he just could not get outside his own head and his own ideas. Although most of us don't like to admit it, we often all get wrapped up in our own ideas, not because we are idiots but because we are human. It's natural to think our ideas best, especially when we're the boss.

14

The too-proud-to-see variation on the *good boss gone bad* syndrome involves three problem-bound behaviors:

1. Letting yourself get so tied to an idea that you won't let it go

2. Refusing to heed the advice of others

3. Relying on your past successes at the expense of weighing different patterns, options, or solutions

All three of these behaviors not only damage performance and productivity but also can undermine your credibility as a leader. Avoiding them requires a strong dose of self-awareness.

THE WHY

"We don't see things as they are; we see things as we are."
—ANAIS NIN

In 1979, Charles Lord, Lee Ross, and Mark Lepper ran an experiment at Stanford University that has given us terrific insight into human psychology and interaction. The researchers selected forty-eight undergraduate students to participate in the experiment. Half favored the death penalty, with the other half opposed. Both groups believed research supported their views. When the researchers showed the participants excerpts from two fictitious studies, one supporting a deterrent effect for capital punishment and one showing a lack of deterrence, the students saw the supporting study as valid and the study that contradicted their personal views as flawed.

The students then evaluated the procedures and methods used in each study. Not surprisingly, each group found the study that supported their preference to be well constructed and properly interpreted by the researchers. These results suggest that people set higher standards of evidence for thoughts, hypotheses, or beliefs that go against their current positions.

Interestingly, at the end of the experiment, the students said that their opinions had actually become more firmly entrenched. This phenomenon, called the *confirmation bias*, causes us to seek out information that supports our views or beliefs and to give more weight to confirming information, while discounting or not noticing information that contradicts our point of view. Confirmation bias is even more likely when people have publicly committed to their position.

Confirmation biases include:

- *Biased search:* The brain cherry-picks its input, accepting confirming data and rejecting contradictory data.

- *Biased interpretation:* The brain interprets data in ways that match its preferences.

- *Biased memory:* The brain stores details that fit its opinions and discards those that don't.

Katie believes swarthy men commit most purse snatchings. When she witnesses such a crime in a crowd, she recalls a dark-skinned, bearded purse-snatcher, while other witnesses claim they saw a fair-skinned, shaven man. She can describe the swarthy man in great detail but does not even remember the fair-skinned man.

These biases tremendously influence our lives, especially when our brains become saturated with sensory information. To filter it all out and operate more efficiently, the mind resorts to shortcuts such as confirmation biases to help it interpret the tsunami of incoming messages.

Confirmation bias has started and sustained wars, prompted consumers to buy things they neither want nor need, and led to some of the worst (and best) business decisions ever made. You'll find no better example of confirmation bias than in the emotionally charged world of political opinion. In 2009, three Ohio State University researchers—Heather LaMarre, Kristen Landreville, and Michael Beam—used the satirical show on Comedy Central, *The Colbert Report*, to investigate the subject. Stephen Colbert parodies conservative politics and pundits, pretending, for example, to have launched a run for the presidency. The researchers asked 332 participants in the study to describe Colbert's point of view. Those who held liberal opinions viewed him as a liberal and his show as pure satire. Conservatives, on the other hand, saw him as a conservative pundit expressing honest conservative opinions through his satire. In short, the participants' own views strongly colored their perceptions of the comedian.

Our own perceptions also affect our assessments of personality. Mark Snyder, in discussing our hypotheses about others, describes studies where subjects are asked to describe the personality of an individual they would soon meet. Some of the subjects are told that they would encounter a shy, quiet, timid individual (introvert), while others are told they would meet an outgoing, sociable, gregarious person (extravert). When the subjects later assessed those they met, they described personalities that matched the initial descriptions.

What do these studies tell us about the too-proud-to-see variation of the *good boss gone bad* syndrome? They underscore the basic human need to be right. Whether we realize it or not, we naturally tend to cling tightly to our beliefs and look for information that confirms our beliefs while disavowing information that contradicts them. This can wreak havoc, however, when we are managing other people because it can prevent us from making accurate and effective judgments and decisions. Confirmation bias interferes with our ability to gather all sides of an argument, consider all possible points of view, and weigh a situation with a cool, objective mind. It diminishes what psychologists call *situational awareness*.

Suppose you must evaluate the performances of two direct reports, John and Sally. John has a tendency to disagree with you constantly, which drives you crazy. On the other hand, you love working with Sally because she often sees things just as you do. You may judge Sally's performance higher than John's simply because you find her more likeable, despite the fact that both people have turned in exactly the same numbers. If John complains when Sally screws up, you dislike him even more and ignore Sally's mistake. In the end, John leaves the company and you hire someone more agreeable to fill his spot on the team. Now you have doubled down. Not only has confirmation bias affected your evaluations, but it has also led you to populate your team with like-minded folks who will always agree with you. You have become the emperor who wears no clothes.

Here's where a trusted adviser can save the day. Everyone needs to seek the views of someone who will offer the unvarnished truth about your behavior. You can't see yourself favoring Sally, but a trusted colleague or mentor will. It all comes down, as usual, to gaining that all-important self-awareness of our own behavior, an awareness neuroscience can bolster.

THE BIAS

According to a 2004 study conducted by Drew Westen and his colleagues at Emory University, when it comes to opinions, emotion easily trumps reasoning. Westen and his team used functional magnetic resonance imaging (fMRI) to scan the brains of fifteen hard-core Republicans and fifteen equally hard-core Democrats during the course of the 2004 presidential campaign. The fMRI brain scans occurred while all the subjects were watching clearly self-contradictory statements by the two candidates. As you might expect, both groups found ways to reconcile the inconsistencies to support and further polarize their beliefs.

The brain scans confirmed that the parts of the subjects' brains associated with reasoning registered little activity while they weighed the inconsistent statements. In contrast, the circuits associated with the regulation of emotion, as well as those responsible for resolving conflicts, got quite busy. In addition, once the participants found a way to explain the inconsistencies to support their original positions, the part of the brain involved in reward and pleasure became active. Bottom line: Motivated reasoning triggers our emotional centers, and once that happens, we cannot easily change feelings, opinions, and decisions. In fact, we get pleasure out of finding consistencies and agreement. Most bosses feel pretty sure of themselves. Over time, they feel even more so, as their opinions of themselves become more and more deeply ingrained.

A 2011 study by researchers Bradley Doll, Kent Hutchison, and Michael Frank, published in the *Journal of Neuroscience*, took a look at how genetics might contribute to the human propensity toward confirmation bias. The researchers focused on two genes that influence the neurotransmitter dopamine, which helps facilitate learning in the prefrontal cortex and the striatum of the human brain. The prefrontal cortex helps us store and process explicit instructions, such as, "Take your daily vitamins." The striatum helps us garner lessons from our experiences, such as, "When I don't take my daily vitamins I seem to get sick."

The researchers concluded, "findings suggest that the striatal learning process is modulated by prior expectations, and that the resulting associative weights cannot be easily 'undone' after the prior is rejected" (p. 6197). In plain English, our own perceptions of what we should do take strong precedence over the instructions and advice of others.

Yikes! This state of affairs does not bode well for someone hoping to cure the too-proud-to-see variation of the *good boss gone bad* syndrome. However, you can take some proven steps to conquer a tendency toward ignoring advice, refusing to let go of your opinions, and feeling smug about your status as a leader.

THE CURE

First and foremost, understand that this tendency is hardwired into our brains, so we have to fight automatic thinking processes to change it. Backsliding naturally occurs, but that does not grant you permission to ignore the tendency. The more you keep a wary eye out for it, the more likely you can keep it under control and prevent it from interfering with your leadership. Look for the symptoms. Ask advisers to alert you to its presence or to backsliding once you are making progress. Never assume you have built up immunity.

You can also learn a lot by paying close attention to this behavior in others. The minute you start to look for it, you will see it everywhere and it's not a pretty sight. Just noticing its negative effects on other people's lives will prompt you to minimize it in your own life. Try playing a little game called, "Don't go down to the basement!" Have you ever watched a scary movie, where the heroine hears a creepy noise in the basement, then, astonishingly, quickly runs downstairs to investigate? You want to yell, "Don't go down there!" Watch for an example of too-proud-too-see behavior in the news or in a film or novel. Then tell yourself, "Don't go there." This little exercise can bolster your primary defense against confirmation bias: self-awareness.

You can also learn something from a spirited debate. Despite the advice that you should never argue about religion or politics because these topics can ignite the most deeply felt opinions, doing so with a good friend or family member can also shed light on your too-proud-to-see tendencies. Find someone who holds an opposing opinion or belief. Challenge it, but then look closely at both your behavior and that of the other person. Does the discussion arouse passion? Do either of you stubbornly defend your strong position despite facts that support a different perspective? Do either of you begin to raise your voice? Does listening grind to a halt? Does one person interrupt the other a lot and even finish the other person's sentences?

Whether you are analyzing one of your own recent leadership acts, a scene you have witnessed involving other people, or a recent argument over a sensitive issue, step back and ask yourself:

- Did the difference of opinion launch the battle?

- Did the parties marshal facts to support their respective positions?

- Did either side ever strive to separate hard facts from purely subjective opinions?

- Did either party genuinely consider the other's viewpoint?

- Did any new facts alter either party's belief?

- Did either person ever say, "That's a good point"?

- Did the change of heart erode anyone's pride?

- Did the change of heart undermine mutual respect?

Performing this exercise from time to time can ultimately result in better decision making, improved judgment, more satisfying interpersonal relationships, and enhanced leadership effectiveness.

The emphasis on defining points of contention and relying on facts rather than feelings helps reduce the strong emotions that often attend a strong discussion or debate. People respect someone who displays empathy and cares enough about their opinions to listen carefully to them and not constantly interrupt or finish their sentences. A good listener comments on and often praises the other person's point of view, even if the listener holds a diametrically opposed perspective. Far from damaging pride or eroding respect, a thoughtful and receptive approach to differing opinions builds a stronger and more productive relationship.

Good leaders are good teachers. The best leaders are good students, as well. They invite opposition to their ideas, they listen carefully to what others think, and they actually change their minds when the facts convince them to do so. To combat the temptation to fall into the too-proud-to-see trap, remember the "eyes-to-ears ratio" rule: Listen at least twice as much as you talk.

TOO AFRAID TO LOSE

Rich and Ethan, two VPs at a large security firm, pride themselves on their leadership skills. They enjoy the admiration of their superiors, their peers, and their direct reports. Their performance has made each of them valuable assets to the company. Then something surprising happens. The security company has launched a new social media security initiative in order to provide better service to its customers. Rich takes charge of the technology side of the project while Ethan oversees the business side of the project. Ethan and his team spend the next several weeks researching similar initiatives by their competitors, compiling statistics and proposed outcomes and creating supporting documents for their business development initiatives. Ethan hits the ground running and never stops. His highly motivated team follows suit.

Rich, despite his advanced knowledge of the latest technology, feels oddly anxious about the new system. Worrying that all the tricky little pieces will not fit seamlessly together to get the desired result, he finds himself looking over the shoulders of his programmers and getting in the way of his development team as he frets about every little decision. Since he has not behaved this way before, everyone on the project is mystified.

Rich has not suddenly lost his mind; he has come down with a bad case of the final variation of the *good boss gone bad* syndrome: Too afraid to lose. A leader who shies away from certain risks not only hurts himself but also hampers everyone else's ability to forge ahead and get the job done. Call it choking or deer-in-the-headlights paralysis, it often exhibits itself in the sort of micromanaging and second-guessing Rich inflicted on his team. Those suffering from the too-afraid-to-lose variation:

- Worry excessively about failing to get the right result.

- Question and second-guess every step along the way.

- Avoid decisions and commitments that might cause mistakes.

- Get involved in every detail, particularly as deadlines loom.

These toxic behaviors will destroy a leader's credibility. More than the other variations, the too-afraid-to-lose form thwarts creative problem solving and impedes team progress. Rich was behaving paradoxically. On the one hand, he was meddling with the details rather than focusing on the bigger picture. His busybody interferences slowed progress down to a crawl. On the other hand, he seemed practically inert when it came to making key decisions. He was busy micromanaging his team, but he was not busy when it came to making decisions. Good bosses who fall into this trap often worry about appearing weak. They mistakenly associate failure and mistakes with weakness and incompetence. This false relationship causes them to behave stupidly and out of character, micromanaging details or becoming immobile. Those suffering from this common ailment are experiencing a problem with what psychologists call *self-efficacy*.

THE FUEL

Psychologist Albert Bandera coined the term *self-efficacy* to describe a person's belief that she can achieve a particular outcome: "People with high self-assurance in their capabilities approach difficult tasks as challenges to be mastered rather than threats to be avoided" (1997, p. 11). Self-efficacy tends to fluctuate depending on the particular situation. For example, Ashley may behave coolly and comfortably in social situations, where she feels assured that her capabilities in this area will lead to positive results. By contrast, when she steps in front of her peers and manager to pitch an idea, she freezes because she is less sure she can manage this situation toward an effective outcome. In the latter situation, her sense of self-efficacy has abandoned her.

Bandura argued that a person's abilities, cognitive skills, and attitudes constitute that person's self-system, which determines how that individual perceives and reacts to a given situation. You are the engine and self-efficacy is the fuel.

Good bosses tend to possess a strong sense of self-efficacy. However, any number of circumstances can diminish or even destroy it. Suppose you normally oversee your team's work with the utmost equanimity and enjoy a reputation as an unflappable boss. Then, suddenly, in the midst of a make-

or-break project, two of your most skilled people quit to join your archrival, not only removing key talent when you need it most but also making it possible for your competitor to crush you. Goodbye Mr. Cool-as a-Cucumber, hello Mr. Red-Hot-Chili-Pepper.

That's exactly what happened to Rich. Faced with the biggest challenge of his career, he froze in the headlights. Or, to put it another way, his sense of self-efficacy abandoned him at the worst possible time.

When your sense of self-efficacy gets swamped, you immediately sink into too-afraid-to-lose quicksand. You begin to doubt yourself and others, you second-guess every decision, and you start micromanaging every little detail. It's easy to slide into that mode, but it's not so easy to pull yourself out.

THE POWER

According to Bandura, a person's sense of personal capability will influence his or her motivation, learning, performance, and perception of whether a task is doable or not.

Leaders with a strong sense of self-efficacy tend to:

- Maintain a strong sense of commitment.

- Recover quickly from setbacks.

- Accept challenging problems as easily mastered tasks.

- Invest greater effort in achieving specific outcomes.

- Demonstrate high levels of accountability for both setbacks and accomplishments.

- Attribute mistakes to inadequate effort rather than personal weakness.

- Set high personal goals.

- Believe that success depends on hard work.

- Take risks and try new ways of doing things.

- Tend to work well under pressure.

- Feel confident in their decisions and critical thinking skills.

Leaders with a weak sense of self-efficacy, on the other hand, tend to:

- Avoid challenging tasks.

- Worry that tasks/situations lie beyond their capabilities.

- Focus on negative outcomes and personal deficiencies when things go wrong.

- Put less effort into accomplishing tasks/goals.

- Lose confidence in personal abilities.

- Set low personal goals.

- Question whether they can succeed.

- Avoid risks and new approaches.

- Lack confidence in decisions and thinking skills.

- Perform poorly under pressure.

THE SHAPE

According to Bandura's research, four influences contribute to a sense of self-efficacy: past and current mastery experiences, vicarious experiences, verbal/social persuasion, and emotional/physiological states.

Let's look at Rich's case. If he had a track record of tackling challenging tasks in the past, he would likely feel comfortable with this one. If he had gotten to his present position by doing a great job on a series of rather easy tasks, he may soon feel too afraid to lose. To counteract this effect, Rich should step back and assess the nature of this challenge. If he finds it daunting, he should confide those feelings to his superiors and ask for help. A boss who has developed a big ego and resists admitting ignorance ("I don't know") or fear ("I'm not sure") will find it hard to admit that he doesn't think he can handle a particular situation. A trusted confidante can provide valuable insight and make it easier to come to grips with fear of losing.

Suppose Rich has never come to grips with such a challenge but has seen other teams tackle even greater ones. He has, in other words, gained experience by watching other people succeed in similar situations. If he carefully reviews his vicarious experiences, that alone may boost his sense of self-efficacy. "If they can do it, so can I." One-on-one leadership coaching can help someone like Rich adjust to new challenges, but a development program might work even better because it offers more opportunities to learn from vicarious experiences.

Rich's own boss can help or hurt him in this situation. If his boss recognizes that this task will test his limits, she can provide verbal assurance that she believes in him and will keep her door open if he runs into any snags. Rich can even give himself pep talks whenever he begins to experience a fear of losing. Verbal persuasion is a two-way street. We can all use some encouragement from time to time; and we must all remember to give it to others when they need it. Bosses tend to make a habit of providing critical input. After all, they want their people to improve. But it's so easy to forget to stop from time to time and give someone a pat on the back.

Last but not least, Rich needs to become his own self-efficacy physician, learning to monitor his emotional/physiological states. Does this new project make me break out in a cold sweat at night? Does my heart race? Do I find myself tossing and turning in bed, unable to sleep because I can't get my mind on tomorrow's work? He should also keep a wary eye out for any mental and physiological signals that indicate the arrival of too-afraid-to-lose symptoms: worrying excessively about failing to get the right result, questioning and second-guessing every step along the way, and avoiding decisions and commitments that might cause mistakes.

WRAP UP

So, you're just like everyone else in the world, at least those who develop the self-awareness to admit no one's perfect, that even the smartest guy in the room can screw up from time to time. Many screw-ups result from the three variations on the *good boss gone bad* syndrome:

- Too busy to win

- Too proud to see

- Too afraid to lose

Self-awareness begins with admitting that you are human. Becoming a boss does not make you infallible. In today's hectic workplace, where your natural neurological and psychological make-up must cope with huge pressures and crazy demands every minute of every day, you can easily lose your cool. Dealing with so many (burning) trees, you lose sight of the forest. You see what you want to see. Or you start to succumb to self-doubt and feel increasingly powerless and inadequate.

It happens to us all. Screw-ups need not mire you in the quicksand of self-pity or self-destruction. The path back to the ranks of the good boss is paved with self-awareness. Just pausing to cast an objective eye on your maladaptive or unproductive behavior or asking a trusted ally to tell you the honest truth about how you've been acting lately can get you back on track.

Why Don't People Heed My Sage Advice?

2

Why Don't People Heed My Sage Advice?

SEVEN SENIOR VICE PRESIDENTS from a large health-care insurance company have convened to brainstorm the company's future. Diane and Bob, two of those VPs, have worked for the company for three years, both managing large sales teams, which have exceeded their revenue targets every year. They each brought impressive credentials to their current positions. However, when it comes to getting people to back their ideas and push their agendas through to completion, Diane always wins out over Bob. If they seem so perfectly matched, why do they end up with such different results?

"We should set our sights on small business owners," Diane offers at the current meeting. Everyone at the table nods their approval and takes copious notes as she elaborates.

"How about focusing on the marketing departments of our already established mid-sized clients and then expanding from there?" Bob suggests. Two people roll their eyes, one makes a grimace, and the others stare blankly at their legal pads or the floor.

Later in the hallway, Sam, the executive VP who convened the meeting, claps Diane on the back "Way to go, kiddo. Great ideas." Then he glances at Bob. "Weren't Diane's ideas great?"

What exactly is happening here? At first glance it seems like a conundrum.

THE CASSANDRA CONUNDRUM

Most of us cringe when we watch someone fail to influence and persuade other people. The speaker struggles earnestly to capture and hold the audience's attention, only to be met with blank looks, tilted heads, yawns, and confused stares. In Greek mythology, the god Apollo granted the gift of prophecy to Cassandra. In granting this gift, Apollo believed he would win her love. When she turned a cold shoulder to his affection, he let her keep her predictive powers, but with a curse attached. Those who heard her predictions would never heed her words, a terrible conundrum.

Bob suffered from the *Cassandra* conundrum, an ailment that can afflict even the most talented leader. Nothing devastates a boss more than losing the ability to persuade, influence, and motivate others to get results. Imagine yourself cursed with the inability to:

- Resolve conflict or personality clashes.

- Ensure workplace harmony.

- Stimulate high performance and productivity.

- Convince others to accept a new idea or product.

- Win approval of a major shift in strategy.

- Create effective teams.

When it comes to fulfilling these leadership responsibilities, what makes Diane so effective? Why is Bob such a dud? When you drill down through all the research to the basic bedrock issues, you hit two simple but hard facts. You lose your influential powers when:

- People do not buy into you.

- People do not buy into your message.

Before we explore the reasons why this can happen, let's establish some useful terminology.

INFLUENCE, PERSUASION, AND MANIPULATION

Many people use the terms *influence, persuasion,* and *manipulation* somewhat interchangeably. But each carries its own specific meaning.

Influence requires winning the minds *and* hearts of your audience and thus inspires action. It is used in situations where leaders have established a relationship of trust, confidence, and established credibility. Diane strives to know people the first time she meets them in a natural and friendly way, eager to form strong bonds with everyone on the team. Since Bob fails to build such relationships with people, he usually fails to influence them.

Persuasion stimulates a person to action because it makes intellectual sense. It is data driven, not emotion driven, with the burden of proof on the persuader. It succeeds even without a deep relationship with an audience. When Diane wants new clients to sign with her company, she marshals all her supporting facts and statistics, all her research, into a presentation with the goal to persuade.

Manipulation crosses a fine line between persuasion and influence. It replaces the welfare and benefit of the group with the selfish desires of the individual. While it defies easy definition, most people know manipulation when they see it. If either Bob or Diane proposes an action primarily because it will win a raise or a promotion for him- or herself, he or she has crossed that line. Colleagues will know it when they see it.

A colleague recently told me a story about a woman he once managed. "Michelle was one of the friendliest people I ever met. She could go into a room full of people she had never met before and come away with a brand-new network of friends." However, my colleague found something oddly unsettling about Michelle's behavior. "She seemed to see everyone as a means to her own ends, rather than folks she really wanted to get to know." Although his gut reaction told him this was a bad sign, my friend chose to ignore his gut and ended up hiring her.

He noticed, over time, that the people Michelle had befriended began treating her with growing suspicion. Even her admirers sensed that she engaged in relationships not for mutual benefit but for her own good. The signals included curtailing a friendship with anyone who did not give her access to individuals she wanted to meet. She broke off all connections with one person who left the company and the industry and could no longer further her career. One former friend offered, "I like Michelle, I really do. She could charm the rattles off a diamondback. But if you don't let her step on you to get ahead, out come the fangs." At first the superficial schmoozing worked, but the manipulation soon became apparent, resulting in the exact opposite of what she desired. People grew immune to her attempts to persuade and influence them. She earned a tarnished reputation that she couldn't repair.

WHY DON'T PEOPLE BUY INTO ME?

Focus, for now, on influence, because influence hinges on personal buy-in. Why do some people, like Diane, stimulate buy-in so easily, while others, like Bob, find it so hard? The answer is power and its unique relationship with credibility and influence. For purposes of this discussion, we'll define *power* as the ability to exercise influence. You can't achieve influence without power. You can't exercise power without a relationship. This brings us back to the premise that influence occurs within relationships.

Power is not intrinsically good or bad. We ascribe meaning to power and make choices about how we will use it or react to its use by others. Ultimately, power is a responsibility, and it exists as a function of the individual, one's followers, and the situation at hand. The relationship between a child and parent illustrates this point. Children are only as powerful within the family as their parents allow. The child may be loud and demanding or throw tantrums to get attention. By itself, those behaviors do not confer power to the child. The child's power depends on how the parents respond to the child's behavior. If they respond by letting the child get his or her way, the child has exercised power over them.

The range of ways people exercise and respond to power can be complicated. In 1959, psychologists John French and Bertram Raven developed a framework for understanding different types of power. Bertram Raven, Arie Kruglanski, and Paul Hersey, working with Marshall Goldsmith, expanded that original framework into seven distinct types of power:

- *Legitimate Power.* This power arises from one's title or position in the pecking order and how others perceive that title or position. Those with legitimate power can easily influence others because they already possess a position of power. If Diane rises to the position of CEO and her people believe she deserves the position, they will respond favorably when she exercises her legitimate power.

- *Coercive Power.* This power comes from fear. Someone who uses coercive power influences others by threat and force. Failure to comply will lead to punishment. If Bob bullies his people, threatening to demote or fire them if they do not get results, he is wielding coercive power.

- *Expert Power.* This power comes directly from a person's skills or expertise or from perceived skills or expertise. Expert power is knowledge-based. If Diane holds an MBA and a PhD in statistical analysis, her colleagues and reports are more inclined to accede to her expertise. This gives Diane a great deal of influence.

- *Informational Power.* This power comes from the possession of needed or wanted information. People with high informational power wield influence because they control access. If Bob could access a secure file with a special password, people would defer to him whenever they needed to see that file.

- *Reward Power.* This power motivates people to respond in order to win raises, promotions, and awards. Both Diane and Bob hold a certain amount of reward power if they administer performance reviews that determine raises and bonuses for their people.

- *Referent Power.* This power depends on personal traits and values, such as honesty, integrity, and trustworthiness. People with high referent power can highly influence anyone who admires and respects them. The likable Diane held this type of power; the off-putting Bob did not.

- *Connection Power.* This power creates influence by proxy. People employing this power build important coalitions with others. They influence everyone who wants to gain the favor or avoid the disfavor of those coalitions. Diane's natural ability to forge such connections with individuals and assemble them into coalitions gives her strong connection power.

FIGURE 2-1   Types of Power

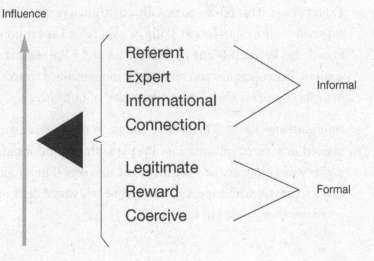

In the workplace, these seven types of power generally fall into one of two categories (Figure 2-1): formal (legitimate, coercive, and reward power) and informal (referent, expert, informational, and connection power). A boss may employ all types of power during a typical workday. When it comes to influencing people without creating potentially negative effects, referent, expert, informational, and legitimate power tend to get the best results. Coercive, connection, and reward power require more careful application because they rely upon a higher degree of trust and risk and can easily become manipulative.

A successful leader often relies on referent power to influence people because it most effectively breeds credibility. As mentioned earlier, there is a strong relationship between credibility, influence, and power. Who will believe in and trust you the most? Who will most likely heed your sage advice? Those people with whom you have built strong, positive relationships.

The effective use of referent power involves developing a number of important and not easily acquired skills, including the ability to:

- Manage boundaries.

- Maintain strength of character.

- Make a clear and compelling presentation.

- Adapt communication to the listener.

- Forge trust.

- Display empathy.

Diane does it so well. She makes it look easy, effortless, and invisible. She draws distinct boundaries between what people can and what they cannot do within the relationship. Every day she strives to hold true to her values. Before she presents her ideas, she crafts a presentation that will make her points clearly and convincingly. She adapts the presentations to her audience, and she really knows her audience. Since she understands that no one will buy into her ideas if they don't trust her, she not only "talks the talk" but also "walks the walk." Every morning before she goes to work, she reminds herself that whenever she encounters a problem with one of her people, she will stop and put herself in that person's shoes.

THE POWER OF REFERENT POWER

Analyzing influence includes looking at both the influencer and the receiver. Think about your worst boss. What was it that made that person so insufferable? How well did you perform under that person's leadership? Now think about your best boss. How did that boss behave? How well did you perform under that person's leadership? I'll bet my doctorate that the best boss made you feel respected and valued. The worst one made you feel unimportant, like a replaceable cog in a wheel. I wager you performed better under the best boss. What separates the two experiences? Referent power.

When it comes to the quality of influence between two people, it all rests on one of the basic tenants of human nature. We like listening to and are willing to follow those people who sincerely respect and value us and whom we also respect and value. Imagine yourself listening to Albert, the brilliant, highly experienced head of Product Development who boasts about his advanced degrees from Stanford and Yale. Albert is telling you all about the new widget your company will soon bring to market, but he's talking to you as though you were a dim-witted six-year-old child. Your deep dislike for Albert now acts as a block, preventing you from hearing what he's saying. In fact, you pay so little attention to his presentation that when it comes time to explain the new product to clients, you stammer and stutter through your dreadful performance. Give the relationship a zero on the influence meter.

Now, imagine the opposite. Albert treats you as a trusted peer, taking care to explain the more complex features of the new product, invites questions because he truly finds no question too dumb to ask, and establishes a comfortable rapport. You soak up information like a sponge and sell a gazillion widgets. Score 100 on the influence meter.

IT'S NOT THE PhD, IT'S THE EMOTION

Referential power, in its most basic form, aims at establishing rapport, a relationship of mutual trust and emotional connection. If you type "how to develop rapport" into your search engine, you'll find over 700,000 sites promising you the secrets to building such a relationship. These include:

- Engage in mirroring behavior.

- Make eye contact.

- Match tonality and rate of speech.

- Listen carefully to sum up what the other person has said.

- Breathe at the same rate.

- Learn the other person's name and use it throughout the conversation.

- Find common ground and engage in small talk.

These are "tricks," but don't dismiss their effectiveness. They work well when practiced with sincerity. Make sure you are never just "going through the motions," as that undermines credibility, power, and influence.

Jason, who ran an executive search firm, believed he was as sincere as the day is long. He sincerely wanted to impress others. He sincerely believed he was a skillful leader. He sincerely believed he was down to earth. He sincerely believed he was a caring boss. But when his employees watched Jason in action, they cringed. "He had a list in his head telling him exactly what to say and do at all times—like a robot. You could almost hear the gears whirring," said one employee to me, barely able to stifle a laugh.

REAL VS. "HOW TO" RAPPORT

You do not build real rapport by applying some simple technique when you need something. It comes from a heart-felt choice to treat people well, from a deep-seated philosophy that governs your approach to relationships. Some people choose to apply rapport as a means to accomplish their own ends, as we saw Michelle do earlier, whereas others, like Diane, naturally build rapport because they truly respect and value the needs of others. The manipulative Michelle got people to comply, but she cannot make them fully commit. Expecting a reward or fearing punishment, people may comply with an order, but they do not commit to it 100 percent unless they have bought into the order and really want to do it. When people feel fully committed to doing something, they will always get better results than if they simply go through the motions. Diane knows this so well, she will never resort to manipulation. Michelle's approach probably came from a self-help book; Diane's comes from her heart. Which will more powerfully move the organization forward?

This does not mean you must become some sort of softhearted, touchy-feely New Age Pollyanna to influence people. A good boss cannot act like everybody's BFF (Best Friend Forever), because all bosses must make a lot of tough calls, talk candidly with underperforming people, and make a fair share of difficult and unpopular decisions. However, the good boss who maintains genuine rapport with people always empathizes with them when making a tough call. As mentioned earlier, with great rapport comes responsibility.

"But," you might argue, "I'm not here to make friends. Leadership is not a popularity contest." Okay, fair enough. You do, however, owe it to yourself and your people to relate to them in a way that engages them to do their best work (a topic we will explore more deeply in Chapter 8). When you just tell people what to do, without engaging their hearts and minds (i.e., by influencing them), you lose them. You certainly lose their commitment to do their best; they may comply in the short term, but you may very well lose them as they walk out the door to join a competitor. Even in the military, where every recruit must follow orders, the best leaders build rapport and exercise tremendous influence. As the old adage goes, "Attitude reflects leadership."

Peter, a CEO with a distinguished career in the British Special Forces, described to me his experiences with two talented superior officers. Jim was a strictly by-the-book officer, studiously following every rule. Equally talented Mick, friendly and laid-back, would brighten a room when he walked in the door. His soldiers respected Mick for his military skill but also for his innate humanity, his knack for making them feel valued. Jim's soldiers, while respecting his military skills, attributed his success to self-serving interests. Something about him never felt genuine, never quite real. Adding insult to injury, Jim was oblivious to his men's perceptions.

Jim and Mick went through the grueling Special Forces selection process at around the same time, and both performed superbly well on the physical aspects of the role. But when interviewers weighed the candidates' personalities, Mick passed and Jim failed. As Peter offered, "Which one would you rather be working with if it hits the fan? Someone whom you know has your back 100 percent or someone who seems like he's only out for himself?"

OUR BRAINS ON OXYTOCIN

So far, we've examined influence from a business perspective, discussing how social awareness and relationship management help leaders develop authentic influence and referent power. Now let's look at it through the eyes of science. Scientists believe that oxytocin, a neurotransmitter and hormone, plays a major role in prompting empathy, trust, compassion, and generosity, to name just a few human traits. They have nicknamed it the "bonding" hormone.

In 2004, Paul J. Zak, Robert Kurzban, and William Matzner reported on a groundbreaking study they conducted to determine how oxytocin affects trust building. During the study, participants played the *Trust Game*, in which two players receive $10 just for participating in the game. Neither player can see the other. At the start of the game, Subject 1 (Keisha) can transfer any amount, from $0 to $10, to Subject 2 (Tom). Whatever amount of money Keisha sends to Tom, Tom actually receives triple that amount. Thus, if Keisha decides to transfer $2 to Tom, Tom receives $6 on top of his original $10. Tom, in turn, can then choose to return any portion of the total amount, or none at all, to Keisha. Immediately after the subjects make their decisions, the researchers administer a blood test to measure the players' oxytocin levels.

Zak and his fellow researchers identified the initial transfer of money from the Keishas to the Toms as a measure of trust, and the return transfer from the Toms to the Keishas as a measure of trustworthiness. They found that Tom's brain produced oxytocin because he felt the donor trusted him. They also discovered that the more money Tom received, demonstrating greater trust on the donor's part, the more oxytocin his brain released. Tom's brain also produced more oxytocin when he gave money back to Keisha. The more he gave back, the higher his oxytocin levels, indicating higher levels of trustworthiness.

Interestingly, oxytocin release did not occur in Keisha's brain when she first gave money to Tom, which supports the conclusion that oxytocin release happens only during social interaction. Rises in levels (not the beginning levels) indicate developing trust and trustworthiness. According to Zak, in a 2008 article published in *Scientific American*, "One can therefore think of positive social signals and interactions as the flipping of a switch to an 'on' state: When the switch goes on, the human brain says, 'This person has shown that he or she is safe to interact with'" (p. 91).

Basically, Zak and colleagues found that the presence of oxytocin increases our likelihood to trust others. He pointed out that while humans are "wired" to trust each other, sometimes their life experiences adjust this neurotransmitter to a different "set point." When we feel safe and nurtured in our relationships and environments, the release of more oxytocin supports our ability to trust others. When we feel unsafe and disregarded, a lower level of oxytocin diminishes our ability to trust others.

Given our natural tendency toward trust, this shows why we respond so positively to referent power, which depends on personal traits and values we admire. As discussed above, influential relationships thrive in the presence of referent power.

WHY DON'T PEOPLE BUY INTO MY MESSAGE?

Even if people admire a leader's personal traits and values, they might still ignore the leader's message. Perhaps they find it irrelevant. Perhaps it poses too daunting a challenge. Maybe they just didn't speak loud enough to be accurately heard. In most cases, the breakdown occurs because, somehow, people did not find the message compelling. How, then, do you create compelling messages that always get through?

TELLING STORIES

On May 16, 2011, Assistant Surgeon General Ali Kahn posted a warning about the Zombie Apocalypse and Zombie Preparedness on the Centers for Disease Control (CDC) website blog "Public Health Matters." This idea came from a communications staff member who noticed that traffic spiked whenever someone mentioned zombies on the Center's Twitter account during the post-tsunami nuclear crisis in Japan. Kahn thought that a posting with the word *zombies* in it would get people thinking about preparedness for natural and man-made disasters. He was right. Not just the word itself, but the associations people make in their minds with zombie stories such as *Night of the Living Dead*, drew so much traffic that the Center's website crashed.

Why do stories carry so much weight? First, they make a dry or boring topic more interesting. They create pictures in people's minds. You can't really picture "John loves Mary" in your mind, but you can see John sweeping Mary off her feet and kissing her passionately. People could not "see" an emergency, but they could picture zombies attacking. The CDC posting relied on the fact that in emergency situations, our brains often freeze up (see Chapter 3), preventing us from logical thought. The moral of a good story, like the point of a parable in a fairytale, becomes deeply ingrained and helps us remember what to do. The CDC posting offered advice on coping with a pandemic flu, but tacking it onto the compelling picture of hungry zombies made the point harder to forget.

Nothing can help a leader become more convincing than coupling an important message with an unforgettable story.

FILLING IN THE BLANKS

Every person brings to a social situation a unique set of experiences and beliefs about himself, about others, and about the environment. And every person with whom a leader interacts enters the conversation with a whole set of preconceived ideas, values, and beliefs that may differ dramatically from those of the leader. As we saw in Chapter 1, people see things the way they want to see things, not the way the boss tells them to see things.

A story provides common ground where people can share an experience with others. Although each person may interpret the story differently, everyone gets the point. Despite subtle differences in interpretation, everyone gets the point of the fable about the scorpion and the frog.

A scorpion decided she wanted to cross a deep river, but she knew she could not swim such a long distance. When she spied a frog sitting nearby, she asked him if he would give her a ride across the river. Of course, the frog said no, "You will only sting and kill me." The scorpion insisted, "No, no, if I did that,

I would fall into the water and drown." The scorpion convinced the frog to agree to the deal. The scorpion hopped on the frog's back, and they began their journey. Halfway across the river, the scorpion suddenly reared back and thrust her stinger into the frog's back. "You fool!" croaked the frog, "Now we shall both die! Why on earth did you do that?" The scorpion shrugged and said, "I could not help myself. It's my nature."

As a universal connector, the story triggers different parts of our brain, including our emotional powerhouse (the amygdala), from those stimulated by a simple presentation of facts and figures (i.e., the prefrontal cortex, which controls our working memory). It helps us make sense of our world. When someone hears or reads it, her mind fills in the blanks until she can see it all happening in her mind's eye. Don't believe it? Try this little mind teaser:

Aoccdrnig to rsaerech at an Elingsh uinervtisy, it deosn't mttaer in waht oredr the ltteers in a wrod are, olny taht the frist and lsat ltteres are at the rghit pcleas. The rset can be a toatl mses and you can sitll raed it wouthit a porbelm. Tihs is bcuseae we do not raed ervey lteter by ilstef, but the wrod as a wlohe.

You figured it out, right? That's your brain taking shortcuts to fill in the blanks or connect the dots. In the same way, our minds complete stories and experiences for us. *It's in our nature* to complete a story and come under its influence. It makes us feel comfortable and trusting.

In 1944, Fritz Heider and Mary-Ann Simmel, two psychologists at Smith College, showed subjects two images: an animated pair of triangles (one small blue one and one large gray one) and a pink circle moving around a square. The researchers asked the participants to describe what they saw. In their descriptions, subjects ascribed human qualities, such as motivation and intention, to the animated shapes by saying, "The circle is chasing the triangle" or "The small blue triangle and the pink circle are in love" or "The big gray triangle is trying to get in the little blue one's way." How cool is that? Presented with a simple image, people tend to embroider elaborate stories that help them make sense of what they see.

Scientists have traced this tendency for people to create narratives back to our evolutionary roots. Early humans used storytelling to teach, empathize with, and connect to others. Throughout human history, people have relied on stories to pass along traditions, legends, and teachings. The Bible, the bestselling how-to book of all time, teaches its lessons through stories, which people remember far more easily than they would an abstract philosophical principle. The developmental psychologist Jean Piaget argued that people tend to reason from the concrete to the abstract, rather than from the abstract to the concrete. If you want to make a memorable point, tell a story. That will drive home the moral more surely than the most well-reasoned abstract argument.

Psychologists refer to this natural human trait as *theory of mind*. From early childhood on, people refine the ability to attribute mental states such as intentions, motivations, and thoughts to others (as the subjects did when describing the triangles and circle). This helps us understand the actions and behaviors of others. Theory of mind explains empathy, seeing events from another person's point of view, and ascribing cause and effect and sequencing to those events. Storytelling provides a reliable medium for taking complex ideas and processes (such as cause and effect) and communicating them to others in a way they can understand. Stories simply make it easier to get inside the minds of others.

A 2007 study performed by Jennifer Edson Escalas of Vanderbilt University found that subjects responded more favorably to advertisements that told a story than to advertisements that required subjects to think about the arguments for a product. Taking this notion a step further, in 2006, the researcher Melanie Colette Green and others showed that labeling information as "fact" increased critical analysis, while labeling information as "fiction" reduced critical thinking. This means that people will find it easier to accept a story at face value, while they may question an abstract argument.

Some interesting research argues that storytelling increases neural connections between people. In 2010, Princeton University neuroscientists Greg Stephens, Lauren Silbert, and Uri Hasson found that when one person tells a story, the brains of the listeners tend to synchronize (i.e., light up in the same ways). The researchers measured the neural activity of two speakers (one English speaking and one Russian speaking) as they each told a long, unrehearsed story. Then they measured the neural activity of twelve English-speaking individuals as they listened to recordings of the two storytellers. Stephens and colleagues found that successful communication, (i.e., the listeners actually understanding the story told in English) resulted in neural coupling (i.e., activation in the same parts of both the speaker's and the listener's brains). Although these general findings require more research, they do support the idea that communicating through storytelling creates a mental dance between a speaker and an engaged listener.

Bottom line: If you want people to pay attention, to learn from and remember something important, tell them a story, as the surgeon general did with the zombie apocalypse metaphor and as Martin Luther King, Jr., did when he shared his dream with the world.

LEVELS OF BUY-IN

When you wish to influence people by shifting attitudes or changing behavior, you need them to buy into the change, by providing them with a powerful message. You can increase the odds of attitudinal and behavioral change by addressing the three different levels of buy-in, each of which plunges more deeply into the narrative and has the potential to increase commitment.

At Level One, the most basic level where persuasion holds sway, people buy into your idea intellectually. Here you put facts and figures to work.

Anyone who has recently ridden in a taxi has seen the sign BUCKLING UP IN THE BACK SAVES LIVES. You probably processed that bit of factual information and promptly ignored it. It did not modify your behavior because it lacked emotion. Even coercion does little to force compliance. The threat of a $50 fine also goes unheeded.

Cold, hard facts don't tap into emotion. Stories do. Facts don't personalize influence. Stories do. Facts don't inspire. Stories do. Unlike facts, stories allow the human mind to capture and relate to the personal essence of the matter and take it to heart.

At Level Two, emotions come into play and begin to influence the outcomes. The facts weave themselves into a verbal or visual tapestry, triggering the emotional centers of our brains. The message is now more powerful, more memorable, and more influential. Here's a new take on the importance of buckling up. The news reported a sad story in 2001 about a young woman named Cindy Jay-Brennan.

> Cindy, a young woman who had won a jackpot in a Las Vegas casino, was recently married and getting ready to enjoy a belated honeymoon with her husband. She was driving home with her sister after a night out and neither of the sisters were wearing seatbelts. They were stopped at a red light when a drunk driver hit their car. Cindy's sister died and Cindy was left paralyzed.

Maybe now just reading that story may fully convince you to buckle up the next time you hop into a car.

At Level Three, a story told from personal experience by another person, carries the greatest influence. During a recent taxi ride in Las Vegas, my driver told me this story.

> I used to work with this lovely woman in her early twenties. She was a cocktail waitress at the restaurant where I worked. She was just a beautiful, sweet young woman. On her way to meet her boyfriend one night she put a few bucks into the Megabucks slot machine and she won millions of dollars. It was amazing. Anyway, one night she was driving down the strip with her sister and was at a red light and this drunk driver hit her. Neither had their seatbelt on. Her sister died and she was instantaneously paralyzed. I saw her recently and it was devastating. She can't even feed herself.

My eyes became teary as I asked if he saw a lot of drunk drivers in Vegas. He replied, "Oh, yeah, tons." I *immediately* buckled up. Personalizing an influential message not only motivates behavior, it can also shift values and attitudes. I have made bucking up in cabs a habit.

Don't overdo storytelling to the point where people cringe, fearing you are about to reel off another shaggy-dog tale. The best storytellers tell their stories judiciously, tailoring them to the context, personalizing and adapting them to themselves and their audience, and making sure they deliver the right message.

DELIVERING THE MESSAGE

We all know people with whom we can easily chat about anything. We can also name people who make us feel uncomfortable and with whom we'd rather not discuss anything. It all depends on communication styles. Some styles pull us like magnets. Others push us away. In general, like attracts like. Suzanne is a tall, Harvard-educated, diehard Red Sox fan. She will more likely find herself attracted to former baseball-playing Boston University grad Tony, who also lives and breathes the Sox, than she will to the five-foot-four plumber with a high school degree who thinks the Yankees walk on water. Dating research suggests that, for the most part, we date people who fall in line with our own looks and level of attractiveness. The same holds true for communication styles, which figure prominently in our ability to influence others.

The best communicators and influencers can read their audience and adapt their presentation to that audience's background and preferences. This *style flexing* is a sure sign of a great communicator. A skillful style-flexer can talk to people both similar and dissimilar in a way that makes both parties feel valued and respected. These style-flexers have mastered the art of *adaptive influence*, adjusting their influencing style in a way that accounts for the varying expectations, abilities, and personalities of their audience.

Researchers have contributed a lot to our understanding of communication. For our purposes, we will concentrate on the notion that communication preferences can fall along a spectrum of directness and sociability, each with high and low dimensions. Each interacts with the other to create four primary styles of communication.

Figure 2-2 illustrates how Diane, from our earlier story, communicates a schedule change to four people on her team. Two members of her team have been with the team for quite a while and prefer a direct style of communication. One demonstrates high sociability (Carroll), the other low sociability (Jasmine). The other two people, both of whom have only recently joined the team, prefer an indirect style of communication, with one demonstrating high sociability (Joe), the other low sociability (Liz). Keep in mind that while we've placed the team members in neat boxes, people in real life do not fit into such black-and-white categories.

FIGURE 2-2 Communication Styles

Direct

Low Sociability	Jasmine, you're working over the weekend so you can meet your deadlines for this project	Carroll, as you know, we are in a difficult situation with a lot of hard deadlines on Monday. We need everyone to pitch in over the weekend. Let's discuss what works best for you so you can both get the work done and still have an enjoyable weekend.	High Sociability
	Liz, we need this project done by Monday and your contribution is necessary to meeting our deadline.	Joe, I know you have so many plans this weekend. We really need to have this project done by Monday and of course you are essential to the project. What are your thoughts?	

Indirect

Diane could have communicated more directly with everyone on her team if she enjoyed strong, influential relationships with all of them. However, she employed an indirect approach with the newer team members, Joe and Liz, with whom she has not yet built a close relationship. With Carroll and Jasmine, the more veteran team members who have grown to admire their boss, she can just speak her mind more easily, though she will fully respect nuances in their communication preferences. In the months to come, Diane will take special pains to make sure Joe and Liz also know that when she communicates an important message she has their best interests at heart and understands their unique needs, valuing them as individuals. In the real world, however, some people who prefer indirect communication will never welcome a direct approach, no matter what you do. *It's in their nature.* Keep all your communications options at hand.

RELATIONAL PHILOSOPHY

It takes time and effort for anyone to change, including yourself, especially when it comes to altering the way you relate to people. Old habits die hard. It's always easier to rely on what you've always done, even when your approach causes problems and undermines your leadership. Nevertheless, we can all benefit from becoming better at forming productive relationships and more effectively influencing our peers, direct reports, and even our superiors. Doing so requires replacing the sort of unconscious behavior everyone tends to rely on to get through the day with a conscious relational philosophy built on heightened social awareness and more skillful relationship management. This means having what we call a *relational philosophy*. It means thinking of others every time you interact with them, not just some of the time. A good relational philosophy:

- Builds consensus and support.

- Inspires others and arouses enthusiasm.

- Recognizes, values, and appropriately rewards people's strengths.

- Tactfully addresses areas requiring development.

- Challenges others and promotes critical thinking, innovation, and creativity.

- Recognizes different perspectives, resolves conflicts, and brings people together.

- Collaborates and promotes a collaborative environment.

- Maintains empathy and promotes awareness of emotional cues.

- Facilitates listening to and hearing others.

- Demonstrates trustworthiness, conscientiousness, and perceptiveness.

- Fosters internal and external relationships.

These characteristics describe great bosses who wield tremendous referent power. Think about the best boss and worst boss you recalled earlier in this chapter. How many of these characteristics did the best boss display? How many eluded the worst boss?

Also ponder the fact that a boss can misuse these characteristics by applying them in a manipulative way. If Diane pretends to build consensus and support but insists that everyone do it her way, or if she insincerely promotes a collaborative environment but does not really take other people's suggestions to heart, people will see her as a manipulator lacking social and relational awareness, and they'll relate, or not relate, to her accordingly. Leaders who consciously, truly, and sincerely wish to relate to their people must actively listen to them before they themselves speak.

LISTENING

Anyone can learn to listen, really listen. Try this exercise with a few people at lunch. First you tell the story, perhaps using a saltshaker, a coffee cup, a sugar packet, and a water glass to represent the characters in the story:

A beautiful woman named Alice (A) lives in a small cabin on the side of a wide and treacherous river. She has fallen head over heels in love with Bob (B), a handsome and wealthy man who lives on the opposite bank. One day she puts all of her money in her purse and asks Chris the Ferryman (C) to row her across the river. After the ferryman tells her that the trip costs twice as much as she can afford, he offers to charge half-price if she will take off all her clothes and leave them on the riverbank. Shocked, she refuses and dashes home. But she longs so desperately to reach the man she loves, she returns the next day, disrobes, and clambers into the boat.

Once across the river, she scampers naked to Bob's house and knocks on the door. Of course, he lets her into the house and for five days enjoys her company. On the sixth day, he admits that he never loved her and unceremoniously throws her out of the house. Naked and broke, she approaches the ferryman, who just laughs and rows away.

Knowing that Bob's neighbor Don the Woodcutter (D) has always been desperately in love with her, Alice knocks on his door and begs him to give her shelter. "I have been watching you this past week," Don tells her, "And you have so completely compromised your virtue that I cannot possibly let you into my house." With that, he slams the door in her face.

The naked and despairing Alice runs into the nearby woods, where she is killed and eaten by a bear.

Now ask your audience to rank their approval of or respect for each character (A, B, C, and D) in descending order. The rankings will differ widely. Ask each person to explain his or her ranking. A lively debate will ensue. Each person's interpretation will tell you a lot about his or her values. Rather than offering your own interpretation and engaging in the debate, listen carefully to what the others say. Most likely this will turn into a rather difficult exercise because, like politics and religion, morality and values invoke strong feelings and a natural tendency to dismiss others' points of view.

You can use this exercise in active listening to exercise your ability to suspend judgment and really hear what others are saying. Not only does this strengthen your listening muscle, it also develops your empathy muscle, a core quality of a great leader.

Five Steps for Active Listening

Step One: Remember the 2-to-1 ratio of ears to mouth discussed in Chapter 1? Shut your mouth and open your ears. Turn off the voice in your head that constantly makes assumptions, judges the speaker, and contemplates what you will say next. Don't finish the other person's sentences or interrupt their train of thought.

Step Two: Listen for feelings. People do not always express their feelings or concerns directly, especially to their bosses. Pay attention to words that express feelings or needs and to nonverbal behaviors that may reflect how someone feels.

Step Three: Acknowledge what you think you heard by paraphrasing what the person just said. Paraphrasing helps you check for accuracy and understanding. Clarify any emotions you think you saw the person express in their verbal expressions or body language. Caution: Do not parrot, as it can be perceived as mimicking and disingenuous.

Step Four: Add your own opinion after acknowledging the other person's contribution. Do it without judgment. When you feel tempted to criticize or dismiss someone else's opinions or feelings (something we all do regularly), STOP! Doing so reduces empathy and relationship building.

Step Five: Pay attention to any change in body language, verbalization, or emotion that was made after you added your own opinion. Acknowledge anything you have noticed and check for accuracy and continued discussion.

BODY LANGUAGE

I recently worked with Joel, a software engineer, who was the product expert on a sales team. Joel came off as a nice guy with a sharp mind, who knew his product inside and out. He offered a wealth of information to the team and its customers. Despite his reputation as the "go to" guy for product questions, customers would frequently contact the team's leader or other members of his team with questions about the product. This frustrated everyone on the team, especially Joel. That's why he had come to me for a little coaching.

It became obvious, upon my first meeting with Joel, why some customers went over or around him when they needed answers to their questions. He speaks forcefully with a loud tone of voice, leaning forward, making aggressive hand gestures to drive his points home. You get the message. When you ask a question, he sits back in his chair, folds his arms across his chest, frowns, and frequently sighs. His body language and paraverbal communication (e.g., tone, volume, inflection, sighs, gasps) had gone from forceful and aggressive to closed and unreceptive. You don't need a PhD in psychology to see what's going on, and how neither was appealing.

After our exchange, I asked Joel if I could videotape one of our sessions. He agreed and toward the end of the next session, we watched the videotape together. Even he could see that his physical posture and gestures were intimidating and off-putting to his customers. "Holy cow, I look like I'm so pissed off!" he blurted.

Everyone knows that communication involves more than mere words. We convey strong messages with our bodies, especially our facial expressions, hand gestures, and postures, not to mention the tone and inflection of our words. If you take away the nonverbal component of communication, you create a fertile ground for misunderstanding and misinterpretation of a message. Suppose your dog were just hit by a car and died, a virus crashed your computer and obliterated your carefully prepared report, and your weekly migraine headache has been ripping your head open. When your best friend walks up to your desk and asks how you're doing, you say, "Fine, thanks." She can tell by your slumped posture, pained expression, and limp tone that you feel the opposite of fine. Despite your words, she offers you her sympathy and support.

Now imagine that a client asks you the same question in an instant message and you type the same answer. The client will take your words at face value and go blithely on with the chat. Most of what occurs on your screen just flies right by you, compounding your misery. Communication soon breaks down, though the client does not know why. She cannot see your body language or interpret your paraverbal communication in an IM.

As a leader, you must pay close attention to body language and paraverbal communication cues, both your own and those of your people. This does not just apply to face-to-face communication. You need to pay attention to it in electronic communication as well, because the tone of phone and email chats can cause a lot of serious (and unnecessary) misinterpretation.

As with so many of the issues we have discussed in this book, it's always easier to notice the body language and paraverbal communication signals in others than in ourselves. Friends and associates can raise your self-awareness, of course, but so can a video recording, which makes problematic body language and paraverbal communication painfully obvious. Interpreters of body language and paraverbal communication scrutinize hundreds of different cues, but you should begin with two basic ones: Do certain cues suggest that you or someone else is *open* or *closed* to communication?

- *Closed-off body language and paraverbal communication:* crossed arms, crossed legs, jittery body movements, monotonous or bored tone of voice, diverted eyes, preoccupation with surroundings or a handheld device.

- *Open body language and paraverbal communication:* leaning toward you, body still and in an attentive posture, natural gestures, open tone, good eye contact, open arms, and no preoccupation with surroundings or a smartphone.

Most likely you have exhibited and experienced both situations. Have you taken the other person's body language and paraverbal communication into account when trying to convey an important message? Have you ever caught yourself presenting closed body language, then adjusted your signals? In either case, you can always ask yourself a few key questions about body language and paraverbal communication displays in face-to-face situations:

- How do I or the other person feel at this moment?

- How do I sit or stand?

- How do I reveal myself through facial expressions?

- How do I decide what outcomes to expect?

- How do I speak and move to achieve my outcome?

In electronic communications ask yourself:

- How might the tone of my spoken or typed message affect the receiver?

- How will different formats (boldface, caps, italics) and emoticons affect my reader?

- How do salutations, pauses, sounds conveying emotion, and background noises add to or detract from my listener's experience?

- How can I avoid sending a message the receiver can easily misinterpret?

It's hard to ask such questions in the heat of the moment, but you can certainly pose them right after a communication has concluded. More effectively controlling your own signals and more accurately assessing those displayed by others will greatly enhance your interpersonal interactions, your face-to-face communications, and your influence over others.

WRAP UP

Boiling it all down to its pure essence, we see that good bosses exercise strong, positive influence over others. They shun manipulation, insincerity, and inauthentic trust and confidence. They gain influence by establishing and nurturing relationships grounded in true trust and confidence. As a result, people buy into them and their messages.

A skilled influencer recognizes that her greatest power stems from the sincerity and genuineness of her relationships, which spring from a conscious decision to embrace a life philosophy based on how she interacts with people rather than what she can get from people.

Humans are hardwired to form relationships, the foundation of which is trust and mutual influence. Insincerity, the misuse of power, and manipulative attempts to gain influence quickly crack that foundation. If you focus on treating your people with kindness and respect, and let them know that you value them and their work, you will receive the same in return. Your influence will grow, and so will your personal and business success.

3

Why Do I Lose My Cool in Hot Situations?

HE HAD PREPARED HIS PEOPLE for what he believed would be the inevitable terrorist attack, but Rick Rescorla, Chief Security Officer for Morgan Stanley at the company's World Trade Center offices, could not have imagined its scope. Specialized military training, serving in both the British and U.S. armed forces, had made him intimately aware that when confronting stress, a leader's own behavior could cost him and his men their lives.

After the unsuccessful 1993 truck-bomb attack on the WTC, Rescorla strongly believed that terrorists would attack the buildings again. Warning Morgan Stanley's Board of Directors of the threat, he urged them to consider moving their offices to another location. When he learned that a long-term lease prevented that move, he set about training the company's 2,700 people to deal with an emergency. To make sure they would behave as predictably as possible during a crisis, Rescorla conducted surprise emergency-evacuation drills every few months. Rescorla didn't give a damn if a stockbroker was closing a multimillion-dollar deal; he would, if necessary, personally grab the guy by his tie and drag him bodily down forty stories to safety. On the morning of September 11, 2001, Rescorla's training saved all but fourteen of Morgan Stanley's 2,700 employees. Rushing back into the building to help others evacuate, he failed to escape before the tower collapsed. He lost his life that day.

This amazing man knew that under extreme stress, survival depends on a person's ability to face hard facts and seize control of the situation. Whether you are dealing with sudden acute stress or ongoing chronic stress, only knowledge and training will see you through it all. In post-9/11 interviews, many survivors of the attacks admitted that they did not know exactly how to evacuate the building and thus they lost valuable time trying to escape. Others described hearing orders to remain in their offices, while still others said they became frozen in place because no one was showing decisive leadership. In sharp contrast, Rescorla's annoying drills taught Morgan Stanley employees the life-saving behaviors they needed to enact when the alarm bells sounded.

When frightening, highly stressful situations occur, 1,400+ physiological changes sweep through our brains and bodies. It's hard to remain cool, calm, and collected when our minds and bodies are going crazy. Rescorla knew that he could overcome that natural tendency only with careful preparation. People who cope well with stress know that. Even people who seem naturally "mellow" have actually taught themselves to stay cool in hot situations.

In our fast-paced, change-filled business world, you will deal with an astonishing amount of stress. That stress builds up, day after day. It's a constant fact of corporate life that's nonnegotiable. But your reaction to stress *is* negotiable. You need to learn how to cope with it.

Why should you learn stress-coping skills? Because *unmanaged* stress— the most underestimated constant in the workplace today—can strangle your company to death. Leaders who do not manage it well make more mistakes under pressure and tend to rationalize their mistakes with the old, familiar excuse, "Oh, I was under a lot of stress at the time." Make that excuse often enough and it soon becomes an addictive habit. You earn a reputation as a *stressed boss* or a *boss who cracks under pressure*, labels that, in the end, will cost you the respect of your people and, potentially, your job.

GOOD STRESS, BAD STRESS

Stress comes in two distinct forms: *eustress* (good stress) and *distress* (bad stress). You experience eustress from a positive experience, such as standing at the starting line for your first 10K, or signing the mortgage on your first house. Distress, on the other hand, occurs during a negative experience, such as seeing the fin of that great white shark circling your surfboard. Unmanaged distress leads to life-threatening physical and mental health problems, taking its toll in the form of heart attacks, strokes, anxiety, depression, or worse.

Managed effectively, stress can be a good thing. It sends a signal that you must do something to deal with the situation. Implementing the right response leads to survival. The right response to stress has kept the human race alive for millennia. Never forget: *Stress is not bad.* A healthy dose of it can motivate us to respond effectively to challenging situations. Focused, immediate, surmountable stressors can help people accomplish goals and get the job done.

The same physiological and psychological systems that aided our ancestors in their survival still keep our species alive and alert today. However, the threats to our survival *have* changed. The human mind and body come wonderfully equipped with mechanisms for dealing with sudden and immediate dangers. Think of the startling appearance of a brown bear on a camping trip or the unexpected blizzard—clear instances of what we call acute stress. We react immediately. But our coping mechanisms do not work so well with the less life-threatening, continuous hassles and obstacles that characterize modern life—what we call chronic stress. Quite often, the unyielding mental, financial, social, environmental, interpersonal, and technological stressors that plague us 24/7/365 tax our systems relentlessly.

How do you manage it all? More important, how do you *think* you handle it all? Whether it's the apocalypse or a flat tire on your daily commute to the office, when the perceived level of challenge begins to exceed your perceived ability to cope with the stressor, you will likely find yourself battered by a perfect storm of emotional, cognitive, and physical chaos. Your face flushes, your heart races, and your brain stops functioning properly.

Even if you fancy yourself a cool cat under pressure, the stressors in your daily life can create a physiological and psychological cacophony in your head. Take New York City Mayor Rudolph Giuliani, who remained calm and collected throughout the extreme pressure of 9/11: He converted the chaotic noise into an orderly symphony. You can learn ways to turn even the messiest and disordered internal racket into your well-orchestrated symphony.

Psychologists know that people perform well under stress if they possess the information they need to take effective action. Under stress they feel they can take control of, or at least strongly influence, what happens next. In order to learn how to do that, you must gain some understanding of the neurological and psychological fire alarms that start blaring inside your mind and body whenever you experience the negative effects of stress and pressure. Before you experiment with the stress-management tools described later in this chapter, you need to learn why they might or might not work in given situations.

In this chapter you will discover what happens in your brain regarding your thoughts and emotions when the stress alarms start blaring. You will learn about resilient brains and why exceptionally cool cats react so well, it seems, in even the craziest and most nerve-wracking situations. Does this mean you will never lose your cool in a hot situation? No, losing your cool is a natural part of being human. That's how you know you're alive. And that's a *good thing*.

WARNING, WARNING

You're driving in your car, windows rolled down, on a beautiful Tuesday morning. You've already gotten your workout in, you feel great, you've just eaten a healthy breakfast, and you look forward to the wonderful day ahead. You are listening to your favorite song and singing along. Suddenly, screaming sirens shatter the quiet morning as two police cruisers appear in your rear-view mirror.

You know how such a situation makes you feel. Your heart practically jumps out of your chest, your stomach flips with a nauseous sensation, and your ears begin ringing. What do you do next? Keep driving, speed up, pull over and stop? You're a law-abiding citizen, so you pull over. You can still feel the blood pounding in your ears, your breathing grows a bit shallower, and your sweaty hands grip the steering wheel for dear life. You have just experienced the physiological impact of sudden and immediate or acute stress—what psychologists call the *short-term fight/flight responses.*

That response activates over a thousand physiological changes in your body that occur when an unexpected siren blast pierces your ear. Any sort of surprise event, from a change in temperature to a bolt of lightning, causes a fairly predictable reaction as our "sensing" organs (eyes, ears, nose, skin, and tongue) take in the new information. In the case of the traffic stop, your ears receive the first jolt, which triggers a series of neurological and bio-chemical reactions in the brain and body.

The sound of the siren activates a process in the brain that triggers the hypothalamus (the part of the brain that keeps your body's systems stable) to get your systems moving to protect you. The hypothalamus first activates the hard-wired neuron system—the autonomic nervous system (ANS), which controls all of the body's operations you don't think about, such as your breathing, heartbeat, temperature regulation, and digestion. It alerts every other system in the body that the situation demands action. It uses the sympathetic nervous system (SNS), which powers up and speeds up the body's systems during the fight/flight response. It promotes the release of adrenaline and noradrenalin. These biochemicals stimulate nerve pathways to initiate reactions. The hypothalamus also activates the endocrine system, which releases dozens of other hormones into the bloodstream, including mood-altering cortisol.

Milliseconds after a siren blast, cortisol, adrenaline, and some forty other hormones prepare every cell and nerve in the body to make an all-out effort either to fight the threat or to run away from it. Once the police switch off their sirens and you sit there waiting for an officer to approach your car, the parasympathetic nervous system (PNS), otherwise known as the "rest and digest" system, helps switch off the fight/flight response and return the hormones, organs, and systems back to pre-stress levels.

You get the picture. The siren sounds, your body accelerates like mad, you slowly realize the smiling officer approaching your car won't kill you, and your body starts calming down. In today's work environment, countless situations can initiate this sequence: A boss asks for an urgent meeting, the fire alarm sounds, three co-workers suddenly lose their jobs, a major customer threatens to go elsewhere. No matter how scary the situation, it will pass. Simply reminding yourself of this can do a lot to help you stay cool in a hot situation.

It's worth noting, however, that the effects of any adrenaline-fueled alertness and "rush" linger long after the threat has passed. Stress presses the pedal to the metal in a flash, but it can take a long time for the brake to bring the body back to a complete standstill.

We are hardwired to respond to acute stress in a highly effective manner to ensure our survival. The wiring operates best if the body does not employ it too often. Our prehistoric ancestors faced the occasional marauding saber-toothed tiger. Today, not many saber-toothed tigers pop up in the office, but a bewildering array of ankle-biting Chihuahua dogs attack us throughout the workday. Ongoing psychological, social, and financial problems, constant and accelerated change, overwork, job dissatisfaction, information overload, and all the other "low-grade fevers" characterize today's business environment. Our physiological response, although amazingly suited to deal with the sudden onslaught of acute stress, does not fare so well with chronic stress, the endless little yipping Chihuahuas that prompt what psychologists call the *long-term fight/flight response*.

The long-term response depends on hormone secretion (especially mood-altering cortisol). Our *perceptions* of a given threat determine the type and amount of hormones the endocrine system will dispense. A steady bombardment of blinking lights, phone beeps, email alerts, and personal and professional obligations build a chemical cocktail that keeps our bodies in a constant state of edginess, impairing memory and learning. Left untreated, this blockage increases the odds that we will end up with serious mental health problems like severe anxiety or clinical depression. In addition to memory and mental health problems, prolonged exposure to stress hormones stimulates the liver to elevate glucose levels. The body cannot sustain these high levels for long periods of time without suffering an adverse reaction, such as diabetes. In addition, long-term stress can cause narrowing of the arteries and elevate cholesterol levels, boosting the chances of succumbing to heart disease, heart attack, and stroke. It can wreak havoc with the reproductive system and weaken the immune system. Not surprisingly, these common ailments, reflected in Figure 3-1, afflict most contemporary workers, from corporate C-suites to company cubicles.

THE STRESSED BRAIN

Physiologically, your body, for the most part, reacts automatically and predictably to acute and chronic stress. Your brain does not. Our perceptions and beliefs strongly influence which situations stress us out and how we respond to the high-pressure ones. Natural disasters and wars affect everyone, more or less. Most people feel a certain amount of stress when they see news reports of post-Katrina damage in New Orleans or human suffering in faraway Somalia. When it comes to all the little stressors (or big ones that impact us personally), demanding deadlines, noise pollution, and relationship problems, we bring a unique set of beliefs and perceptions to those situations. They cause reactions that run the gamut from a minor grimace to a full-scale meltdown.

If you want to manage your own, unique stress reactions more effectively, you must start with a heightened self-awareness. You can change old habits or develop new ones, but not without the same kind of commitment and effort it takes to stop smoking or lose 20 pounds. Leaders who want to solve the problems that keep them up at night would be wise to begin with a thorough inventory of their *stress personality*. It all starts with perception.

FIGURE 3-1   The Signs and Symtoms of Stress

Cognitive Symptoms	Emotional Symptoms
Lack of concentration	Moodiness and restlessness
Indecisiveness	Agitation/short temper
Poor judgment	Tension and anxiety
Negative attitude	Feeling overwhelmed
Loss of objectivity	Sense of isolation
Forgetfulness	Depression or sadness

Physical Symptoms	Behavioral Symptoms
Headaches or backaches	Eating more or less
Muscle tension and stiffness	Sleeping more or less
Diarrhea or constipation	Relationship conflict
Nausea and dizziness	Abuse of alcohol, cigarettes, or drugs
Insomnia	Nervous habits like nail biting, pacing
Chest pains, rapid heartbeat	Teeth grinding, jaw clenching
Weight gain or loss	Overreaction to unexpected problems
Skin reactions like hives, eczema	Combativeness
Sex-drive diminishment	Inattention/high distractibility
Colds	Procrastination, neglected responsibilities
	Overdoing activities like exercising or shopping

Source: Adapted in part from the Cleveland Clinic website "Recognizing Signs and Symptoms of Stress," *http://my.clevelandclinic.org/healthy_living/stress_management/hic_recognizing_signs_and_symptoms_of_stress.aspx.*

PERCEPTION

You work as Vice-President of Marketing for a new competitor in the eBook reader industry. Fierce competition and bugs in the company's initial offering have slowed the organization's penetration into this fast-growing market. Stories in the business media suggest that Maureen, the CEO, will soon slash the payroll. If you keep your own job, you may soon find yourself eliminating the jobs of some good friends.

This situation will affect each of us differently. Everyone will see the threat of job loss, but each of us will bring our own life experiences to that threat. For Maureen, it may be business as usual. As a seasoned CEO, she has been there and done that. You, a young recruit who has risen rapidly up the corporate ladder, may take it as a blow to the solar plexus.

Psychologists and researchers Richard Lazarus and Susan Folkman offer their *Transactional Model of Stress* to explain this phenomenon. The model describes the interaction among a stressor, an individual's view of the stressor, and that person's perceived ability to cope with it. Many factors—beliefs, a tendency toward pessimism or optimism, sense of control over a situation, and one's degree of hardiness—figure into a particular person's response. You can learn to cope with these variables to some extent and thereby exercise more control over them and change them over time. Before you try to do that, ask yourself two basic questions:

- How am I threatened by this event?

- How do I cope with that threat?

Maureen may occasionally wake up in the middle of the night, fretting about the next day's downsizing initiatives, but she will quickly calm herself, knowing she will end the day with her job and company intact. She's experienced such stress before and has learned how to handle it. You, on the other hand, a novice, will lay awake all night, tossing and turning, scared to death that you will lose your job or, almost as bad, will be forced to dismiss people who have become like family to you. These two different people maintain two different perceptions. What accounts for that?

CORE BELIEFS

It's Monday morning. Maureen walks past your office without saying a word. Her shoulders are hunched over and she has a scowl on her face, so you know she's in a foul mood. You wonder, *Is she avoiding me because she doesn't want to lose her concentration or her temper? Or worse, Is she shrinking from greeting me because she will have fired me by the end of the day?*

Your reaction to that situation would depend on your core beliefs—all the ingrained positive or negative thoughts that influence how you think and feel about yourself and the world around you. While the positive ones can keep you in control of your emotions, the negative ones can undermine your ability to handle stress effectively. Common core beliefs, reflected in Figure 3-2, that affect responses to stress include:

FIGURE 3-2 Common Core Beliefs

Destructive Core Beliefs	Constructive Core Beliefs
I always get the short end of the stick.	I know that there is both gain and loss in life.
I must be perfect at all times.	I try to do my best.
I can never change.	I will constantly evolve.
I must only look out for myself because no one else will.	I care for myself and others.
I am not a people person.	I like and enjoy other people.
I am never listened to or respected.	I feel respected and appreciated.
I must strictly adhere to my plans.	I know the best-laid plans require adjustments.

A negative core belief that might spike your stress level quite often reveals itself when you mutter the old, *shoulda, woulda, coulda* mantra. The bad-belief family of telltale words also includes the cousins *must* and *ought* and their grandparents *always, never,* and *can't.* In order to get a handle on your own core beliefs, you need to listen carefully to the positive or negative self-talk that goes on in your head.

Don't beat yourself up over the negative words. They do not mean you're nuts. Quite to the contrary, you began drawing these valid conclusions as a toddler. Your DNA, along with all of your interactions with your caregivers, your environment, and your social circle, shaped your answers to these basic questions:

- Who am I?

- What can and can't I do?

- What belongs to me?

- What way should I react to people, experiences, and situations?

- What do I expect from myself and of others?

- What is my measure of success?

Your answers can only make you crazy if you let them. It's not so easy to replace negative feelings with positive and optimistic ones, because a person's self-perceptions build up and solidify over the years. You need to chisel them down to size. Unless discovered and diminished, core beliefs tend to solidify and resist change. The pessimist looks for reinforcement of her negative beliefs and ignores evidence that would contradict them. If you start with the belief that most people don't like you, you will take Maureen's demeanor as proof of that fact. Following your core beliefs, if she greets you with a warm hello and bright smile, you'll think she's just faking it.

You can easily get trapped in a block of concrete. Yet, despite the almost granite-like nature of many core beliefs, you can soften and even break them down.

OPTIMISM AND PESSIMISM

Maureen prides herself on her optimism. She thinks Murphy's law ("If anything can go wrong, it will") was made to be broken. That does not make her a Pollyanna, unflinchingly cheerful in dire circumstances. It means she always seeks information that will remedy her situation. You, on the other hand, think Murphy was an optimist.

Our world has not grown more psychologically safer than the world of our ancestors. Sometimes there is a good reason to feel pessimistic. Sometimes a proper amount of pessimism reflects healthy reality testing. But if that pessimism becomes unrealistically persistent, when it turns into chronic negativity, then it shuts out options and possibilities you need to deal with debilitating stress. Bereft of workable options, you may quickly lose confidence and your ability to trust others. If you start out with the belief that people don't like you, you will react to their bad moods with unrealistic pessimism. Over time, your pessimism irritates to the point that your prophecy comes true and people really don't like you.

Optimism does not mean putting on blinders or plunging yourself into denial. Realistic optimism enables you to make the best of a less than perfect situation. A realistically optimistic person maintains hope, even in dire circumstances, by planning to make things better. The father of positive psychology, Martin Seligman, found that optimistic people have positive core beliefs and engage in positive self-talk. They maintain better physical and psychological health than their pessimistic cousins. They become the hardy souls who control their own fate.

CONTROL AND HARDINESS

In the late 1970s, Dr. Susan Kobasa, a clinical psychologist at the City University in New York, studied executives at the Bell Telephone Company who were experiencing high levels of stress due to the government-mandated restructuring of the company that broke up the monopoly of "Ma Bell" into the many "Baby Bells." She found that three personality traits could actually protect someone from the negative health effects of prolonged stress:

- *Commitment:* Maintaining a purpose in life and nourishing your social and community involvement. Positive beliefs foster successful reactions to stress.

- *Control:* Perceiving control over a situation. People can choose how they react to a stressor and thus exert some degree of control over it.

- *Challenge:* Viewing stressful events as problems or opportunities. Those who cope successfully with stress tend to look at the silver linings as well as the clouds.

Kobasa found that executives with (a) a strong sense of commitment; (b) a belief they could exert control over their situation, and (c) a tendency to see the opportunity inherent in a problem experienced a 50 percent decrease in their risk of developing a stress-related health problem compared to their more pessimistic counterparts. The three traits had increased their hardiness, their ability to weather a stress storm. They felt stress, but they did not let it drag them down into despondency. Anyone can develop this sort of learned optimism.

ANTICIPATION AND WORRY

You and Maureen may feel differently about the looming layoffs. She might feel sadness when she delivers the bad news; you might lie awake at night, worrying that she will fire you or a good friend. Or, the reverse might be true. She could worry herself sick about all the impending drama, while you, having anticipated the bad news, have already begun looking for a new job.

Like stress, anticipation and a certain amount of worry help ensure our survival. They force us to do our homework, save our money, buy insurance, and when a major hurricane comes roaring up through the Gulf of Mexico, purchase massive amounts of duct tape, plywood, and bottled water. But excessive worrying can make us sick. It can increase stress and reduce resilience. Merely anticipating stress or a stressful situation, whether it befalls you or not, and even if you only imagine it, can trigger a physiological stress response. What do most people fear more than death itself? It is public speaking and the anticipation that they might make a fool of themselves in front of other people.

Anticipatory worrying may not only contribute to or trigger the stress response, it may also burn up the cognitive energy that you should invest in actually performing the dreaded task. Sian Beilock and Thomas Carr researched this aspect of worry in 2005. They gave ninety-three undergraduates a specific amount of time to complete a tough math test, telling them that their colleagues would film them as they worked. It turned out that the students who had previously displayed the best working-memory capability under nonstressful conditions (not timed and not filmed) performed much worse under the stress-induced conditions (filmed and timed). Worry may not only make you sick, it may also make your worst fears come true.

ASSUMPTIONS AND EXPECTATIONS

At 9:30 A.M., Maureen sends you an urgent email about an important 1 P.M. meeting you must attend. For the next several hours you slowly worry yourself into a bundle of nerves. You assume she's called the meeting to chop off your head. As 1 P.M. rolls around, you rush into the room, red-faced, palms sweaty, body shaking. To your surprise, you see three other VPs sitting in Maureen's office. It's not an execution, after all, but you're still a basket case.

The old saying "Never assume because it makes an ASS out of U and ME" perfectly applies to the psychological stress response. Human beings make assumptions and set expectations all day long. Some make sense. Some don't. The ones that don't not only distort reality but also prevent us from gathering the information we need to react properly in a given situation, especially a stressful one like that 1 P.M. meeting.

Have you ever sat in a theater watching a horror film like *A Nightmare on Elm Street* and joined the audience in yelling at the screen, "Don't go down to the basement! The slasher will get you!"? Hollywood has conditioned us to make certain assumptions and set certain expectations about certain situations. We do it in our everyday lives as well, writing scripts in our heads about what we will or will not do in certain situations. Thoughts about love create our own personal romantic scripts. Fears of stressful situations create our own horror-film scripts. We base them on our own experiences, but also on what we see other people do.

In the case of stress, our scripts include what has happened to us in the past ("I got fired the last time the company laid people off, so I'm going to get fired this time, too"), what happened to Dennis ("Dennis worked there for five years and still got fired; I've worked here for six years, so I'm going to get fired, too"), or something we read in a book or saw in a movie or television show ("Julia Roberts got fired in that movie, so I'm going to get fired, too"). We can't help but draw conclusions from what happened to us or other people in the past, even if this time the slasher does not actually lurk in the basement or our name does not actually appear on the list of employees getting the axe.

No matter what script you have previously written for dealing with stress, when stress actually strikes, you may or may not follow that script. Unimaginable physiological and psychological factors can, and usually do, interfere with even the most well-crafted scripts. Although we would like to think we can read other people's minds and deduce their behavior, we're not very good at it. Predicting the outcome of a situation involving another person almost always tests our assumptions and expectations. Nevertheless, we cling to them like ragged but comforting security blankets without realizing that they may ultimately prevent us from taking in all the important information we need in order to respond effectively to an impending crisis. Scripts are, by definition, fiction. Fiction never fully reflects reality.

CONTAGIOUS STRESS

Benjamin, a nurse at a respected teaching hospital, relates his experience with his head nurse. Denise, an academically accomplished, eminently experienced and credentialed nurse practitioner, had worked hard to earn her position. However, Benjamin thought she lacked the right leadership skills. She would habitually arrive late to meetings in a terribly stressed and disheveled state with a lame "the dog ate my homework" type of excuse. She regularly blamed her tardiness on her husband or kids or a traffic snarl or bad weather. Her frantic appearance put everyone on edge.

Once the meeting began, she would talk incessantly, interrupting others and finishing their sentences. People began to tune her out. This was a sad development, because the students in the training program could have learned a lot about nursing from her. Her perfectionism also led her to jump in and perform procedures herself, not always with good results. This tendency not only thwarted learning, it often taught the wrong lesson. While her skills were top-notch, her behavior also affected patients adversely; her anxious bedside manner did nothing to reassure them. No wonder everyone around her, from her peers and students to administrators and patients, began avoiding her at all costs.

Denise's credentials, accomplishments, and talent could not overshadow her inability to handle the stress of her job. Those around her never focused on her obvious skills with patients; they only noticed her stressed-out behavior around them. It's only natural to pay more attention to unpredictable or stressful behavior. Moreover, even a rare incident of erratic behavior makes an indelible impression on those who witness it. One outburst can earn you a reputation as a volatile personality. Do it a lot, and you'll soon find yourself labeled as *that* guy or *that* gal or worse—out on your ear.

Neuroscience backs up the notion that people find it hard to work for leaders who do not handle stress effectively. Everything that goes on in our work environment affects the brain's limbic system (the brain's emotional center). Jovial people make others feel jolly. Like a contagion (discussed in detail in Chapter 7), frantic people make other people feel frantic. When it comes to leaders, their behavior affects everyone around them. Those who stay cool in hot situations manage to get outside of their own heads and set the right tone, the right example, for handling stress. The less sabotaged and preoccupied you let yourself feel when the tiger jumps out of the jungle, the more likely you will set an example for honesty, transparency, clear communication, compassion, and empathy. You also provide a model for setting the right priorities, forming workable plans, and achieving goals. The bottom line is this: Effective stress management makes you and everyone around you more efficient and productive.

While this may seem self-evident, what you may not think about is that the converse holds true. If you allow yourself to feel unsettled and paralyzed, you set the wrong example: Your behavior tells those around you that they can lie, cover up or spin the facts, blame others for the problem, rationalize bad behavior, lower their standards, and ignore other people's feelings. You will win a reputation as someone who cannot set the right priorities and execute the right plans.

In order to set the right example consistently— especially if, like Denise, you have dug yourself into a pretty deep leadership hole with your people— you will want to master the art of stress and leadership resiliency in a world increasingly characterized by acute and prolonged stress.

RESILIENCE

The host of the television show *Man vs. Wild*, Bear Grylls, served in the British Army's Special Forces. In spite of a parachuting accident during his military career, which resulted in a broken back, Grylls went on to set many records for physical endurance. He became the youngest British climber to reach the summit and successfully descend Mount Everest. He jet-skied around the entire perimeter of the UK. On his television show, this modern-day adventurer presents worst-case scenarios that would push most of us to the breaking point. He shows the more timid among us how to survive various disasters, whether man-made or natural. Like many first-responders, emergency-room doctors and nurses, police and fire officials, and effective leaders, Grylls possesses an uncanny ability to operate with grace under pressure—what can be called resilience. Resilient people share a number of traits:

- A belief that they can influence life events (internal locus of control)

- A willingness to always hold themselves accountable for their circumstances

- A knack for finding meaning and purpose amid life's turmoil (optimism)

- A wisdom to learn from and tolerate positive and negative consequences

- A flair for adaptation and flexibility

- A sense of confidence and self-esteem (positive core beliefs)

- A reliance on social support and connection

- A habit of obtaining the information and experience that helps them respond

Resilient people generally maintain an optimistic outlook and strong core beliefs about their abilities, and they rely on their experiences, wisdom, and connections with others during times of stress. They tend to avoid, or at least recognize and adjust, what in the 1960s psychologist Aaron Beck called thinking errors—false assumptions and negative anticipation. This doesn't mean that resilient people don't get stressed. It means they deal with it as adroitly as Bear Grylls so often does. Remember, your reaction to stress is negotiable. If you want to negotiate a better response—the sort that serves Bear Grylls so well—you should first perform a 180-degree shift in the way you react to stress.

A 180° SHIFT

Jacqueline is Vice-President of a successful and fast-growing company that provides financial and accounting services to hospitals. She runs a large department with 250 employees and four directors who report directly to her, each with leadership strengths she validates and liabilities she hopes to modify. Her peers and colleagues think highly of Jacqueline, who enjoys a reputation as an excellent problem solver. Her boss has even asked her to teach other VPs her problem-solving techniques. As a result, Jacqueline has begun spending most of her work day helping other people solve their problems, with little time left over to tackle her own.

Over the past two months, she has found herself starting her day at 6 A.M., three hours before anyone else comes to the office, and turning out the lights at 8 or 9 P.M., long after everyone else has gone home, and still she ends up taking work home, spending weekends trying to catch up. Her personal life has evaporated. She has broken up with her long-time boyfriend. She has become short-tempered in meetings. She resents her less-driven colleagues and often treats them with disdain or outright anger. She has stopped going to the gym to work out and has started packing on weight. She eats dinner out of a bag every night and looking in the mirror has become an avoided activity.

Does Jacqueline's story sound familiar? If so, tape this motto to your desk: I CANNOT STOP STRESS. Striving for success, balancing work and personal life, dealing with the intense pressure that characterizes most workplaces, and just living in this revved-up, high-pressure world with so many people and devices vying for our attention will create stress. Count on it. But also tape this motto beside the first one: I CAN CONTROL MY REACTIONS TO STRESS. You can minimize the adverse effects of stress, the meaning you attach to stressful situations, and your poor responses to the inevitable stressors that come your way. In other words, the stress response is negotiable. But don't wait for stress to force that shift. Begin working on it now, during the calm before the storm, when you can apply your best effort to the task without the anxiety that attends stress-producing events.

TALKING TO YOURSELF

If you see a well-dressed executive walking down Fifth Avenue, muttering and shaking his finger, he may be closing a big real estate deal on his Bluetooth, or he may be preparing himself to cope with stress. Given an average of 50,000 to 60,000 thoughts per day, we all talk to ourselves from time to time, but few of us do it strategically. Talking to yourself does not mean you have lost your mind. It's perfectly natural. Our prehistoric ancestors probably did it all the time. However, most of our thoughts just keep repeating themselves in an endless loop. That explains why we get so comfortable with our self-talk that we don't stop to think about what we are really saying to ourselves. If we did, we'd find that our mutterings range from quite positive to very negative. Not surprisingly, negative self-talk can prompt our stress response because negative musings often distort reality. Psychologists have sorted the most common cognitive distortions into categories (Figure 3-3):

FIGURE 3-3   Cognitive Distortions

Cognitive Distortion	What Is It?	Example
Thinking in Terms of of Black or White (Polarized Thinking)	You see people, yourself, and things as either all good or all bad, with no in between.	I am a total success or I am a total failure.
Overgeneralizing	You draw very broad conclusions based on a single, negative event.	I did not get the promotion; therefore I will never be successful in this company or in this industry.
Expecting the Worst-Case Scenario (Catastrophizing)	You automatically think the worst will happen.	He didn't call to check in so he must be dead.

Filtering	You magnify the negatives and downplay all of the positives of a situation.	You receive a strong, positive performance review containing one constructive criticism, and you harp on the criticism but ignore the praise.
Personalizing the Situation (Personalizing)	You assume that everything people do or say represents a reaction to you, which makes you think you cause events in which you actually played no big role.	If I had worn my red baseball cap, my team would have won.
Global Labeling	You extrapolate one or two qualities into a negative global judgment.	Since she hates me, everybody hates me.
Jumping to Conclusions (Mind Reading)	Lacking sufficient information, you assume that you know how someone feels and why they act the way they do (specifically toward us).	He yawned when I was talking, so he thinks I'm boring.
Letting Emotions Overrule Logic (Emotional Reasoning)	You believe what you feel must be true.	I feel stupid and uninteresting; therefore, I must be stupid and uninteresting.

(continues)

FIGURE 3-3 Cognitive Distortions *(continued)*

Cognitive Distortion	What Is It?	Example
Expecting Others to Change First (Fallacy of Change)	You think other people should change to suit your needs, usually through blaming, demanding, withholding, or trading.	Don't ask me to do a better job managing you; get your own act together first.
Assigning False Control (Fallacy of Control)	Externally, you think your happiness depends on outside forces (external control). Internally, you feel totally responsible for other people's happiness (internal control).	Nothing will improve until I get promoted. *or* It's my fault that Jill is failing; I have not provided enough support.
Using Fairness as an Excuse (Fairness Error)	You judge other people's actions according to personal rules of fairness and get upset when people do not follow your rules.	If my teammates really wanted me to succeed, they would do a better job.
Asking "What if?"	You worry about all sorts of problems that probably won't occur.	If our marketing budget declines second quarter, we'll certainly go out of business.

Insisting That You Are Always Right	You demand that people never question your judgment and do not question it yourself.	Don't contradict me because I have never made a mistake about this issue.
Thinking Egocentrically	You rarely put yourself in other people's shoes but expect them to walk in yours.	Everyone thinks the way I do.
Dreaming of Future Rewards (Heaven's Reward Fallacy)	You expect your sacrifice and self-denial to pay off later, and you feel bitter when the reward doesn't come.	My boss is such a jerk, I'll put up with her for now because I'm sure I'll have her job in 10–15 years.
Making Unfair Comparisons	You feel you always fall short when you put yourself up against others.	She is so much smarter than I am. I'll never succeed the way she does.

All of us fall victim to distortions from time to time. Those of us who cope well with stress more often listen to an inner voice that serves as a friendly inner drill sergeant, encouraging us to suck it up, push harder, stop whining. That's a good thing. But taking orders from an unfriendly inner drill sergeant—one screaming at us to crawl back into bed, bury our heads under our pillow, and cry our eyes out—doesn't do us any favors.

Jacqueline generally felt comfortable in her own skin. Yet sometimes she couldn't help but scold herself when, for instance, she took on an assignment that she knew would stretch her beyond her breaking point or snapped at a co-worker for no apparent reason or failed to finish a report late Sunday night. After paying close attention, she realized that such harsh scolding did her no good at all and that doing so had become a bad habit she needed to break, before it added even more stress to her life. She did not want to turn into the screw-up described by her scolding voice. She was not a screw-up; she was an accomplished person who had fallen victim to an ever-growing web of self-doubt.

Negative self-talk or cognitive distortions can resist even our best efforts to change them. They can become so deeply ingrained and habitual that it takes an almost superhuman effort to break their hold on our mind. Fortunately, you can do what that executive strolling down Fifth Avenue was doing. You can take the following practical steps to get that unfriendly drill sergeant out of your head:

Step One: Become cognizant. Listen to that inner voice; does it talk to you in a way that you would not tolerate if a friend spoke those words? Would they wound a friend if you yelled them at her? Pay close attention to your exact words and write them down. Three questions will help you recognize those words. Consider how Jacqueline answered them:

a. What triggered the event? Missing a deadline.

b. What negative thoughts popped into my head? I'm a total screw-up.

c. What emotions did I experience? Stress, helplessness, anger, sadness.

When you start analyzing your negative self-talk you should begin to appreciate how the perceptions they express instigate or further a stress response. Jacqueline's unchecked script of negative thoughts caused her great distress; they were actually impeding her ability to live up to her reputation as a skillful problem-solver.

Step Two: Obliterate the negative thought. Once you identify the negative thought(s), you can ask another series of questions to help change them. Look at the way Jacqueline answered them (Figure 3-4):

FIGURE 3-4 Challenging Negative Thoughts

Ask Yourself	Answer Yourself
What is my negative thought?	I'm a total screw-up. I'm going to lose my job.
What evidence proves this thought true?	I finished a few reports after they were due, which is not okay.
What evidence proves this thought false?	The CEO praises me as the company problem solver and even calls me his right-hand woman.
What unhealthy feelings and behaviors does this thought cause?	I feel totally stressed out. I'm always on edge. I'm having trouble focusing. I'm snapping at people.
What will eventually happen if I continue thinking this way?	It will damage my professional reputation and cause long-term stress-related health and psychological problems.
What advice would I give a friend who feels this way?	I would tell them to snap out of it, that they are making a mountain out of a molehill. I would tell them to begin delegating more.
What conditions should I accept right now? What won't change?	I need to accept the need to maintain my workload until I figure out a way to make it more manageable.
What can I do to make my thinking more positive?	I need to cut myself some slack, better organize my time, and focus on my own core work.

(continues)

FIGURE 3-4   Challenging Negative Thoughts *(continued)*

Ask Yourself	Answer Yourself
What words will express my new healthy thought?	I enjoy a successful career and the friendship and respect of my colleagues and my boss.

If you find it difficult to do this objectively, ask a trusted colleague or adviser to assist you. Since we seldom see ourselves the way others do, we can benefit from inviting people we trust to help us gain much-needed objectivity.

You may also find it extremely difficult to effect a change if your negative thinking involves a core belief that has become deeply engraved in your mind. It takes more time and effort to deal with these stubborn, inflexible rascals. When they prove intractable, try learning your ABCs.

THE ABCs

After a weeklong conference in Chicago, John and Peter, both senior executives in the financial services industry, meet in the American Airlines lounge at O'Hare Airport. As they prepare to go to the boarding area, they hear an announcement that their flight to Los Angeles will not depart for another two hours. John drops his briefcase, kicks his carry-on bag, and utters profanity that turns every head in the room. Pete lets out a long sigh, dials his wife to explain his delay, and gathers his briefcase and suitcase. Then he heads to the airport restaurant for a leisurely meal and a careful review of the notes he took at the conference.

Why does John lose his cool while Peter remains calm and collected? Both face the same irritating situation. The answer, of course, resides in their heads. Let's take a peek at how they apply their stress ABCs.

A = Identify the activating event. John and Peter's plane is delayed.

B = Determine the core belief or ingrained thought process. John believes that these types of inconveniences always happen to him and he takes it as a grave personal insult. Peter believes this sort of inconvenience comes with the job and views it as an opportunity to do something productive.

C = List the behavioral consequences. John feels enormous stress and displays his anger with physical and verbal abuse. As a result, he will not accomplish anything productive during the two-hour delay; by contrast, he may stew and feel restless the entire time. If you ever react to a stressful situation the way John did, you should move on to the letter D.

D = Dispute the belief. If a given belief causes you a lot of grief, you should try disputing it the way John did (Figure 3-5):

FIGURE 3-5 Dispute the Belief

Ask Yourself?	John's Answers
What is my problematic belief?	Bad stuff and inconveniences always happen to me.
What evidence supports my belief?	The evidence is that the plane delay is an inconvenience to me.
What is a better explanation for what happened?	The inconvenience is not just happening to me, it is happening to everyone on this flight.
What are the consequences of this belief?	Anger and stress have sent me into a tailspin.

(continues)

FIGURE 3-5 Dispute the Belief *(continued)*

Ask Yourself?	John's Answers
What would happen if I changed my belief right now? Permanently?	I could enjoy a nice dinner and catch up on some work and calls at the airport.
What are my new core beliefs?	S--t happens! I can manage inconvenience better.

If you conclude that you would gain some real benefits if you changed your belief, you can finish this exercise by delving into E.

E = Imagine more effective ways to deal with stressors.

- *Control what you can.* Since you cannot change many aspects of stressful situations, focus on what you can change. For example, John could brainstorm and then act on more productive ways to use the two-hour delay.

- *Go away.* Try removing yourself from a stressful situation by taking a walk, leaving a room, or just doing something else. A temporary break can refresh your mind and help you gain a more positive perspective.

- *Breathe.* Breathe with your diaphragm. Use your belly to pull in a deep breath. Hold it for ten seconds, then let it out slowly. Repeat at least five times. Taking a few deep breaths won't abolish the stress, but it will counteract some of the adverse physiological effects of stress and buy you a moment to reset your thoughts.

- *Hydrate.* Drink plenty of water. Most of us live in a regular state of mild dehydration. Stressful situations can further dehydrate you, and dehydration contributes to a bad mood. Stopping to sip water not only increases your mood in the moment, it may also distract you from the stressor, albeit momentarily. That brief distraction might buy you just enough time to gain some perspective on the situation.

Once you move yourself to a place where you do not feel so all consumed by your emotions and can think a little more clearly, reframe that negative core belief into a more positive one that won't send you flying off your rocker in the future.

If you have disputed the negative core belief and accept the fact that it causes you problems, you will automatically find yourself coping more effectively. In John's case, he recognizes that his negative core belief that "inconveniences and bad things always happen to me" has created a lot of physiological, psychological, and reputation problems for him. With this in mind, he can reframe his core belief. In addition, John can use this specific "freak-out" to remind himself that such behaviors do not work for him when he encounters a stressful inconvenience.

THE MARATHON

Over a two-month period, Hilary, a Regional Director for a large retail chain of fifteen stores in the Midwest, experienced the perfect storm. Teenage mobs disrupted two stores, with one unruly participant punching a pregnant store manager in the stomach when the manager tried to stop him from shoplifting merchandise; corporate headquarters fired her own beloved boss; three of her direct reports had begun shirking their responsibilities; her most reliable lieutenant abruptly left the company to join a competitor. All the while, she was overseeing the construction and staffing of a new store and the dismantling of an underperforming one. Phew. It was enough to blow a weaker woman's cool.

While Hilary had never flinched under pressure, she had never faced such a marathon of woe. If you have ever engaged in an endurance sport, you know what it's like to reach a point during the competition when you hit the wall—when you feel you cannot run, jump, pedal, or swim one second longer. If you have ever started a company or worked as a manager of an enterprise, you've undoubtedly felt the same way when you hit a wall in the form of a cash-flow problem, the loss of a key customer, a staff rebellion, or that huge project that keeps mushrooming out of control.

How does the marathoner scale the wall? She sets small, incremental goals she can accomplish: left foot, right foot. Ten more steps. Just to that next stop sign. Okay, now to that bend in the road. That enables her to cover the last mile and throw herself across the finish line. Leaders can learn a lot from that response to acute physical stress by breaking down the accumulation of stressors at work into bite-sized, manageable bits.

In Hilary's case, the stress-buffeted executive could not afford to let the perfect storm blow her over the edge. Rather than viewing it all as the end of the world, she converted it into a motivator and began setting small, manageable goals. At the end of every day, she would email herself and her coach a "to-do" list of micro-accomplishments she expected to achieve the next day. This approach meant that Hilary had to set aside her usual perfectionism and settle for successfully taking one step, two steps, or ten steps forward, left foot, right foot. Long story short, she weathered the storm, but, more important, she learned a new set of skills for dealing with stress in her work and life.

REALITY CHECK

Ronny, the CEO of a mid-size graphic-design firm in Atlanta, fancied himself the type of boss any of his people could approach with a problem. He believed that everyone at his company admired his sincerity, honesty, and caring support. He always took the time to listen to and address even the smallest concerns his people raised. So, imagine his shock when a consultant, hired by the company's board to observe Ronny's leadership, bluntly told him that most everyone who worked for him joked behind his back that, while he was a nice guy, he was a thoroughly incompetent boss. Although he did spend a lot of time listening to people, Ronny never provided the advice and resources people needed to get the job done on time and within budget. It was that shortcoming that had led the Board to hire an outside coach to work with him.

Clearly, Ronny needed a reality check. Most leaders succumb from time to time to certain illusions about themselves, thinking that just because they occupy the top rung of the corporate ladder, they can do no wrong. Worse, they can fall prey to the Emperor's New Clothes syndrome, believing all the praise they hear from people who can't bring themselves to tell the boss the truth.

You may think you handle stress like a veteran rock star while, in reality, you are more a one-man band with a broken snare drum and a tuneless kazoo. On the other hand, you may think you never deal with stress as adroitly as you should—while, in fact, people cannot believe how cool-headed you remain when a forest fire breaks out. As a leader, what you think of your own behavior matters far less than how others perceive you, especially in times of great stress. With a little help from the coach, Ronny eventually learned this important lesson. To paraphrase an old adage, "We see ourselves as a combination of our thoughts, fears, and intentions, but others just see our behavior."

Once you accept a position of leadership, you should make conducting a reality check an ongoing process. Otherwise, you can quickly succumb to illusions that, in the end, will embarrass you or cost you your job. After every project, sale, presentation, review, difficult conversation, or any other potentially stressful incident, you should ask yourself and, at times, other people involved in the situation:

- What worked?

- What did not work?

- What got in the way of getting desired results?

- What helped me/us achieve desired results?

- What other, perhaps better, ways could I/we have approached the situation?

- What have I/we learned from this situation?

Although this may strike you as a time-consuming task, doing it on a regular basis will help you discern patterns in your leadership style and your ability to cope with stress-inducing situations. In addition, it starts separating your false assumptions and beliefs from the reality of how others view and react to you. This was exactly what Ronny's coach advised him to do. Although anyone can coach him- or herself to do it, it often helps to ask a professional coach or even a thoughtful colleague to help you.

WRAP UP

A leader suffering chronic stress can't manage other people as effectively as she would hope in stress-inducing situations. She might get some initial results, but for all of the expended effort, eventually the undertaking becomes hopeless.

Stress management does not mean stress obliteration. Rather, it means learning how to negotiate your own reactions to the stress that inevitably occurs every day of your life as a leader. Choosing to mind what's going on in your head and observing your body's physiological responses and how others' perceive you mark the first sure steps toward coping effectively with stress.

CHAPTER 4

Why Does a Good Fight Sometimes Go Bad?

JANET AND BRAD have known each other since their college days at Brandeis, then at Harvard Law. So close is their relationship, they have often thought of each other as brother and sister. And, like most siblings, they have often engaged in friendly competition, first in the classroom, then on 5K runs, and now as attorneys working at one of the leading law firms. Equally talented and at the top of their game, they are both leading teams of associates. While remaining competitive with each other, they have kept their friendship strong through mutual respect. Their respectful competition fuels their productivity and motivates their teams to go the extra mile.

Brad and Janet stand head and shoulders above their peers. They consistently have won cases, their teams excel, and the firm's partners generously reward their performance. The senior partner, Wayne, fondly refers to them as "rock stars."

Wayne tells them that the partners expect to add one of their names to the marquee. What he doesn't tell them is that the partners, who understand their competitive relationship, expect that relationship to make each of them fight harder for the promotion. As the days, weeks, and months pass, tension between the two escalates. When Brad scores a victory, he gloats a little. When he suffers a setback, Janet takes a little guilty pleasure in his defeat. She also beams when she succeeds and winces when he chuckles over her own setbacks. Soon their once-friendly competition has deteriorated into an intense rivalry, keeping Brad awake at night, making him irritable and mistake-prone, and causing him to push his teammates to unreasonable lengths. He soon develops a deep resentment and spends a lot of time thinking about ways to keep his once good friend from gaining an advantage. His unhappiness rises as his team's productivity declines.

Janet, who has managed to keep her thoughts about Brad from turning toxic, wins a huge case, bringing several million dollars into the firm. The partners reward her with the promised partnership. Brad's behavior now goes further south as envy dominates his emotions. He loses more sleep, angrily berates his people over the smallest missteps, treats Janet like a sworn enemy, and begins to sabotage her in subtle and not-so-subtle ways. Behind her back, he calls her a cold-blooded shark, "loses" documents she needs for a major case, and hints to clients that she won the promotion by sleeping with her boss. None of this is helping him or his reputation. He has lost confidence in his own ability and is seriously thinking about leaving the firm, even getting out of the legal profession altogether. Brad's doctor expresses concern about his rapid weight gain and high blood pressure.

Most everyone has at one time or another felt a twinge of envy or jealousy about a colleague's success, or delight at his or her failure. It's only human. Interestingly, those feelings can actually contribute to productivity. The healthy competitiveness of a good fight can fuel productivity and innovation. When a good fight goes bad, though, and those feelings intensify beyond control, they can derail relationships and erode productivity.

THE CAIN AND ABEL EFFECT

Perhaps the most iconic story of healthy competition gone horribly wrong comes from the Bible. After God banished them from the Garden of Eden, Adam and Eve went on to have two sons, Cain, who became a farmer, and Abel, who became a shepherd. Like many siblings, the brothers' relationship was close but contentious.

Life was good. To show his gratitude to God, Abel, true to his life's work, chose to sacrifice his first and best lamb. Cain chose straw, the product of his own hard labor. Both hoped their offerings would please God.

On the day of the sacrifice, Cain watched as Abel's burning lamb sent fragrant smoke to the sky, while his straw smoldered with the odor of burnt grass. God expressed respect for Abel's sacrifice but not for Cain's. Why, wondered Cain, did God prefer his brother? He had also done his best to please God. It must be Abel's fault. Envy began to consume Cain's heart. Finally, inviting Abel to join him on a walk, Cain grew so angry he struck down and killed his brother.

When Cain realized what he'd done, he at first felt relieved that no one had seen him murder Abel. Then the Lord spoke, "Cain, where is your brother?"

Cain shrugged, "Am I my brother's keeper?"

God then cursed Cain. "Henceforth, your brother's blood will make your land barren, and you shall wander the land a fugitive."

At those words, Cain fell to the ground sobbing. Finally, he felt the full horror of what he'd done.

What causes the *Cane and Abel* effect? What turns a healthy, productive competition into a corrosive battle? It often happens when someone lacks emotional self-awareness and the ability to handle emotional and behavioral stresses. Brad could not see himself as others saw him, and he could not control the temptation to badmouth and sabotage his competitor. Her promotion was his tipping point, enraging him to a level where he could not help murdering his own career and reputation. Managing his emotions seemed beyond his control. His behavior also baffles his boss, who does not know how to deal with Brad's temperamental outbursts. Leaders who encounter the *Cain and Abel* effect, whether in themselves or in team members, always find it hard to manage the raw emotions of jealousy, envy, rage, and the sabotage and backstabbing that accompany them. Digging out the root causes can prove even more difficult. As with all the psychologically fueled leadership dilemmas we have been exploring in this book, the first step involves understanding what's going on in your own brain and the brains of those who suffer from the *Cain and Abel* effect. It all starts with the deeply embedded roots of competition.

NATURAL COMPETITION

In 1954, Leon Festinger, a social psychologist best known for his work on cognitive dissonance, offered his *theory of social comparison*. This theory held that, as natural social beings, we thrive on learning from and growing through our interactions with others. From the cradle on, we learn the rules of behavior from our parents, teachers, and friends. Those rules, which govern our behavior in society, teach us the difference between right and wrong and the social rules society expects us to follow. This natural form of social learning includes *social comparison*, the act of evaluating our opinions and abilities by looking at those held by other people. The comparison tells us to what degree we excel or fall short.

In 1977, social scientists D. R. Mettee and G. Smith summarized it nicely. Social comparison is "our quest to know ourselves, about the search for self-relevant information and how people gain self-knowledge and discover reality about themselves." Research on the theory of social comparison has flourished over the years and has shed light on all the different ways it affects our lives. Sometimes we compare ourselves to people who seem superior to us (upward comparison). At other times we compare ourselves to people we deem inferior (downward comparison). At still other times, we compare ourselves to people we perceive as more or less like us in various ways (proxy comparison or model).

There are many different reasons we compare ourselves to others. A social comparison can help us evaluate our relative standing in a particular area (self-evaluation), or it can supply information about how we might improve our performance (self-improvement).

Think back to the story of Janet and Brad. Early on in their friendly competition, they compared themselves as equals and used the results to heighten their self-awareness and to fuel improved performance. Somewhere along the way, Brad perceived himself as inferior to Janet. That perception created feelings of jealousy and envy that took his eye off the need to improve his own performance. Despite the natural tendency for people to compare themselves to others, most people don't like to admit they do it. In a classic 1985 study, Joanne Wood, Shelley Taylor, and Rosemary Lichtman found that cancer patients initially denied engaging in social comparison with other cancer patients. In later interviews, these same patients proved that they had, in fact, compared their own coping strategies or abilities to others.

That's not surprising. Admitting that you are comparing yourself to someone else seems a little self-serving or unseemly. On the other hand, we find it perfectly acceptable to talk about "keeping up with the Joneses." The former gets more directly into interpersonal stuff, while the latter involves inanimate objects, what the "Joneses" own, their cars, clothes, and houses. The cancer patients felt reluctant to admit to the personal stuff. Think about some of your own recent social interactions. Have you ever found yourself eyeing the slick new iPhone 5 in your fellow traveler's hand? Have you ever watched a colleague lose her job and think to yourself, "Whew, I'm glad it wasn't me"? Just recalling the many social comparisons you make each day will raise your self-awareness of the role they play in your life and work.

You will come to understand that comparisons at work, whether you have just begun a new job or have served as the leader of a few dozen people for many years, can and do create strong feelings, just as they did for Brad. They spring up because social comparison breeds competition and competition brings out both the best and the worst in us.

GOOD FIGHTS VS. BAD FIGHTS

From the dawn of the human race, survival has depended on competition. Whether gathering life-sustaining resources or gaining the affection of a mate, we have always felt compelled to make ourselves faster, stronger, smarter, and more attractive. We want to win the blue ribbon, cross the finish line first, knock the other guy off his perch, or score highest on that crucial exam. Sometimes that pushes us ahead and sometimes it just enables us to keep on playing. Competition stems from our natural tendency to pay attention to what surrounds us. According to Stephen Garcia and Avishalom Tor, both negative and positive comparisons carry tremendous meaning. Our wish to widen or reduce the gap between ourselves and those around us often triggers competitive behavior to protect our feelings of superiority or reduce our feelings of inferiority.

Like most deeply rooted human behavior, competition is perfectly normal and healthy. It is also necessary in human evolution because it drives natural selection and "survival of the fittest." Competition can make the office an exciting and rewarding place to work, as it did for Janet and Brad early in their rivalry. Conventional wisdom insists that cooperation and collaboration work better than competition, but the inevitability of social comparison argues quite the contrary. Comparison is the mother of competition. And competition is a fact of corporate life. Harness its power as a good fight, or risk seeing it metastasize into a bad fight. The benefits of healthy competition include:

- Greater innovation

- Increased motivation

- Improved productivity

- Increased self-improvement

- Enhanced teamwork

- Boosted engagement

- More fun!

That's the power of a good fight. Unfortunately, what begins as healthy competition can quickly shift into ugly, corrosive competition, as it did with Brad and Janet. Corrosive competition can burn everyone in its path by:

- Sapping motivation

- Killing collaborative processes

- Stunting performance and productivity

- Poisoning team and organizational culture

- Reducing engagement and commitment

- Increasing stress and insecurity

- Ruining reputations

- Robbing work of fun

Certain warning signals can alert you to the fact that a good fight has slipped over the line and may soon infect the workplace with the *Cain and Abel* effect:

- You resent another's success rather than using it to inspire and motivate you to greater heights.

- You concentrate on your competitor's weaknesses and limitations rather than studying his strengths.

- You justify or rationalize your own limitations and setbacks rather than affirming your own strengths.

- You feel ashamed and humiliated when you lose a battle rather than using it to fuel a more strenuous effort the next time around.

When we watch others succeed or fail, we often compare ourselves to them, and our observations can stimulate powerful emotional and behavioral responses. Many factors influence the nature of our feelings and reactions, including past experiences with similar situations, our level of self-esteem, and our judgment about whether someone deserved to succeed or fail in a particular endeavor. Early success came easily for Brad, even though he secretly doubted his ability since childhood. His early success also meant even a small failure knocked him for a loop. He never dreamed Janet would push ahead of him on the promotion track.

Complicating matters, current social mores dictate that when someone fails, we should sympathize or even empathize with her predicament, and when someone succeeds, we should cheer and offer hearty congratulations. What happens when our reactions run afoul of those social mores? What if we delight in someone's setback or despise his advancement? Then we can easily slide into envy, jealousy, even rage and end up disliking ourselves even more than the target of our ill will. Herein lies the psychological dilemma where the collision of social and self-expectations can shift a good fight into a bad fight.

Emotional self-awareness and effective self-management start with a firm understanding of some often misunderstood emotions that lie at the root of much bad behavior in the workplace. Negative emotions such as envy, frustration, and anger can trigger acts of sabotage, incivility, and bullying—actions that can end up making us feel guilty and ashamed.

You should keep in mind, however, that such negative emotions are part of being human. You can't avoid them; but left unchecked, they not only create turmoil, they can also damage both the target of those feelings and the one experiencing them. They do not pose serious problems or threaten a relationship unless you ignore them and let them fester into a deep psychological wound. The first telltale pinpricks of envy, jealousy, frustration, and anger should provide a clue that you need to pull out the thorn and apply the antiseptic. This applies to all sorts of unsettling emotions we hate to admit we feel, especially schadenfreude, envy, and jealousy.

SCHADENFREUDE

"Whenever a friend succeeds, a little something in me dies."
—GORE VIDAL

Julian could not wait to start his new job. When he gave his two weeks' notice to his current employer, Hugh, at a small graphics shop specializing in Internet advertising, Julian felt both elated and sad. He was elated at the opportunity to join their competitor, a much larger company with an impressive track record for designing award-winning Internet ad campaigns, but he was also sorry to leave behind colleagues and a boss he thought of as a brother. Hugh accepted Julian's resignation graciously, congratulating him on snagging such a plum job and wishing him all the success in the world. Over the next few months, the two men found themselves competing for business, with each one winning an equal number of new accounts. The loser always patted the winner on the back and vowed to learn from the experience and try a bit harder the next time they competed.

A year after he started working for the new company, Julian began to beat Hugh more often than not. At the same time he began to hear some distressing gossip on the industry grapevine. Hugh, it seemed, was now bad-mouthing Julian as an ungrateful and untalented scoundrel who broke all the rules of good sportsmanship to gain business for his new place of employment. Julian could not believe his ears. That did not sound like the Hugh he knew. He decided to confront Hugh at a local trade conference. When he tried to pull Hugh aside for a chat, his former boss just smirked, excused himself, and walked over to a group of executives that included Julian's new boss, Barbara. To his amazement, Julian could hear the sarcasm dripping in Hugh's voice as he told her how lucky she was to have poached Julian.

From that moment on, Julian vowed to bury his feelings of betrayal and confusion over Hugh's behavior and focus, instead, on excelling at his new job. Eighteen months passed before Julian joined a few friends from his old company for lunch. There his former colleagues revealed that Hugh had announced that he was selling to Julian's new company in order to extricate himself from deep financial problems. "You wouldn't recognize the Old Man," said one former colleague. "He's always so stressed out. It looks like he's on the verge of a stroke. He comes in late, leaves early, and doesn't take care of clients the way he used to. A lot of our best accounts have gone elsewhere." As Julian listened, he noticed a familiar yet troublesome feeling brewing in his gut. He found himself feigning a concerned, "Oh, no, that's terrible" look on his face to hide a barely perceptible self-righteous smirk. Julian's real thoughts were "That jerk got what he deserved!" But he says to his friends, "Oh, no, that's awful news. I really hope things turn around for him."

Rarely do we react to the fortunes or misfortunes of others with complete indifference, especially those that involve people to whom we compare ourselves at work, whether peers, superiors, or direct reports. Sometimes we really do take genuine pleasure from someone's winning performance, even if her success came at our own expense during fair competition. We might even experience disappointment over her defeat at our own hand.

In a good fight, you wish the best performer to win, and when he does, you shake his hand, smile, and move on to the next order of business. Other times, we don't want to do any of that. We just feel bitter, angry, and envious over our rival's good fortune or take delight in her misfortune. That's when you know the good fight has gone bad. Just hope you don't take it so far you end up standing over a colleague's bleeding career with a scalpel in your hand.

The difficult-to-translate German word *Schadenfreude*, combining *schaden* (damage) and *freude* (joy), describes a universal human emotion: taking pleasure in the misfortunes of others. It sends a little shiver of delight up the spine. Julian felt it, and so have humans throughout history.

In Dante's *Purgatorio*, the protagonist speaks to a soul stuck in the 2nd Terrace of Hell (The Envious) because "she took more joy in others' misfortune than in her own good luck." Or, as nineteenth-century atheist German philosopher Arthur Schopenhauer put it, "To feel envy is human, to savor schadenfreude is devilish." From Cro Magnum suitors to brilliant philosophers, from kings and presidents, to you and me, this particular emotion can easily get the upper hand when we see another person trip and fall.

Schadenfreude, like all emotions that pop up during competition, stems from our human tendency for comparison. In our contemporary society, where conventional and social media have spawned a multitude of arenas for people to compare themselves with one another, schadenfreude frequently rears its head. For years, Martha Stewart presided as the queen of domestic perfection. In the end, however, her arrogant and condescending behind-the-scenes behavior made her the butt of late-night talk-show jokes and the inmate of a minimum-security prison for lying about her financial affairs. People who had once felt inferior to the domestic diva now experienced a little thrill of schadenfreude at her fall from grace. It's perfectly natural to feel some degree of pleasure when we see someone else suffer, especially a successful person who may have formerly sparked feelings of envy or resentment.

Schadenfreude grows troublesome when we apply it to those closest to us: our colleagues, bosses, peers, and friends. It's one thing to feel schadenfreude toward a person we don't know personally, like disgraced Enron CEO Ken Lay or the queen of the perfectly cooked dinner and grand centerpiece, Martha Stewart; it's quite another thing to take pleasure from a colleague's demotion or a once happily married friend's divorce.

Before you accuse yourself of heartless insensitivity when you feel that little shiver of delight, remind yourself that every other person in the world feels it from time to time. It is as normal as feeling simple happiness or contentment. Unlike those positive emotions, however, it can metastasize into something ugly. Someone falls down a few rungs of the ladder, while you climb a rung higher. Go ahead and feel pleased with yourself. But don't kick the other person off the ladder.

Recent brain research suggests that experiencing the misfortunes of others can trigger the same part of the brain that is triggered when we have sex or eat chocolate, especially if we have a connection to them. In 2009, neuroscientists Hidehiko Takahashi and colleagues used functional magnetic resonance imaging (fMRI) to examine the brain activity of nineteen volunteer subjects. The study involved each subject's reading a story involving four people: a protagonist, who was an "average Joe," and three other individuals, two of them superior to, and one inferior to, "average Joe." The researchers told the subjects to imagine themselves as the protagonist, comparing themselves to the two superior and one inferior individual. One of the superior individuals displayed characteristics that mattered and were relevant to the protagonist while the other did not. As the subjects read the story, the research team scanned their brains to create baseline readings.

Then the researchers scanned the subjects' brains as they read about misfortunes befalling the superior and inferior individuals. At the outset the subjects had stated the degree to which they envied the characters in the story. In the second phase of the study, they cited the amount of pleasure they took from hearing about the characters' troubles. It turned out that the more envious a subject felt about the superior individuals (especially the one who mattered most to the protagonist), the more activity the subjects' brains displayed in the region scientists associate with conflict, social pain, and rejection.

Picture it this way. You're reading a story about Dick and Jane and Spike. Dick is a dolt you would not invite to lunch. Jane is admirable in many ways, but you do not much relate to her superior intelligence. On the other hand, Spike also draws your admiration, but for his good humor and generosity rather than his IQ. When dumb old Dick trips over a log and falls flat on his face, you shrug your shoulders, thinking it's just the sort of accident that happens to him all the time. When Jane slips on a banana peel, you smile to yourself, thinking that it serves her right for being such a know-it-all. But when the fellow you envy the most, good old Spike, takes a hard fall, you take even more delight in *his* misfortune.

Why do we feel pleasurable sensations when something bad happens to someone we envy? It happens because, as fMRI studies show, episodes of schadenfreude spur activity in the part of the brain that contains its reward system and responds to basic pleasures such as sex, food, and drugs. This area also plays a big role in the release of dopamine, a neurotransmitter sometimes called the "feel-good chemical." Humans love dopamine, which explains why we find the pleasures in life so addictive. Schadenfreude can feel just as good to us as the applause that comes after the pitch-perfect delivery of an important speech or the celebratory dinner as a reward for a job well done.

Psychology has taught us that people are highly motivated to protect or enhance their views of themselves, so much so that psychologists deem seeing ourselves positively as a primary drive. One way to protect or enhance our self-view is by comparing ourselves to others who are less fortunate (or who may have been more fortunate but have suffered a setback). The feeling of schadenfreude provides a momentary self-esteem boost. When your good friend stubs his toe, you delight in wriggling your own happy toes.

Think of schadenfreude as a soothing response to the negative feelings associated with envy. Envy triggers that part of our brain that deals with conflict, emotional pain, and rejection—experiences we all find unpleasant. The pain prompts some nasty behavioral responses that can undermine or even ruin trust, team cohesion, interpersonal relations, and the general health of an organization's culture.

Most people make no distinction between envy and jealousy, but the two emotions differ in important ways. Envy rears its ugly head when someone desires a quality or achievement possessed by someone else, whether that person is a close friend or a complete stranger (e.g., "I wish we owned our neighbor's Lexus"). Jealousy arises within the context of a relationship (e.g., John can't bear losing Sally's affection to Tom). In our discussion of these emotions in the workplace, we will talk mostly about envy.

ENVY

Hugh stewed over what he considered Julian's betrayal when he left. However, he masked those feelings and wished Julian great success at his new job. Over the next several months, as the former colleagues became competitors, Hugh's company began losing more and more business to Julian's. Within a year, Hugh found himself in a financial hole. When he bumped into Julian at the trade conference, he could barely control his emotions. He thought, "That traitor looks so happy, I could just spit in his face." Instead of acting on his thoughts, he belittled Julian to everyone he met at the conference. Hugh also resented the fact that Julian was making so much money that he had bought a new house and married his longtime sweetheart, who also once worked for Hugh.

The more Julian's fortunes rose, the more Hugh's sank. Julian had joined the Board of Directors of the local trade association, while Hugh avoided most meetings and stayed home feeling sorry for himself. Hugh felt old, worn out, and depressed. Business deteriorated further, until he could see no way out of the mess but through a merger. This would get the company's rudder back in the water, but it would wound Hugh's soul to turn over the reins to his hated rival. After the merger, Hugh spent more and more time away from the office. He eventually quit and retired from the work he had once loved. Every day he thought about Julian. He either wished "that ingrate" would stumble and fall or imagined himself in Julian's shoes, once again young and vibrant and successful.

Often confused with jealousy, envy holds a special place in human history as one of the Seven Deadly Sins. Like greed, envy arises from an insatiable desire, not for material goods but for the success and good fortune of others. An envious person resents that another person has obtained acclaim and status he or she lacks. It violates one of the Ten Commandments—specifically, "Neither shall you desire . . . anything that belongs to your neighbor." In Dante's Purgatory, those who committed this sin suffered a special punishment. The sinners' eyes were sewn shut with wire because they had gained sinful pleasure from seeing others brought low.

This history helps explain why we tend to keep this all-too-human feeling a deep, dark secret. It makes us feel selfish and ashamed. If we admitted our shame, we would then draw attention to the fact that we are comparing ourselves to others and that our self-esteem has suffered a blow. Envy can also violate an equally powerful desire to see ourselves in a positive light, as a good person who supports others and enjoys their successes, as opposed to a bad person who harbors envious or malicious thoughts about their achievements. The resulting cognitive dissonance (holding two conflicting ideas simultaneously) can create anxiety, frustration, and even lead to clinical depression. We might even, like Hugh, sit alone feeling sorry for ourselves, and imagining the person we envy falling off a cliff while we soar on the wings of success.

Envy occurs when we wish we possessed another person's attributes, achievements, or possessions or wish they did not have them. Hugh desired Julian's youth, happiness, and business success and could not abide his own advancing age and financial struggles. He might also envy billionaire Bill Gates, but that causes him a lot less grief than the envy he feels for Julian, someone he knows on a personal level. We tend to suffer more when we compare ourselves to people nearby and find ourselves on the short end of the stick. In the workplace envy can cause grief because:

- It highlights what others possess.

- It reminds you of what you lack.

- It triggers unpleasant or destructive behaviors.

- It can interfere with successful, productive work relationships.

- It can make you feel ashamed.

Envy sometimes motivates us to do better. Researchers John Schaubroeck and Simon Lam conducted a study in 2004 involving tellers at a bank in Hong Kong. They found that tellers who were not promoted felt especially envious of promoted colleagues they had earlier rated as most similar to themselves. Interestingly, the envious tellers ended up performing better over the next five months, demonstrating the fact that envy can spur people to higher achievement. These motivated individuals were able to transform that envy into "healthy competition," similar to what Janet and Brad did early in their relationship.

For those with a fragile sense of self-esteem, envy can further damage that image as they engage in comparison and competition at work. According to psychologists John Sabini and Maury Silver, envy, unlike other emotions, does not elicit a singular emotional state. Rather, it includes many different unpleasant and uncomfortable psychological states. Inner feelings of inferiority, injustice, longing, and resentment become plainly obvious to others, no matter how hard we try to conceal them. These emotions can fuel outright acts of hostility as our hope for another's failure leads to acts of sabotage.

Hostility tends to erupt in the wake of what psychologists call *self-relevant envy*. The term *self-relevant* describes situations in which the attributes, achievements, or possessions of another seem beyond our reach yet still matter a lot to us. Imagine that you despair of ever moving up to head teller, but define your status in life in terms of your place in the pecking order. Frustration and feelings of worthlessness can cause you to grow sullen, treat colleagues poorly, and lash out whenever you feel someone has slighted you at work. Now envy becomes a truly poisonous emotion that can, ironically, push you further down the pecking order or out of the workplace altogether.

Robert Vecchio, a professor of management at Notre Dame, extensively studied envy in the workplace. He found that competition for rewards, resources, and recognition drives a lot of the envy people feel on the job, much of which stems from a sense of injustice. People most susceptible to work-related envy suffer from fundamentally low self-esteem. Without strong executive brain functioning to mitigate these challenging feelings, they tend to resort to manipulative, self-serving behavior, which can create major leadership problems.

However, research has suggested that effective leadership and strong, connected organizational cultures can help mitigate some of the negative effects of envy in the workplace. For example, two 2012 studies by Michelle Duffy and colleagues demonstrate how a lack of strong interpersonal relationships play a role in the intensity of envy. Investigating the behavior of hospital workers, the researchers learned that envious workers were more likely to report committing sabotaging behaviors when their relationships were weak with co-workers. When they reported closer connections to their co-workers, those who experienced envy reported lower sabotage incident rates.

In a second study, university students completed a series of questionnaires throughout the semester rating their level of envy, the quality of their connections with other members of their workgroup, and the degree to which they or others in the group committed sabotage. Those students who admitted to feeling envious and who did not identify strongly with their workgroup reported the highest instances of sabotage, especially when they belonged to groups that reported high rates of sabotage overall. These two studies suggest that strong workplace relationships don't necessarily alleviate envious feelings, but may mitigate sabotaging behaviors often triggered by envy. The studies also suggest that when workplaces tolerate sabotaging behaviors, it can increase the chances that people will engage in the behaviors if they are feeling envious.

In a survey of more than 100 first-level supervisors conducted by Dr. Vecchio, as reported in an article in the *Windsor Star* on October 2, 2006, it was discovered that feelings of envy ran higher when supervisors demonstrated a lack of concern. These studies all suggest that strong, positive workplace connections and caring leadership can mitigate feelings of envy and malicious behavior.

In the June 18, 2010, issue of *The Guardian*, Hilary Osborne tells the story of an executive, "Lee Smith," who suffered at the hands of an envious colleague. Smith, head of marketing communications for a large American company, began working side by side with "Bob Jones," an older executive at a firm Smith's company had acquired.

Smith recalls that Jones would go behind his back by contacting Smith's direct reports and having them work on his own projects without telling Smith. Jones, jealous of his new partner's position, not only undermined Smith's authority but he made life miserable for everyone else in the office as well. When Smith complained to his American bosses, they refused to deal with the situation and allowed the sabotaging behavior to continue. Eventually Smith threw in the towel and left to start his own business.

Research confirms the notion that schadenfreude, envy, and jealousy— all emotions triggered by competition and social comparison—can grow more powerful in group situations. They serve as bonding agents, making people in the group feel more comfortable with otherwise discomfiting emotions. Since people more freely compete in group settings than in one-on-one situations, they often find themselves behaving on a team in ways they would not behave in individual competition. Playing singles tennis, we tend to compete with greater decorum and sportsmanship; put us on a football team, and we take delight when a star player from the other team gets injured and is out for the season.

What exactly can a leader do to create an environment that minimizes the negative effects of these complicated emotions among both individuals and teams?

COPING WITH THE EMOTIONS
OF A GOOD FIGHT GONE BAD

When you decide to deal with the emotions triggered by a fight gone bad, you must first address that individual's sense of self-worth and self-esteem. These issues lie at the core of a person's identity and involve some of the most raw and most powerful of human emotions. To protect that core, people may use a range of tactics, from playing the victim to acting like a gossipy teenager or even engaging in crippling sabotage. When they play the victim game, they may blame others for what they lack, wallow in self-pity, and refuse to take accountability for their situation. If they go on the attack, they will justify and rationalize their actions or deny that they have done anything wrong. In either case, the powerful emotions that attend these behaviors can blind the envious person to the damage they are doing to themselves, the target of their envy, and anyone else working nearby. This Dante-esque blindness makes it harder than usual to obtain the self-awareness you need to solve psychological problems at work, especially ones involving envy.

You can start by taking a personal inventory. If you have recently felt a little shiver of schadenfreude or have found yourself envying someone else's success, ask yourself:

- Have I been playing the victim? Have I blamed someone else for my own situation? Have I let my victim thinking prevent me from taking action to improve my situation?

- Have I verbally undermined someone whose success I envy? Do I gossip about them or spread rumors that make them look bad?

- Have I acted on my feelings by sabotaging the target of my envy?

- Have I been able to say to myself or, more courageously, to others, "Wow, I feel really jealous"?

You might also pose these same questions to a trusted adviser, coach, or even a psychotherapist who can help remove the blinding wires from your eyes. A colleague or business coach can offer unique, objective insights about behaviors you may not know you display. In any case, a third party can help you take some important steps toward respecting the rules of a good fight before you come down with a full-blown case of the *Cain and Abel* effect:

- Pinpoint the cause of your schadenfreude or envy.

- Measure the strength of your relationship with that person.

- List your emotions: resentment, anger, shame, regret, disdain, frustration, etc.

- Describe your expected outcome before you felt these emotions.

- Pinpoint the events that led up to your feeling out of control.

- Identify the people (intended and unintended) who might suffer from your actions.

- Rate your current sense of self-worth on a scale of 1 (ashamed) to 10 (proud).

- Place your behavior on a continuum from mild to outrageous.

- Consider advice you would give to a trusted friend about coping with similar emotions and behaviors.

- Identify one or two steps you can take right now to rise above your circumstances, take ownership of your situation, and achieve your desired results.

Taking these steps or chatting about them with a trusted adviser provides some of the psychological distance we need in order to regain perspective. Nothing cures a psychological problem like a healthy dose of reality. For example, had Brad done so, he may have been able to alter his attitude and behavior before it started taking a massive toll on his career and health. Identifying his feelings of anger, resentment, and envy may have led him to conclude that these perfectly normal feelings, given the situation, had nevertheless resulted in his low sense of self-worth and all those unhealthy sabotaging behaviors that hurt himself, Janet, and everyone around him. He actually did all he could to win the promotion; Janet just happened, by the luck of the draw, to win a big case first. Has the time come for him to set his sights on the next opportunity for promotion and invest his considerable energy in achieving the results he wants in the future?

PROMOTING GOOD FIGHTS

As we have seen, competitive environments in which people feel estranged from one another encourage malicious, envious behavior. To create a healthier environment that keeps the good fight from going bad, as a leader you can cultivate certain norms:

- *Supportive, Friendly Competition:* As a leader, you do want to cultivate healthy competition, but you do not want people to pit themselves against one another in a destructive way, as Brad and Janet did. Better results, greater productivity, keener motivation, and stronger performance depend on harnessing the good fight in a way that makes people feel good about the competition. Create friendly competition, but not an ultimate "win or lose" challenge among team members. Focus on how everyone's individual efforts help the entire team achieve success. The firm's partners could have reassured Brad that while Janet may have gotten there first, they would make sure he got similar opportunities soon. Janet's winning did *not* make him a loser. Remain alert for signs that people have crossed the line: unwarranted complaints about others, angry outbursts, backstabbing, finger pointing, even sabotage.

- *Transparency:* Maintain an open-door policy that encourages people to speak candidly about their feelings. When you must do something that might cause feelings of envy or schadenfreude (e.g., adding a teammate; promoting, demoting, or rewarding someone), do it openly and make your reasons perfectly clear to all concerned. If someone must win or lose, make that clear to everyone involved. If the partners at the firm had built a transparent culture and wished to retain both "rock stars" no matter who won the promotion, they would have acknowledged the potential problems up front and that would have set the ground rules that would have promoted a good fight instead of a slugfest.

115

- *Mentorship:* In his article, "Managing Envy and Jealousy in the Workplace," Dr. Robert Vecchio recommended placing star performers (who often trigger feelings of envy) in mentor roles, in which they can assuage negative emotions and emphasize the need to create collaborative, communicative team environments. Mentoring opens up the line of communication and reduces preconceived notions and assumptions that can fuel the envy flame. Good mentorship also provides opportunities for the mentor to learn from the student, which further humanizes the mentor and may reduce envy or hard feelings.

- *Balance the Scales:* Cultivate a sense of fairness and justice. Think about it. What will most assuredly incense co-workers? Seeing a colleague get credit for something he didn't do or receiving special (unwarranted) treatment. Make sure everyone understands the reward system and clearly communicate why someone has received a reward and how others can win, too. Look for injustices and swiftly correct them. Again, scan for your own biases and recognize when you unfairly grant a favor or make an exception for one person and not another.

- *Address Conflict:* Nip problems in the bud. A good leader notices the emotional nuances that occur between people. You can usually see malicious envy brewing, which the firm's partners should have seen developing in Brad. Feelings of envy make people uncomfortable, and our discomfort naturally leaks into our behaviors. The minute you see it, address it. When people know their boss really cares about and respects their feelings, they will speak up when the good fight takes a bad turn. If the partners spoke up about the spiteful feelings when they first erupted, they might have intervened before Brad stepped off the cliff.

- *Develop Team Spirit*: Invest time developing a team that "plays nice" and competes cheerfully and positively. Learn about emotional intelligence and the role it plays in teams. Marcia Hughes and James Terrell have written an excellent book on the subject: *The Emotionally Intelligent Team*. Lead the team in socializing outside of work so they can get to know each other better and form closer connections. (Remember, malicious envy will more likely spring up among disconnected people.) Create opportunities for shared responsibility and group incentives so everyone can learn from each other's different work styles and gain confidence that they can count on each other.

- *Hire Intelligently:* Dr. Vecchio suggested spending time evaluating the emotional maturity of candidates during and after the hiring process. Research supports the fact that envy most easily afflicts people who suffer from low self-esteem and have a self-serving approach to life. Look for clues during interviews. How does the candidate talk about past jobs/bosses/colleagues? Note any tendency to disparage or badmouth former teammates. Pose hypothetical situations that would test a candidate's inclination toward feelings of envy. "How would you react if you saw a teammate receive praise for something you did?" Of course, you can also do a little emotional research when you check out a candidate's references.

WRAP UP

What do Cain and Abel, and all of us who strive for success in the contemporary workplace, have in common? They, and we, all suffer from bouts of envy from time to time. Few other emotions create so much trouble. Unchecked, envy in the workplace can quickly turn healthy competition into a knock-down, drag-out fight.

Occasional feelings of schadenfreude and envy do not make you a bad person. They are natural emotions triggered by the same brain chemistry that makes us feel good when we eat our favorite candy bar.

The emotions underlying a good fight gone bad in the workplace often occur as a result of a sense of injustice, contention for resources or standing, or feelings of inferiority. A bad fight can do a lot of damage to individuals and teams. As with most psychological problems that cause damage in the workplace, you must open your eyes and see more clearly. Fortunately, both leaders and those embroiled in the bad fight can take steps to increase self-awareness and arrive at healthy solutions.

5

Why Can Ambition Sabotage Success?

A HIGHLY ACCOMPLISHED, hugely ambitious general has conquered many lands and territories in the name of his people. Clever, politically savvy, well connected, and adored by the men who serve under him, he has embarked on a rivalry of epic proportions. His name is Julius Caesar, and he has agreed to share power over the Republic with his main competitors, Crassus and Pompey. But tensions mount. The delicate balance of power tips when Caesar crosses the Rubicon River with his army. This precipitates a civil war, which Caesar will ultimately win. When he becomes the undisputed leader of Rome, Caesar basks in his glory and lives an opulent life. By declaring himself dictator for life and using traditional signs of power, he alienates the Senate. The Roman Senate frets that Caesar's ambition will lead him to demand that they anoint him King of Rome. This political change could well destroy the Senate, not to mention the entire country and its dominions. Soon, even Caesar's closest friends and allies turn against him and plot his assassination, attacking him on the steps of the Senate. After each assailant thrusts a knife into his body, his most trusted friend, Brutus, delivers the final, fatal blow to the heart.

For all of his miscalculations, Caesar made a wise choice. He picked an able successor, his great nephew and adopted son, Octavian Caesar. Following his father's assassination, Octavian pursues a steady and politically astute course of action, building alliances and demolishing rivals where required. Octavian, by now known as Caesar Augustus, gradually ascends to the position Julius had coveted, serving as the first unchallenged true Roman Emperor. He rules for nearly forty-five years, compared to his father's scant four. Although tremendously successful, Augustus never assumes the trappings of power that in some ways so consumed his adoptive father. He publicly positions himself as an adviser to the Senators, not their boss, while in fact being the true creator of the centralized Roman Empire. The outcome of this after many years of disruptive civil war is the famed Pax Romana—a period of peace for the Mediterranean people that lasts not just for his rule, but for 150 years thereafter. When Augustus dies of old age, his followers believe he has ascended to the ranks of the gods and he is thereafter worshiped as a deity.

Both men possessed great talent and each was tremendously successful, yet one was killed because of his personal ambition while the other harnessed his ambition for the welfare of all the people and won their undying loyalty and admiration. What caused these two equally talented leaders to suffer such dramatically different fates? It comes down to whether or not a leader can:

- Balance ambition with humility.

- Restrain one's ego.

- Treat others with respect.

- Create positive impressions.

- Adopt a long-term perspective of success.

The Julius Caesars of the world often end up failing because they pursue myopic success, a "nearsighted" view that defines success in terms of self-interest. The Caesar Augustuses, on the other hand, pursue *panoramic success*, defining success in terms of the "big-picture" best interests of all.

Like the other leadership issues we have examined in this book, psychology and neuroscience offer some fascinating glimpses into what works and doesn't work in the world of ambition and success. Let's look at the building blocks that can lead to triumph or doom.

SCHEMAS AND EXPECTATIONS

We all create what psychologists call *self-schemas*: personal stories we use to define ourselves. For many of us, our internal monologues are like comfort food. For others, our stories are like swallowing shards of glass, causing such pain and suffering that they interfere with our ability to function. We have all known someone, a friend or colleague, who consistently expects to fail, downplays all accomplishments, views life as a half-empty glass. Then there are those who expect to succeed no matter what the contest, positively glow with self-approval over every accomplishment, and view their life not merely as a half-full glass but as a Baccarat crystal flute brimming with Moët & Chandon champagne. Whether positive and optimistic or negative and pessimistic, our stories become so deeply ingrained, so taken for granted, they cannot be easily changed. Only with deep self-awareness can we detect the patterns and alter them in ways that will help us get more of the success we desire. The pessimist may benefit from a brighter outlook; the perennial Pollyanna may get better results with a needed dose of reality.

Schemas are like little personal instruction books that diagram our worldview. They tell us how to think, act, and relate to others. Our schemas grow out of what happens to us as we progress through life: our experiences, our cultural backgrounds, our environments, the ways our parents and family and caregivers treated us, the teachers who guided us, those we befriended along the way, and so on. Like fingerprints, no two schemas are entirely alike. When you do anything in life, you are operating according to your personal schema, whether you are driving a car, developing a romantic relationship, going about your daily work, or assuming a position of leadership.

Once you form a schema, your brain stores it as a long-term memory it will use to process personally relevant information. Ms. Positive has developed an optimistic schema about the people she meets, and that schema leads her to engage in and manage relationships easily. Ms. Negative is, of course, more pessimistic. Her schema causes her to struggle with her relationships, often missing great opportunities. As we create experiences according to our schemas, they constantly reinforce the correctness of our differing views.

When information comes in or experiences occur that are similar to our existing story, the brain *assimilates* the new information, often reinforcing our schemas. Ms. Negative's colleagues go to lunch without her. Although it was an accidental oversight on the part of her colleagues, because she was in a meeting when they took their lunch break, this incident is assimilated into her already pessimistic schema, which strengthens her view that people do not enjoy her company.

Sometimes, an experience does not fit our preexisting schema and we must make some adjustments. Ms. Positive wrestles with a nightmarish workplace relationship so she may need to slightly adjust her schema. The same holds true for Ms. Negative when she falls into what seems like the perfect workplace relationship. Psychologists call these *accommodations*. We find it easier to remember and incorporate into our worldview assimilated information that reinforces our schema or requires only a little accommodation.

The key word here is *little*. We reject and disregard information that drastically contradicts our schemas. We might say to ourselves, "Oh, that's so rare it'll never happen again." Doing this opens us up to a highly biased, if not distorted, view of reality, which, of course, can get us into a lot of hot water.

Ms. Positive and Ms. Negative's stories create highly biased views of the world. If you listen carefully to someone's reactions to events, you will learn a lot about the speaker's schema and the bias it produces. As we saw in Chapter 1, people tend to practice confirmation bias, interpreting an event in a way that matches their schemas. Over time, we can even distort reality so much we come to believe that an event confirmed our bias when, in fact, it did not. What does this have to do with success and ambition?

SUCCESS SCHEMAS

Given the fact that we construct schemas for everything that happens in our life, it shouldn't come as much of a surprise that we also adopt our own schemas for success. Our schema for success is tightly intertwined with our self-schema, making it a very potent player in our mental outlook and one highly susceptible to bias. Our schemas develop as a result of:

- The obvious and not-so-obvious messages our caregivers convey about success

- The interpretations we make of success, comparing our caregivers to other people

- The way we regard ourselves in relation to others

- The success messages delivered by the media 24/7/365

- The messages of achievement and ambition we learn inside and outside the classroom

I recently co-led a workshop with a group of undergraduate students at a leading business school. Students who graduate from this school often go on to what many would consider highly successful careers as leaders of industry. At the end of the workshop, I conducted a series of one-on-one coaching sessions with the students. We could discuss anything during the coaching sessions, but we often found ourselves chatting about what it takes to build a successful career. Most of these bright and engaging students had set their sights on investment banking. When I probed the origin of their decision, most of the students admitted that they simply liked the idea of making a lot of money or said, "That's the track I'm *expected* to take." They had defined success in terms of building a fortune or fulfilling someone else's expectations. As I dug deeper, I found that few of them could tell me exactly what an investment banker does.

One student, an entrepreneur at heart, told me that before entering this undergraduate program, he had already designed and sold a technology product and a few startup ventures. When we discussed these business experiences, his eyes lit up and he spoke with passion. When we talked about his career plans, he dispassionately said, "Investment banker." When I challenged this goal, he confessed that he had chosen that route because he figured that ten years spent toiling in that job would earn him enough money to do what he really wanted to do in life. "What about your passion for technology startups," I asked? Hadn't he bankrolled a good deal of money doing what he loved to do? He shrugged and said, "What's love got to do with it?"

Many of the students stressed cold calculations about their futures. Emotional attachments to other people and ideas, social and romantic relationships, and other warm, fuzzy feelings would get in the way of fulfilling their ambition.

I also got a chance to talk with a few professors and students from the school's graduate business program. Each one told me that the students who come directly from the school's undergraduate program place less value on their relationships with their peers and tend to obsess over their careers. Basic human traits like empathy and relatedness are devalued, with being the best ranked higher.

Like all schemas, those that governed the lives of the students I met had arisen from an intertwining of social, cultural, developmental, and environmental factors. The resulting powerful neural network of beliefs shaped their definition of success (investment banking = money = success). Those deeply ingrained beliefs will ultimately shape their behaviors (e.g., choosing a profession according to the expectations of others, measuring success with a monetary yardstick, discounting or delaying endeavors about which they feel passionate, and limiting socialization experiences that do not obviously advance their careers). The culture of the business school, the inherent social comparison that occurs among naturally competitive students, and messages received from parents and teachers and mentors, coupled with a general lack of exposure to life and the wider world, led them to adopt rather cold, narrow, and myopic success schemas.

These students, like all of us, will develop their schemas as they evolve and gain more diverse experiences and meet a wider variety of people. While their success schemas can and will assimilate and accommodate new information, they will find them stubbornly resistant to change unless they develop a keen sense of self-awareness. Four psychological principles help explain why bias and distortion tend to make our schemas relatively static:

- We quickly and efficiently process information that matches our current self and success schemas.

- We tend to retrieve and remember information that supports our self and success schemas.

- We tend to resist information that contradicts our self and success schemas.

- We shape our perceptions and expectations of others, our environment, and ourselves according to our schemas.

No wonder we become prisoners of a narrow set of views and actions. As Deepak Chopra once suggested, "We have approximately 60,000 thoughts in a day. Unfortunately, 95 percent of them are thoughts we had the day before." How does a leader break out of this mental jail? It often takes a virtual slap upside (or inside) the head in the form of a life-altering event or an intense commitment to self-awareness.

Three business students stood out from the crowd. They had radically different backgrounds, but they shared one thing in common: Each brought a life-defining experience to his or her definition of success. Roger had lost both of his parents at an early age, Emmanuel had become a student of faith, and Divia had grown up in a culture that placed supreme emphasis on relationship building and respect for others. Although none of them could fully articulate how they saw their career paths unfolding, all three talked about their desires to create change, to inspire and move others forward, and to engage in socially responsible behavior for the good of all. They all, not surprisingly, struggled with the highly self-centered business-school culture. Divia confessed to a frustrating sense of "outsidership" with respect to her peers.

Even if Roger, Emmanuel, and Divia did not rank at the top of their class academically, I'd hire them in a heartbeat. I could happily see myself working for or with any one of them. Placed in leadership positions, they would likely define success more in terms of the general welfare of the group than of their own interests. I call this view of success the panoramic schema. Panoramic suggests a wide and inclusive perspective.

I call the self-centered or focused schema held by so many of the other business-school students, *myopic schema. Myopic,* a word that literally means "nearsighted," suggests a narrow and exclusive perspective. In contrast, a *panoramic schema* encompasses the "big picture." If you imagine a spectrum, with myopic on the left and panoramic on the right, most of us fall somewhere in the middle. Those who live on the far left of the spectrum often find it harder to sustain long-term success than do those who operate on the far right.

MYOPIC SUCCESS

Julius Caesar's myopic approach to success, fueled by his personal schema and a lack of self-awareness, caused him to fail to weigh the needs of "us" required for success in government and business. Unless *all* stakeholders in an organization, including employees, customers, shareholders, partners, the community in which the organization operates, the environment, and the world at large succeed, the leader will ultimately fail.

A myopic approach to success fuels harmful and shortsighted leadership practices and unbridled ambition. It can lead to autocracy, abuse of power, and the violation of civil rights. When it does, the leader eventually suffers the loss of people's trust, goodwill, and energy. In the worst-case scenario, a myopic leader ends up losing the very power he craves, leaving in his wake a weakened and even dying organization.

In a classic example of such a ruinous decline, Sunbeam hired the notorious "Chainsaw" Al Dunlap to take the helm as CEO in 1996, giving the ruthless turnaround expert the mandate to improve organizational effectiveness. Dunlap, who fancied himself "Rambo in Pinstripes," had developed a reputation for issuing withering tirades to underperforming employees and chopping the head off anyone who fell short of his expectations. Corporate boards loved him because he worked tirelessly to benefit shareholders. This time, Dunlap set unrealistically ambitious goals for Sunbeam, then fired all executives who failed to meet them.

Like a wildfire, fear and repression soon engulfed the entire organization. Sunbeam's people became dispirited and disheartened as massive layoffs ensued. Wall Street turned its back on the company. The stock price, after initially experiencing an impressive bump up and hitting its all-time peak, then crashed. Within two hellish years, Dunlap's reign of terror at Sunbeam came to an end. His slash-and-burn behavior earned him a class-action lawsuit on behalf of the shareholders who had initially supported him. *Et tu, Brute?* Accounting fraud uncovered at Sunbeam led to a civil suit launched by the Securities and Exchange Commission (SEC), which ultimately barred Dunlap from ever again serving as chair or director of any public company. The once-mighty tyrant retired to the solitary splendor of his massive mansion, surrounded by sculptures of animal predators. Al's former friends and colleagues rarely saw him anymore, and he no longer had a relationship with his son.

Dunlap ascended to power by stepping on those he should have served. His lack of empathy and his predatory tactics had enabled him for many years to take the reins of many troubled companies and drive them to financial success, but he finally hit a wall. His personal and professional crash epitomizes the hazards of a myopic success schema.

You need not look far to find examples of myopic leadership at work in organizations around the world, both large and small. They often make headlines in the wake of a disastrous self-centered lapse in judgment or a breathtaking abuse of power. A rogue's list could include Richard Nixon, Bernie Madoff, British Petroleum's Tony Hayward, Lehman Brothers' Richard Fuld, Boise Cascade's William Agee. Such behavior should come as no surprise. The *Harvard Business Review*, in citing a 2007 article that appeared in the *Journal of Business Ethics*, noted that, "31 of 34 directors surveyed (each of whom served on an average of six Fortune 200 boards) said they'd cut down a mature forest or release a dangerous, unregulated toxin into the environment in order to increase profits. Whatever they could legally do to maximize shareholder wealth, they believed it was their duty to do."

Serving shareholders' interests and amassing a personal fortune do not a villain make. What turns an ambitious leader into a bad character or even a criminal? More often than not, it's an unbridled drive to serve oneself at the expense of all others. It's not fame and fortune. It's the *path* to fame and fortune. So how do leaders start down the path to wrack and ruin? It all comes down to the lies we tell ourselves.

LIES WE TELL OURSELVES

Have you ever swiped a few Post-it note pads or highlighter markers from work? Or claimed a business expense that really didn't involve any business? Think of an incident where you sneaked a forbidden cigarette, downed one-too-many drinks, broke your diet with a chocolate cake. I'm no Mother Teresa myself, and whatever little transgression I commit, I quickly come up with a handy excuse to exonerate myself. "They don't pay me enough anyway" or "The government already gets enough of my paycheck" or "Just one Marlboro or Heineken or Sara Lee cake won't kill me."

Psychologists call this sort of reasoning *cognitive dissonance*, a concept proposed by Leon Festinger in the 1950s. An extremely powerful psychological phenomenon, it plays a leading role in the development of biases, distortions, self-justification, rationalization, and self-serving myopia. Cognitive dissonance means that our schemas impel us to hold onto our existing attitudes and beliefs while avoiding disharmony (or dissonance). Most of us feel highly motivated to preserve a stable, positive self-image throughout our lives, even when we experience major challenges to our belief that we are at heart good, decent, and reasonable; that we treat others respectfully and honor all relationships; and that we weigh the consequences of our decisions. Dissonance occurs when we encounter a situation that undermines

130

those beliefs. The dissonance produces a feeling of discomfort, which can often lead to an alteration in the basic belief as a way of reducing the discomfort and restoring harmony to the heart. We all know a common example: Betty hits Bernice and, when challenged about this bad behavior, claims, "She *made* me do it when she touched my doll!"

In 1958, Judson Mills conducted a famous study of cheating behavior with a group of sixth graders. Mills administered a test to the group that none could pass without cheating. Before administering the test, Mills measured each student's attitudes about cheating. He then passed out the test to the sixth graders and left the room so they could take it unsupervised, but with a hidden camera recording the session. Some of the students cheated, some did not. Following the test, Mills again measured each student's attitude toward cheating. Not surprisingly, Mills found that those students who cheated grew more lenient in their attitude about cheating, while those who did not cheat felt even more negative about cheaters. The results supported the notion that, in order to reduce cognitive dissonance and feel better about their choice, whether they cheated or not, the students justified their actions to retain their self-concept. Interestingly, the results of the study also suggest that the harshest opponents of a given position may be the ones who were tempted toward that same position at one time. We all know a former smoker who expresses the harshest opinion of anyone who lights up in public. When it comes to rationalization, we all do it.

To cope with cognitive dissonance, we use three different tactics to reconcile disharmony. First, we can change our beliefs ("Cheating is okay"). However, our schemas make it hard for us to alter our basic beliefs and attitudes. Second, we can change our actions ("I'll never cheat again"). While powerful emotional motivators such as guilt or anxiety can encourage us to whip our behaviors into shape, we often tamp down feelings of guilt or anxiety over an action or decision because we can easily train ourselves not to feel that way. Guilt seldom sustains learning over the long haul. The third and most common tactic for resolving cognitive dissonance involves changing our perception or memory of an action ("Since everyone cheated on that test, why shouldn't I?"). Reconceptualizing the behavior provides a pleasant and convenient way to deal with disharmony, and it supports our natural human desire to see ourselves as basically good and reasonable people.

In another famous study conducted in 1956, researcher Jack Brehm asked women to rate various appliances, then to take home one of two they had found equally attractive. Twenty minutes later, Brehm asked each woman to re-rate the products, and without fail, the women rated the chosen appliance higher than the one they had previously rated as equal. Brehm concluded that the women reconciled their post-decision dissonance by distorting their perceptions in a way that would help them feel better about their decisions. Whether you're rating appliances or dealing with a more momentous decision, dissonance tends to prompt attitudinal change in situations where mental conflicts are highly self-relevant, more meaningful, and ultimately can result in the greatest consequences. Since leadership represents one of the most self-relevant, meaningful, and powerfully consequential positions in our world, cognitive dissonance frequently influences a leader's decision making, thinking processes, moral and ethical behavior, and ultimately how she or he approaches ambition and success.

DEFENSE MECHANISMS

Given our imperfections as human beings, our minds have created a whole host of defense mechanisms and biases to cope with cognitive dissonance, including *self-justification*, *rationalization*, and the *self-serving bias*. While we readily observe those behaviors in others, we find it much harder to see them in ourselves. Imagine a company's top executives announcing good or bad quarterly results:

- "Buoyant market forces saved the company this quarter."

- "Weak market forces are responsible for this quarter's poor results."

You never hear the first statement: leaders admitting that market forces, rather than their own skill, produced good results. On the other hand, you hear the second statement all the time: leaders blaming the market rather than themselves for bad results. This type of self-serving bias runs rampant in business as leadership takes credit for success (*self-enhancing bias*) while denying any responsibility for failure. Just like self-justification and rationalization, the self-serving bias protects our egos, enables us to confirm our self-worth, and helps us resolve cognitive dissonance.

Why do we resist admitting failure? Why do we avoid taking full responsibility? When our brains cannot assimilate or accommodate an event or circumstance into neat, happy boxes, especially ones that provoke a state of cognitive dissonance, as failure invariably does, some people will do everything possible to bias their thought process to make themselves feel better. Most of us do it on a small scale, rationalizing a small transgression such as crossing the street against the light "because I didn't see any cars coming." However, some do it on a large scale, like justifying a horrible business decision or a major breach of ethics, "because I was just doing what the Board hired me to do: Make a lot of money."

We naturally use both internal and external self-justification to defend our minds from dissonance. With *internal justification*, a decision maker justifies the decision to herself ("I stole that pack of gum because the store overcharges for it and won't miss one tiny sale"). With *external self-justification*, a person wants to appear rational to others in order to save face ("You're right, I did forget to pay for the pack of gum, but it's too late to go back now"). In the first instance, you apologize to yourself; in the second, you apologize to your companion. In both cases, the decision maker ducks responsibility for any wrongdoing. "It's not my fault" or "She made me do it" or "Everyone else does it" or "It's no big deal."

Self-justification usually involves rationalization, concocting a "logical" explanation for a behavior in order to make the action more compatible with our self-image and our beliefs, values, or opinions. We can rationalize our own behavior or the behavior of others, spinning our own or our companion's little shoplifting spree to make it seem like a perfectly rational thing to do. In addition to behaviors, we also rationalize feelings, beliefs, and values, providing logical explanations to ourselves and everyone else. We strive to make ourselves and those close to us look decent and good at all costs. "Jane and I may have made a little mistake, but at heart we are exemplary human beings."

As natural as eating and sleeping and breathing, these defense mechanisms enable us to live with ourselves by adjusting our perceptions of what we do to match our positive image. The more skillfully we manufacture the self-justification or rationalization, the less likely we will suffer the pain of dissonance. Some people will go to great lengths to justify and/or rationalize their thought processes and their actions. A colleague of mine, Ben, recently told me about a leader, Paul, with whom he was conducting a 360-degree assessment and follow-up coaching. Paul had come to Ben because his people had begun rebelling over what Ben called "personality issues." The results of the 360-degree assessment told the story: Paul's direct reports, peers, and even his own boss described him as "difficult," "uncaring," "arrogant," "ineffective as a leader," and a "terrible decision maker." Ben, the very soul of tact, shared this feedback with Paul. As Ben told me later, "Paul just sat there stone faced, except for this tiny smirk." As the session progressed, Ben realized that nothing he said was getting through to his client. When he more forcefully nudged Paul to respond to the feedback, Paul launched into a long-winded explanation of the reasons the shortcomings of other people made him act the way he did and that his people were fools for not appreciating his excellent, if stern, leadership style. It all boiled down to, "I'm right; they're wrong." His self-justification and rationalization had become so rock-solid that he never did alter his behavior and soon ended up looking for a new job—and a new coach.

No matter how much bad behavior, faulty decisions, abusive leadership, and unethical practices some leaders commit, they will not change their ways. They will, instead, do whatever it takes to preserve their positive view of themselves. Although the lies we tell others and ourselves, from little white lies to great big whoppers, reflect natural human tendencies, they can do a lot of harm when wrapped in the cloak of a myopic schema. See what happened to Nixon, obsessed with "me, me, me," and Al Dunlap, hell-bent on serving a relatively small group of stakeholders. By contrast, those who go about their business according to a panoramic schema, as Augustus did, working on behalf of "us" rather than "me," enjoy a built-in control over leadership abuses and the havoc they wreak on an organization.

PANORAMIC SUCCESS

*"If I can see further than anyone else, it is only
because I am standing on the shoulders of giants."*
—ISAAC NEWTON

Leaders who work with a panoramic view of success do not operate with total selflessness, but they do define their own success within the context of the bigger picture. If "we" don't succeed, "I" don't succeed.

Researchers Harold Harung and colleagues found that top-performing leaders demonstrated a higher integration of electrical brain activity, more mature moral reasoning, and more frequent peak experiences than their underperforming counterparts. To support their findings, they quoted Joan Marques's 2006 article entitled "Wakefulness: The Decisive Leadership Skill," which appeared in the journal *Management Services*: "An awakened leader maintains a high level of alertness in every regard." According to Marques, a top-performing or "awakened" leader has a deep understanding of his or her own drives and motives and how they impact and relate to all aspects of an organization, from tasks to people to an entire organizational culture.

With regard to psychological development, Harung and colleagues highlight the difference between conventional (80% of today's adult population) and postconventional (10% of today's adult population) stages of adult ego development (the remaining 10% exist at the preconventional/ stunted development stage). The theories of adult development generally describe how our existing schemas evolve, or don't evolve, over time and inform an increasingly complex perception of our world, others, and ourselves. According to psychologist Susanne Cook-Greuter, each stage of development emerges from the synthesis of doing (coping, needs and ends, purposes), being (awareness, experience, affect), and thinking (conceptions, knowledge, interpretations), with each new level containing the previous one. As we advance in age, our brains acquire and integrate more and more information, which in most cases increases our psychological awareness. Harung describes the greater awareness that arises during the progression from the conventional to the postconventional stage by poignantly stating that a leader evolves "from efficiency (doing things right) to effectiveness (doing the right thing)."

The best leaders evolve from a myopic view (conventional) to a panoramic (postconventional) view as they gain more experience. Researchers David Rooke and William Torbert presented groundbreaking research on this topic in an article published by the *Harvard Business Review* in 2005. Rooke and Torbert, utilizing twenty-five years of research into the accomplishments of thousands of leaders working in a wide range of industries across America and Europe, identified seven leadership transformations that loosely correlate to the different stages of adult development. They found that leaders exhibit a wide range of "ways in which one interprets their surroundings and reacts when their power or safety is challenged." They found that leaders who have reached a more advanced and comprehensive stage of development (loosely tied to the postconventional stage of adult development) "showed a consistent capacity to innovate and successfully transform their organizations." The researchers also found that only a small percentage of leaders actually attain these levels, because reaching higher levels of self-awareness requires tremendous effort and personal risk.

Why do so few leaders adopt a panoramic approach to success? Part of the answer lies in the fact that every leader must deal with so many competing forces and priorities, both internal and external. When you are working inside a tornado, it's hard to step back and see yourself, your stakeholders, and your situation clearly. Not only must you engage in a certain amount of self-preservation in order to retain your position, you must also look after the best interests of your employees, your organizational culture, your customers, your shareholders, your board, your community, and even your planet. In a lot of cases, making a decision to satisfy the needs of one will disappoint another. Justifying and rationalizing all those tricky decisions allows for relative peace of mind. Too little rationalization may drive you crazy; too much may drive everyone else crazy. Welcome to the leadership tightrope.

It takes a keen sense of balance to stay on the tightrope, and a keen sense of balance depends on taking personal responsibility and public accountability for your actions.

RESPONSIBILITY AND ACCOUNTABILITY

"If you could kick the person in the pants responsible
for most of your trouble, you wouldn't sit for a month."
—THEODORE ROOSEVELT

In 1973, Ray Anderson began building the company that would eventually become Interface, Inc. While specializing in modular floor coverings for business, industry, and the home, the company used a traditional industrial model and grew rapidly through acquisitions and growth. In 1994, something changed. Anderson was preparing to speak at a meeting when he found inspiration in Paul Hawken's book *The Ecology of Commerce.* Hawken blamed business and industry for the decline of the biosphere, and suggested that only the destroyers wielded enough power to extricate the human race from its eventual demise. Hawken's ideas so impressed Anderson that he wove them into his speech the following day, challenging himself and the company to develop a strategic commitment to sustainability that would create a new, postindustrial business model. Anderson then practiced what he had preached. He adopted "a cyclical model mimicking nature" with which Interface would only take from the earth what could be renewed naturally and rapidly. Proclaiming his new motto, "Take nothing, do not harm," Anderson began leading as a "recovering plunderer."

Since its founding, Interface has grown into a billion-dollar corporation, operating across four continents and selling to 110 countries. A major force in sustainability, it has won accolades from *Fortune* magazine as one of the "Most Admired Companies in America" and the "100 Best Companies to Work For." Ray Anderson died in 2011, leaving behind the lasting legacy of a better company and a better world. His personal transformation proves that a leader can successfully evolve a myopic approach to business into a more panoramic one that promotes a much broader definition of success. Such qualities, as outlined in the company's vision and mission statement, included:

> Vision: To be the first company that, by its deeds, shows the entire industrial world what sustainability is in all its dimensions: People, process, product, place and profits—by 2020—and in doing so we will become restorative through the power of influence.

> Mission: Interface® will become the first name in commercial and institutional interiors worldwide through its commitment to *people, process, product, place and profits.* We will strive to create an organization wherein all people are accorded unconditional respect and dignity; one that allows each person to continuously learn and develop. We will focus on product (which includes service) through constant emphasis on process quality and engineering, which we will combine with careful attention to our customers' needs so as always to deliver superior value to our customers, thereby maximizing all stakeholders' satisfaction. We will honor the places where we do business by endeavoring to become the first name in industrial ecology, a corporation that cherishes nature and restores the envi-

ronment. Interface will lead by example and validate by results, including profits, leaving the world a better place than when we began, and we will be restorative through the power of our influence in the world.

Anderson's panoramic leadership brought success to employees, shareholders, the environment, and the bottom line. He served his organization as a good steward. In fact, we might use "stewardship" to refer to the panoramic approach to leadership.

Morela Hernandez, professor at the Foster School of Business, defines stewardship as:

> Attitudes and behaviors that place the long-term best interests of a group ahead of personal goals that serve an individual's self-interests. It exists to the extent that organizational actors take personal responsibility for the effects of organizational actions on stakeholder welfare. The issue of balance is a key part of taking personal responsibility; in working toward communal welfare, organizational actors aim to balance their obligations to stakeholders inside and outside the organization while upholding a broader commitment to societal and universal moral norms.

Note the emphasis on *balance*, a term that applies to so many of the leadership attributes and problems we have discussed in this book. Responsibility also characterizes the most effective leadership styles. For our purposes here, responsibility refers to an *internal* sense of obligation to ensure the welfare of all stakeholders. The well-balanced leader feels the need to juggle many balls, balancing the leader's own success with the success of the people the leader serves. Accountability, on the other hand, refers to the *external* forces that measure the degree to which the leader keeps all those balls in the air: "I take responsibility for the welfare of the group" versus "I accept accountability for the results of my actions." The two form an alloy that is stronger than its independent elements. If a young woman named Bethany accepts an assignment to lead her work team, she must:

- Expand her understanding of group and social dynamics and increase her self-awareness in order to become increasingly adept at responding to the ever-changing nature of her own, her team's, and her organization's needs.

- Challenge the natural psychological processes that strive to protect her ego, ameliorating the typical biases of justification, rationalization, and other forms of self-protective thinking.

- Generate new ways of thinking and approaching problems and solutions by balancing her own feelings and ideas with those of her teammates.

- Accept the positive, negative, and even unintended consequences of her decisions and actions.

- Develop a holistic vision, taking ownership of the needs of all stakeholders, yet making an unpopular decision when the situation requires her to do so.

- Commit to a team culture that emphasizes responsibility and accountability at all levels.

- Track accountability for results for both herself and her team.

When Bethany takes personal responsibility for her behavior and decisions she will find herself resorting less frequently to the lies we tell ourselves. In fact, her expanded self-awareness will help shape a more accurate self-image. Her commitment to personal responsibility also enables her to do the right thing as well as just do the thing right. When she takes true accountability and responsibility for both the way she goes about her job and the results she seeks, she will more willingly accept the fact that she and her group will be called to account for *all* their actions and choices.

COUNTERACTING THE LIES

Shifting from a myopic to a panoramic approach to success and leadership takes a lot of willpower and an extreme commitment to counteracting the lies that we tell ourselves. Some of these lies are not bad or unproductive, especially the "little white lies" that motivate us to arrive at good panoramic decisions. However, some of the lies prevent us from doing our jobs in the way we need to be doing them.

It's no easy task. Most of us spend a lifetime preserving our self-image by ignoring the negative consequences of our thoughts, beliefs, perceptions, and behaviors. We grow so comfortable in the cocoon of self-protection we have built for ourselves we cannot easily step outside and see the larger world. To gain perspective, you need to look for the clues that reveal that a self-protective belief or behavior does more harm than good. And you need to ask yourself, "Why do I do what I do?"

UNCOVERING MOTIVES

The self-protective lies we tell ourselves tend to hide in the dark corners of our mind, making it quite difficult to shine the bright light of self-awareness on them. It usually helps to invite a mix of trusted people to help you do it. Select people who know you in different contexts: your colleagues, direct reports, boss, family members, spouse or significant other, friends, personal trainer, or (ahem) therapist. Tell the person you want absolute honesty, then ask the simple question, "What do you think motivates me?"

I can't overemphasize this point: Make sure your crew of respondents understands that you require complete candor. As you record their answers, note the context. Your mother will see you differently than will your long-time colleague at work. But this is also true: People will color their answers with their own self-protective biases, distortions, and rationalizations. Still, whether you like what you hear or not, perceptions can influence people as much as pure reality. If someone perceives you as a control freak, you must deal with that perception, even if you know it does not usually describe the way you operate. The *appearance* of impropriety is as bad as impropriety itself. Resist your natural urge to defend yourself.

In the spirit of "Physician, heal thyself," I'll let down my guard and share my own experience with this exercise. Before I began, I jotted down what I think motivates me:

- To influence people and the world on a large scale

- To help people understand themselves

- To earn credibility in order to do so

- To live my life passionately and fully

I believe that these four motivations have translated into the work I do and the professional and personal challenges I take on. However, when I posed the question about my motivation to trusted advisers (friends, family, colleagues, employees, people who have attended my professional presentations), I received both expected and surprising feedback:

Phrases Describing Nicole's Motivation

- Seeking accomplishment for accomplishment's sake

- Seeking thrills

- Fixing problems for people by offering creative problem solutions

- Fearing complacency and stagnation

- Keeping busy

- Creating drama and drawing the attention of others

- Connecting with and helping people

- Needing a constant sense of striving and achievement

- Helping people overcome their true or imagined limitations

- Uniting people

- Desiring control

- Seeking power

- Loving coffee

- Seeking recognition

- Influencing people and the pleasure that comes from that

- Respecting professionalism

- Attracting the love and respect of others

- Honoring the loss of her parents with her ambition to succeed

While I found all of the positive comments reassuring, I initially resisted those that did not perfectly match up with my perception of myself. Me, a control freak? Not me. Someone who must keep moving just for the sake of keeping busy? No way. A woman driven by childhood loss? I don't think so. Drama queen? Give me a break. The more I thought about it, though, the more I came to understand why those around me had developed those perceptions. I vowed to keep a closer eye on my behavior, reducing actions that center on "me, myself, and I" (the myopic view) and cultivating those that revolve around "you and we" (the panoramic view).

Whatever your beliefs about your own motivation, no matter how much they parallel or diverge from the honest opinions of others, you should spend some time contemplating your motivations with an eye toward making desired adjustments in your thinking and behavior. As a role model (you can never *not* lead), your actions send signals to your people about the behaviors you and the organization encourage and respect. If you grow, your people grow.

USING COGNITIVE DISSONANCE AS A TOOL

Cognitive dissonance offers a fine tool for making mental adjustments. When you chose to engage in self-reflection and ponder the ways you naturally or willfully distort reality, you have taken the first crucial step toward greater self-awareness. Self-awareness always precedes any transformational change in thinking and behavior. Do you ever find yourself explaining and defending your actions, justifying your behavior, rationalizing the negative consequences of your actions, making excuses, finger pointing, or saying to yourself and others anything that suggests you might be ducking responsibility and accountability?

"Yeah, but I…"

"It's not my fault…"

"It's beyond my control…"

"It was bound to happen anyway…"

"I'll let it slide just this once…"

"This is the way I always do it…"

"She made me do it…"

"I can't do that…"

"I see everyone else doing it…"

When you spot your defense shields going up, pause for a minute. Listen carefully to what you said. Can you think of a way to discuss the situation that replaces the old perpendicular pronoun "I" with the more inclusive "we"?

"Let's see if we can figure out what went wrong…"

"It's time we stop playing the blame game and get back on track…"

"Since we own this problem, let's take steps to solve it…"

"We need to learn from this…"

"We can do better…"

Once you catch yourself in the act of self-defense in the wake of failure, try using this simple exercise to get yourself thinking in a more panoramic manner:

Step One: Challenge your assumptions. Try to disprove, rather than prove, your hypotheses. Since confirmation bias makes it incredibly hard to do this, bring the decision to your trusted advisers, asking them to spot potential roadblocks and offer alternative solutions.

Step Two: Consider the impact of this particular decision on all the stakeholders involved, including your employees, the organizational culture, the customers, the community, the environment, and your shareholders.

Step Three: Get feedback from the people most deeply affected by your decision. Again, fight your urge to explain away the feedback. Remember the old saying, "We have two ears and one mouth for a reason, use them proportionally."

I offer one last piece of advice. Never shy away from saying, "I was wrong." Leaders hate to admit their failings, but doing so makes people respect you more than all the rationalizations and justifications in the world.

WRAP UP

Imagine you have reached retirement age and plan to sail off into the sunset next year. What legacy will you leave in your wake? Or, suppose your career will abruptly end in fifteen minutes. How would people remember you, as a Julius Caesar or Al Dunlap type or an Augustus Caesar or Ray Anderson type?

In either case, your footprints will be imprinted on that path to success. It comes down to the choices you make. Do you let unrelenting internal and external forces, your schemas, defenses, financial, political, and social pressures, lead you down the myopic path to self-fulfillment and, possibly, self-destruction? Or do you harness those forces for the greater good of all?

6

Why Do People Resist Change?

IN ITS 131-YEAR HISTORY, Kodak's brand name and products became integrated into our life and language with memorable moments captured on film as a "Kodak Moment." This industrial giant completely dominated its industry. Consistently rated as one of the country's most valuable brands, Kodak held a 90 percent share of film and 85 percent share of camera sales in the United States. As early as 1917, the company boasted, "If it isn't an Eastman, it isn't a Kodak."

In 1975, Kodak innovators developed one of the first digital cameras, an accomplishment that should have positioned the company to extend its dominance to the new world of digital photography. Larry Matteson, a former Kodak executive, wrote a detailed report in 1979 outlining how the market would switch from film to digital, beginning with government reconnaissance, progressing to professional photography, and ultimately, to the mass market by 2010. His report proved prophetic. Yet, despite Kodak's extensive expertise, massive resources, and unrivaled past success, Sony, a major competitor, seized the lead by launching its digital camera in the early 1980s. It took Eastman Kodak almost twenty years to make a serious foray into the digital market. Although its EasyShare line enjoyed some modest success, the digital market zoomed past Kodak. The next evolution of digital photography and high-quality camera phones would deliver the knockout punch.

Dr. Ziggy Switkowski, who worked at Eastman Kodak from 1978 to 1996, and served as the chairman and chief executive of Australasian operations from 1992 to 1996, summed it up in a January 6, 2012, interview with *The Australian*: "Kodak's biggest failing was not identifying that the future of the high-margin chemical imaging business was going to end. You had a company whose leaders were all from that side of the house and whose strategy was to optimize returns ultimately for a business that would become extinct." He goes on to say, "To make the call to go into new businesses when your legacy business is in terminal decline is a breathtakingly difficult one to make—but when your business is in that position, then you must adapt in order to survive."

Kodak filed for bankruptcy in January 2012. Why did this once-mighty giant become a timid mouse, blindly resisting change and failing to see its future?

One major reason: The mentality of Kodak's leaders could not get past "This is the way it's always been done." It's deeply ingrained in human nature to develop and hold onto habits, both good and bad, because they provide a warm, comfortable cocoon of safety. We find it amazingly easy to turn our backs on compelling reasons to change, whether it's a threat to our health from eating junk food and smoking cigarettes or to the danger posed to our business by market shifts or declining revenue. In their book *Immunity to Change*, Robert Kegan and Lisa Lahey outline the basic human processes related to our universal resistance to adopting a new way of thinking or behaving. They argue that the reason change is so difficult is that we develop habits that are adaptive over time. By that they mean beginning in childhood, we tend to shed habits that don't serve us well but hang on tightly to those habits that provide us comfort or safety. These persistent habits are able to endure even the most vicious assaults long past their expiration date.

When it comes to changing almost anything (a belief, a prejudice, a hairstyle, or even friends), basic psychology and the way the brain works can interfere with critical thinking and decision making.

It happens because:

- We seldom welcome change gladly.

- The brain's hard wiring predisposes us to habitual, routine behavior and decision making.

- We let psychological biases influence our reaction to change and our ability to make decisions that cause change.

Fortunately, you can learn to feel more comfortable with change by changing your brain and altering your biases. Of course, as Kegan points out, you'll find it a lot harder to do with habits that have become as comfortable and familiar as an old pair of slippers. As with every other topic we've discussed in this book, arming yourself with heightened self-awareness and knowledge of what makes you and other people tick will give you a leg up when it comes to challenging yourself and others to make important changes.

RESISTANCE

In the May 1, 2005, issue of *Fast Company*, Alan Deutschman wrote a fascinating article, "Change or Die," describing the IBM conference "Global Innovation Outlook," where leading thinkers proposed solutions to big problems. Deutschman highlighted Dr. Edward Miller, dean of the medical school and CEO of the hospital at John Hopkins University, as he addressed the crisis in health care, talking about patients with the type of potentially fatal heart disease for which heart surgeons routinely perform bypass surgery. Around 600,000 patients undergo this surgery every year in the United States, while another 1.3 million receive angioplasties that open clogged arteries.

According to Dr. Miller, of those who undergo coronary-artery bypass surgery, half will experience arteries that clog up again within a few years. Those who receive angioplasties will develop blockages within a few months. Both conditions will lead to further surgery. Not good odds. A patient could lower those odds by adopting a healthier lifestyle. Research has consistently shown that 90 percent of people who have undergone coronary-artery bypass surgery do not change their lifestyle, despite the fact that they have just received the scare of their lives. Change, it would seem, scares people more than death. The same holds true for other personal habits: smoking, poor diet, sedentary lifestyles, not buckling the seatbelt, and texting while driving. Even when faced with life or death, most of us will still resist change. Why would leaders find it any less scary to change bad corporate habits?

Kodak's resistance to change puts it in a pretty big club that also includes Blockbuster Video. On September 23, 2010, Blockbuster, the company that provides home video and video game rentals through brick-and-mortar rental shops, filed for bankruptcy. In the firm's heyday, its customers recognized its big blue and yellow sign, expecting and receiving a reliable and enjoyable shopping experience. Then along came Netflix. By the time Blockbuster reacted to the threat in 2004 with an online DVD rental delivery service, it had already put one foot squarely in the grave.

Why do individuals, teams, and entire organizational cultures resist, avoid, or even fatally delay changing "the way we do things around here"? The reasons may include toxic and inert cultures, myopic decision making, poor information, financial fear, and ignorance or neglect of market demands, to name a few. Organizations, like all living organisms, function as complex systems with unique characteristics. Although you can make some changes easily, you will find others challenging because some deep-seated psychological and neurological factors cause resistance, avoidance, or delay, even when the change makes perfect sense. In many cases, no matter how compelling the case for change, people will naturally fight it tooth and nail.

THE CURMUDGEON AND THE GYMNAST

The mere prospect of change can create psychological discomfort. The discomfort arises from two main brain systems: the basal ganglia (our old curmudgeon) and the prefrontal cortex (our mental gymnast). The basal ganglia allows us to put on our socks before we put on our shoes, drive our usual route to work without thinking, and perk up our ears when we hear the music of the ice cream truck. It's both a blessing and a curse. The same system causes you to automatically drive home from work along your normal route when you had promised to swing by your friend's house first. In it reside our ingrained memories (which can afflict us with cognitive errors), facts and information we need to get on with our daily functioning (which can lock us into ruts), participatory traditions (which can make us stubbornly resist change), and structured routines (which can compromise our potential for peak performance).

The old curmudgeon lives in our forebrain between the cortex and the brainstem, where it can access both the cognitive area of the brain involved in decision making and the one that controls movement. In other words, the basal ganglia links thought with action. Learning something as simple as tying your shoes takes a tremendous amount of initial brainpower, but once you get the hang of it, it consumes very little.

The formation of such habits involves one particular part of the basal ganglia, the dopamine-rich input station for messages from other portions of the brain called the striatum. As we master routines, dopamine rewards us with feelings of pleasure or avoidance of pain, helping us perpetuate the routine.

By contrast, the prefrontal cortex, a highly active component of the forebrain, functions as the brain's captain and can perform all sorts of mental gymnastics. It houses our short-term memory and governs complex cognitive thought and behavior, such as abstract thinking, short- and long-term decision making, mediation of conflicting thought choices between right and wrong, expression of personality, planning and strategizing, outcome prediction, and moderation of social behavior. Because the prefrontal cortex helps us focus our thoughts, it also plays a role in attention and learning. Imagine it as a control center that receives data, processes it, and determines actions in accordance with our internal goals. Not surprisingly, this part of the brain requires a lot of conscious mental energy, which is hard work.

The prefrontal cortex also connects to the amygdala, part of the limbic system that serves as the brain's emotional center. It facilitates emotion and memory and is also responsible for our fear circuitry, which helps produce the "fight/flight" response in our brains and bodies (see Chapter 3).

Brain analysis technology has proven that change activates the prefrontal cortex. However, analysis has also shown that, because the thinking part of the brain connects to the emotional part, an assault of unfamiliar information can upset the emotional part of our brains. The mere prospect of change can ignite a firestorm of emotions (intense fear, anger, depression, fatigue, anxiety) that make us want to fight for the comfort of the status quo. As we learned in Chapter 3, the fear response can cause impulsive, shortsighted decision making that impedes performance.

MENTAL BARRIERS

In 1992, a day didn't pass without an America Online (AOL) trial disk landing in your mailbox, falling out of a magazine, or beckoning your eye on the counter of your local grocery store. In the brutally competitive early days of the digital Wild West battle to draw the public into the Internet frontier, the original Internet service providers (ISPs) such as Prodigy, Genie, and CompuServe fell under the onslaught of AOL's massive and expensive advertising campaign. AOL's revolutionary graphical user interface (GUI) and "walled garden" approach (keeping information self-contained within AOL) made Internet access available to even the most nontechnical user. Suddenly, everyone from the stay-at-home mother in Bayonne to the PhD economist in Palo Alto could easily access a recipe for boeuf bourguignon or the gross national product of Transylvania.

As AOL added chatrooms, then instant messaging, the company firmly became the industry's undisputed leader, the gold standard for Internet access. Then, in 1993, Netscape entered the fray with the first easily accessible Web browser, Mosaic. Two years later, Microsoft released its own version, Internet Explorer. The "browser wars" had begun. Despite AOL's reluctance to enter the new battlefield, it claimed a whopping 3.6 million subscribers in 1997. In 1998–99, AOL's stock prices rose over 600 percent, and by 2002, AOL, then worth $200 billion, boasted 34 million members.

As Internet users began incorporating the Web into their daily lives, with the browsers and websites becoming more and more refined and user friendly, folks began to wonder why they needed the closed garden approach of AOL when they could access the same information on the World Wide Web from many sources. Among both the tech savvy and the average user, AOL had become a joke: "the Internet with training wheels" and "the company that sends you free drink coasters."

No matter, AOL steadfastly clung to its business model: expensive and pervasive marketing combined with a simplified user experience, one for which users paid a premium for stuff they could get elsewhere for free. As the online community mushroomed, AOL steadily lost ground. By 2006, membership had declined by 50 percent, and AOL's worth had shrunk by 90 percent. As of this writing, AOL has evolved into a primarily free service, offering an online news aggregator with some exclusive content. Their paid subscriber base is down to 4 million users. The faithful holdouts may be sticking with the company purely out of their own change resistance. In a 2011 article in *The New Yorker* magazine, a former AOL executive said, half-jokingly, "The dirty little secret is 75 percent of the people who subscribe to AOL's dial up service don't need it."

AOL had appeared to welcome change back in 1998, when it bought Netscape, the most popular Web browser at the time, and when it subsequently merged with Time Warner in 2000. The company clearly had the potential to lead the ranks of ISPs. Instead, they experienced a spurt of brilliant growth followed by a rapid descent, clinging to a dated model. More powerful browsers outperformed Netscape, and the marriage of AOL and Time Warner ended in a bitter divorce, with both companies losing reputation and value.

Leading the pack for so long, why would the Internet giant avoid rocking the boat to do things differently, even when it became apparent that only change could save their business?

Obviously, AOL's leaders could not get on board with change even though they should have seen it coming. They're not alone. No matter how much clear writing you can see on the wall, you can easily succumb to the powerful forces of psychological biases that can blind you to the need for change. Many cognitive biases can immobilize us, but sometimes it simply comes down to mental exhaustion.

EXHAUSTION

New and unfamiliar routines and choices challenge the comfort zone of our ingrained habits. When you effect a change, you force yourself out of that comfort zone. It takes a lot of energy, and it can wear you out. In the same way that your muscles eventually give out during a strenuous workout, your mental muscle starts to lose function at full speed, hampering your ability to care, make choices, maintain motivation, weigh decisions, and ultimately take action. Psychologists call this *ego depletion*, a state of mind where you can lose critical elements of your self-control and all the other mental processes that require focus and conscious effort. As we saw in Chapter 1, a chronic level of ego depletion can make you "too busy to win."

In 1998, researcher Roy Baumeister and colleagues investigated this phenomenon by asking people to sign up for what the participants thought was a taste-perception experiment. The researchers formed three groups: radish eaters, chocolate eaters, and noneaters (the control group). They asked that the participants skip one meal and arrive hungry for a scheduled appointment. When the radish and chocolate eaters arrived for the appointment, they could smell freshly baked chocolate-chip cookies. On the table before them they found a bowl of radishes and a plate of freshly baked chocolate chip cookies and chocolate candies. The radish eaters were instructed to eat two or three radishes, avoiding the chocolate. The chocolate eaters could eat two or three cookies but no radishes. The noneaters did not participate in this part of the experiment.

Once the participants had finished eating, the researchers asked all three groups to solve an unsolvable spatial puzzle. The subjects could abandon the task at any time. Who quit first? The radish eaters. The chocolate eaters and the noneaters stuck with the task longer and for more or less the same amount of time. The early quitters, the radish eaters, reported feeling more exhausted than the other two groups.

What can we conclude from the results of this experiment? Since it takes a lot more self-control to avoid the temptation of mouthwatering chocolate than it does to shun a bowl of radishes, resisting temptation took a bigger toll on the radish eaters. That resistance depleted the mental energy needed to tackle the puzzle and caused the radish eaters to abandon it more quickly. On the other hand, subjects in the chocolate and noneating conditions depleted fewer mental resources maintaining self-control and could more easily spend additional time with the puzzle.

If resisting cookies can make your mind weary, imagine what resisting a big change in the workplace can do to you, after adding in all the other stuff you do every day. Triple the effect for a hardworking leader. Everything you do and every decision you make at work, at home, at the gym, on the tennis court, at a parent-teacher conference, and during a business dinner requires an investment of willpower, and that investment steadily diminishes your mental resources. Sorry, dear reader, but even Einstein started the day with a finite tank of mental fuel. Once he drained the tank with all that daily calculating, he felt as weary as you do at the end of your long day. Now throw change into the mix. Einstein relocates from Germany to Princeton, all the while trying to put the finishing touches on his special theory of relativity. It's enough to make a grown genius cry.

That's the bad news. What's the good news? While you were forming your habits and routines, you got a lot of feel-good dopamine rewards, but once you settled into those routines, the dopamine stopped flowing. Change fires it up again because it creates the sprouting neuronal pathways that electrify new parts of the brain. Imagine forks of lightning flashing from the sky to the ground: The more new ways of thinking and doing you adopt, the more forks you create for lighting up the brain. You also gain new pathways for the dopamine receptors, which start flowing again.

That boost of good feeling can help you persevere with change and, to some degree, counteract the effects of exhaustion. Happily ensconced at Princeton, Einstein gets back to the hard work of calculating the speed of light. At the end of the chapter we'll look at ways you can tackle exhaustion by taking a creative break from your routine.

Before we do that, however, let's turn our attention to some of the less obvious reasons we can end up fighting change.

COSTS

We invest so much mental energy in our decisions that we find it hard to admit when we make a bad one. We invest even more time and energy to make our bad decisions look right. Remember confirmation bias from Chapter 1? Seeking out and paying attention to data that support our opinions and beliefs reflects this "latching-on" tendency. Cognitive dissonance, discussed in Chapter 5, also comes into play as we struggle to avoid the discomfort of holding two conflicting ideas at once. These mental tricks help us turn a blind eye to, or justify, this stubborn behavior. Another psychological bias makes it even more difficult to let go of people, processes, and ideas in which we have invested a lot of time, money, and resources. It's called sunk costs and mirrors the saying, "Throwing good money after bad."

Once we make an investment (time, money, emotion), we have incurred a sunk cost. When you sink emotion into an activity, you have invested so much in it that you can't easily let it go. Imagine buying a pair of jeans at the mall. You may decide, when you get home and try them on again, that you don't like them after all. While you can return them and get your money back, you have still sunk time into driving to the mall, making the purchase, trying them on, then driving home and putting them away in your closet. Driving back to the mall and exchanging the purchase requires additional investment. All of that investment may persuade you to live with the new jeans after all. And if you do exchange them, you will never recoup those investments you have already made. Thus, any investment binds us to the investment, and the greater the investment, the more tightly we hold onto it.

AOL had invested so much money, time, and effort into their tried-and-true strategy that they simply could not let it go. Logic perhaps told the executives to move on and think differently, but sunk costs overruled that logic, creating a state of corporate inertia. The reluctance to change in an efficient and effective way costs more time and money, reinforcing the inability to change. It's a sad cycle, but one that happens over and over when leaders refuse to heed all the signals that they need to change. This is what happened with the Aerospatiale-BAC, in what Richard Dawkins and T. R. Carlisle dubbed the "Concorde fallacy."

The Aerospatiale-BAC supersonic transport (SST, more famously known as the Concorde), jointly funded by the British and French governments, was an impressive but extremely costly achievement. The jet dazzled the eye with its sleekness and the mind with its swiftness. It became increasingly apparent, though, that the Concorde would never achieve a return on the huge costs the two governments had sunk into it. So what did the two governments do? They sank even more money into the project. Losses mounted in a cycle as sad as my own management folly that I discussed in the introduction to this book until, finally, in 2003 and 2004, Air France and British Airways finally decided to cut their losses.

If you think about it, you can come up with your own examples of the Concorde fallacy, from the little ones that happen every day in your personal and work life to the big ones that happen when countries go to war or companies make spending decisions that send them hurtling toward a financial cliff. This is one of the many reasons we may hang on tightly to the status quo.

STATUS QUO

AOL executives, like so many corporate leaders throughout history, fell so deeply in love with the status quo that they couldn't change, even when it became apparent that only change could save their business. Rather than move boldly and better their strategy, they sat back, muttering, "Let's not rock the boat" or "Our approach got us on top, it will keep us on top" or "Let's just hunker down and weather the storm." Psychologists call this *status quo bias*.

According to a 2007 study by Katrin Burmeister and Christian Schade, instead of considering all available information when making a decision, people tend to rely on information that represents the current state or on previous choices that created current conditions, whether they or someone else made those choices. Status quo bias includes the natural tendency to:

- Refrain from action altogether because you'd rather do nothing than make a mistake.

- Favor a current routine over new options.

- View current conditions favorably because that provides a measure of comfort.

Status quo bias affects both large (AOL) and small (your breakfast) decisions. AOL stuck with its business model, you eat a bowl of vanilla yogurt with sliced banana in the morning, every morning. When Google rockets onto the scene or you find nothing but a bagel in the fridge, the tendency to prefer the status quo causes both stress and reluctance to change the old habit. That's when you can easily close your mind to potential opportunities.

Psychologists refer to this aspect of decision making as *loss aversion*. When you contemplate making a decision that involves change (leaving a job or taking a new one, withrawing support from a failing project, or adapting to changing market forces), you worry about a potential loss (you won't find a better new job; the new job will turn into a nightmare; the project will get back on track tomorrow; the new market force represents a fad, not a genuine shift). Will the decision rob us of current benefits? Will desired benefits actually materialize? What if we bet the farm and end up losing it? What will people think if we fall flat on our face? These questions quite often convince us to stay mired in the mud of status quo.

Then along comes the *endowment effect.* In 1980, Richard Thaler conducted a seminal study at Cornell University, in which he presented half of the students in a class with coffee mugs. The lucky recipients could sell their mugs to students who had not received one. It turned out that the mug sellers set their prices so high and the buyers set theirs so low that very few transactions took place. Briefly owning the coffee mug influenced the sellers to overvalue it and inflate the price to compensate for the potential loss; buyers did not want to lose much money on a mug they might wish they had not bought. Thaler chalked it all up to loss aversion. Everyone, it turned out, could more easily live with the status quo than with the possibility of loss. If we hold on tight to something as inconsequential as a coffee mug, imagine how steadfastly we will cling to something really valuable.

Ironically even when corporate decision makers make a big change and bet the farm on a new direction, their customers may hang onto the status quo. In a July 2011 working paper entitled "A Model of Flops," Patrick Hummen, John Morgan, and Phillip Stocken describe Coca-Cola's major marketing blunder with its introduction of "New Coke." The authors write that in 1985, the former CEO of Coca-Cola, Robert Goizueta, resolved to do something about Coke's steady loss of market share to archrival, Pepsi. After exhaustive investigation into its customers' preferences, Coca-Cola created a new formula for its soft drink. "New Coke" would replace "Old Coke." Taste tests had revealed that consumers really did prefer the sweeter taste of the new coke formula, but when "New Coke" hit the market, customers objected strenuously, going so far as to launch a class-action lawsuit to force Coca-Cola to restore the original recipe. Seventy-nine days later, the company returned to the original formula and removed the new one from the shelves. If people will fight a change in a favorite soft drink, imagine what they will do when they think a change in the status quo will threaten their livelihood.

It seldom makes sense to change just for change's sake, but studies have consistently shown that people tend to overvalue and overrely on the status quo, which can result in major missed opportunities. Just ask our friends at AOL, Blockbuster, and Kodak. In fact, behavioral economists have demonstrated that the same applies to decisions about personal finance and investment. Back in 1988, William Samuelson and Richard Zeckhauser conducted a series of studies involving 486 students enrolled in economics classes at Harvard and Boston universities to demonstrate the status quo bias. The researchers used two slightly different questionnaires about finance, only one of which included questions offering a status quo alternative. The students were asked to consider this situation: "You are a serious reader of the financial pages but have lacked funds to invest. When you inherit a fortune from your great-uncle, you can finally put your financial learning to work. Do you invest in a moderate-risk company, a high-risk company, treasury bills, or municipal bonds?" Some questionnaires describe the uncle's preference (i.e., the status quo), others did not. More often than not, the students who received the former elected to stick with the status quo.

This kind of decision-making behavior happens all the time. People just naturally lean toward protecting themselves by making safer choices, conserving their energy, and avoiding risks that might end in disaster. That's fine, until you face a choice where sticking with the status quo will end in disaster. How do you tell the difference?

FRAMES

It depends on how you frame the change. In 1993, Eric Johnson and colleagues described an interesting phenomenon that occurred when both Pennsylvania and New Jersey made identical changes to their auto insurance laws to reduce costs. Each state gave drivers a new option that offered them lower insurance premiums in exchange for agreeing to a limited right to sue after an accident. Consumers embraced one law but objected to the other.

It all came down to the different ways the states framed the change. In New Jersey, drivers could choose the full right to sue; in Pennsylvania, they could choose to give up the right. Note the striking difference in the default (status quo). Most New Jersey drivers went along with the change (it sustained their status quo); most Pennsylvania drivers did not (it violated their status quo). As a result, Pennsylvania lost approximately $200 million in expected insurance and litigation savings.

Other research by Kahneman and Tversky has shown that behavior depends on the framing of change. Different ways of framing a challenge can produce different behavior, even in the case of otherwise identical options. Loss aversion drives humans to bet aggressively/take greater risks (not necessarily intelligent ones) when faced with a potential loss than when faced with a potential gain. In business, this tendency argues that anyone proposing a change should frame it as a great opportunity, so people will less likely see it as a potential threat.

In 2002, Harvard Business School professor Clark Gilbert examined how the newspaper industry responded to the threat of the Internet in the mid to late 1990s. He found that those who framed the issue as a threat to their existence responded by pouring dollars into the Web, but simply replicated their hard copy online. Other newspaper publishers, who framed it as an opportunity, responded more adaptively but, ironically, seldom allocated sufficient resources to their Internet presence. The most effective organizations initially assessed the Web as a disruptive threat, but then they framed it as an exciting opportunity that could revitalize their business.

In general, when organizations encounter real or imagined threats, they go into crisis mode. Just as happens to an individual who runs into a bear along the forest path, fear ignites the leaders' freeze/flee/fight response. All three options reduce the flow of innovative ideas, open-minded decision making, and swift, appropriate action.

In this era of accelerating disruptive change (game-changing technology, social media, instant media exposure, and globalization, to name a few), change has gone from an exception to the rule. Customers want one product or service today and a far different one tomorrow. In 1995, Joseph Bower and Clayton Christensen published a fascinating article in the *Harvard Business Review* entitled "Disruptive Technologies: Catching the Wave." In the article, the authors posit that companies often fail because their preoccupation with satisfying today's customer needs causes them to pay too little attention to developing what the customer will need tomorrow. The authors define two types of technology: sustaining and disruptive. With sustaining technology, a company merely updates and enhances what the customer already owns and loves. "If you love our sleek sports car, you will want these new bells and whistles." That may work for the short haul but not forever. With disruptive technology, a term first coined by Clayton Christensen in his 1997 book, *The Innovator's Dilemma*, a company pursues a technological innovation, product, or service that eventually renders the existing dominant technology or product obsolete. How many can you name besides the printing press, the light bulb, and the World Wide Web?

According to Clark Gilbert, organizational leaders who frame change as a threat invest too many valuable resources adding bells and whistles. Those who frame it as a golden opportunity invest their resources in designing a sports car that operates via mind control.

As we discussed in Chapter 5, when it comes to mental models, you must know when to hold 'em and know when to fold 'em. The now-defunct Borders bookstore chain held onto its model too long. Borders, like Barnes and Noble, offered a vast variety of books in a single store, where customers could browse the aisles and sip a double-espresso latte. Early on, Borders embraced technology and developed a superior inventory system that could optimize and even predict what consumers across the nation would buy. The chain flourished. However, in the mid-1990s, as the whole world was going digital and businesses needed to frame the appropriate response to it, Borders tenaciously clung to its initial model. While Barnes & Noble quickly developed its own Nook eBook reader and invested heavily in competing with upstart Amazon for online sales, Borders was investing in their merchandising, focusing on CD and DVD sales in addition to books and coffee. To make matters worse, Borders expanded its physical plants, renovated their brick-and-mortar stores, and outsourced online sales to Amazon.com. Instead of creating their own e-reader, Borders offered other devices, such as the Kobo and Cruz, neither of which at the time seriously challenged Amazon's Kindle or B&N's Nook. Borders' investment in shoring up the past rather than inventing a new future eventually led to its painful demise in bankruptcy court.

Although I cannot climb inside the brains of the Borders leadership team, I can say with certainty that the way they framed the digital challenge contributed a great deal to the company's failure, while the way B&N's leaders framed it led to at least temporary success. How they fare in the future against Amazon and Apple will depend on how they frame that challenge.

My friend and literary agent Michael Snell cites independent bookstores as another example of good and bad framing. While most mom-and-pop bookstores kept selling a limited selection of the same books offered by the superstores, some clever entrepreneurs reinvented themselves by developing unique brand identities and transforming themselves into attractive destinations for targeted book buyers. Some focused on parents, setting up reading rooms for children and designing events and activities that would attract parents and kids. Others developed niche specialties. The bookstore owners who went out of business clung to the old way of doing business; those that survived and even thrived remade themselves as attractive alternatives to the big-box stores. All leaders must eventually make the same choice when change strikes.

PLASTICITY

Given all the forces that conspire against a decision to paddle through unknown waters, what's a poor leader to do? You get yourself a plastic brain. No, not one made of polymers, but one that lends itself to learning new tricks. Research into brain plasticity (also known as neuroplasticity or cortical remapping) has shown that the brain can change and adapt as a result of learning and experiencing new behaviors, environments, and neural processes. Leaders who want to move forward can take the following steps to survive the rapids.

CHALLENGE BIASES

Review what we have learned about sunk costs and status quo biases. Simply recognizing their existence will not make them go away. But recognition and self-awareness mark an important step in ameliorating their negative effects on change behavior. Bear in mind that a team and an organization develop a culture and that a culture can perpetuate and even intensify these two biases. The culture has bought into and owns the status quo. "We've invested a lot in doing the things we always do around here." When change slips into town, a leader must confront it head-on. Bring together all the people who feel a sense of ownership in the status quo and encourage them to ask and answer some key questions:

- How do we define our status quo?

- What investments have we made in our status quo?

- What benefits have we derived from our status quo?

- How are we limited by our status quo? Would we choose to make the same investments?

- What is our major competitor's status quo? How has it worked for them?

- How do we imagine our future and our competitor's future next year? In five years?

- Which business forces require a bold response?

- What specific changes can we make to ensure a bold response?

- How much time, money, and emotion must we invest to make desired changes?

- How will we benefit or not benefit if we make these changes?

- How will we manage the change process to maximize buy-in from the rest of the organization? From our stakeholders?

Simply guiding yourself and your people through this Socratic process will shake up people's minds, get them thinking in a forward direction, and loosen the shackles of the status quo. Slowly but surely the power of the group begins to counteract the cognitive biases of both individuals and the team. Now you can properly reframe the challenge.

REFRAME

Begin by describing the current challenge in one simple sentence. Let's suppose you run a small restaurant that specializes in local seafood. When a national chain opens a Tuna Charley down the street, you suffer a sharp drop in customers owing to Tuna Charley's inexpensive and standardized fare. You write down the challenge: "Our carpetbagger competitor wins customers with charming advertising featuring Charley the Tuna." Framing the challenge that way might tempt you to spend a lot more on advertising but otherwise make no significant changes in the way you do business. Now let's try reframing the challenge: "A standardized chain has threatened our territory; what can we do to compete?" Now you might think about ways to combat the challenge, possibly by redesigning your menu to appeal to a gourmet clientele while enhancing your reputation for using fresh, local ingredients. The former frame favored the status quo; the later spurred creative and productive problem solving and decision making.

Here's a strategy I like to use with clients who are wrestling with decisions about confronting change.

- Gather people with similar and different business interests into a room.

- Write a one-sentence summary of the business challenge on a white board.

- Invite people to offer different ways to state the challenge.

- Cross out all value-laden terminology; fair, smart, dumb, beneficial, and problematic.

- Reframe the question in a neutral sentence.

- Ask different stakeholders to frame the challenge from their particular point of view.

- Help the group analyze gains and losses from each point of view.

I worked with a membership-based organization that targeted educators in higher education. This organization was challenged with stagnant membership for several years, a challenge made worse by the recession. The leadership team displayed all the telltale signs of a classic stick-in-the-mud organization: strong emotional attachment to their organization and their brand, oversized egos from former successes, and a bad case of status quo and "confined to the box" thinking. Before I came on the scene, the leadership team had conducted a formal survey of the organization's existing members. They asked them what they valued about the organization and what they would like to see enhanced (from a list of existing offerings).

When I asked the leadership team to state their business challenge, they agreed on this statement: "We offer our members so many benefits, but an increasing number of less competent competitors have robbed us of members and the recession has cost us even more." Note how they blamed everyone but themselves for their predicament. Before delving in, I asked them to brainstorm some solutions. Not surprisingly, they came up with nothing more than variations of the same old story coupled with "Our members just don't appreciate all that we do for them." That's like the ostrich saying, "I can't see because of all this sand in my eyes," rather than "Maybe I ought to pull my head out of the sand."

When we set about reframing the challenge by editing out the emotional and value-laden elements and the stubborn pride in past accomplishments, the new statement became "Evolving customer needs and economic realities require new approaches." Notice the absence of emotion. Note also that the new frame does not blame others but accepts responsibility for a better future. It begins to close the door on the status quo and open a window for creative problem solving. It did not take long for the team to come up with a host of new ideas, from adopting a more customer-focused approach to business development and a clearer focus on the organization's target audience, young professionals, and students.

Effective reframing shifts emphasis from symptoms to causes. It replaces a Band-Aid with the antibiotics to heal the infection. Like treating the root cause of an illness, reframing takes a lot of skill and hard work. Changing the way the culture thinks and operates means asking tough and sometimes painful questions.

In the case of the organization I worked with, the leaders needed to figure out what present members and prospective members thought of the organization. They found it painful to admit that they had unwittingly built a reputation as a professional "old boys club," a stodgy place where wrinkled veterans gathered to pat themselves on the back for all their achievements and awards. Education programs and gala events would do nothing to counteract that perception and might even reinforce it. Once the leadership saw the real cause of their problem, they could do something about it. No, they did not totally abandon the status quo, because they needed to retain the old guard. But they could come up with ways to entice the new guard with such offerings as a mentoring program, a networking center, and nuts-and-bolts business seminars. They could also address the new guard's preference for using new technologies and social media in their professional practices with online services and online educational programs. With these and other initiatives, they hauled themselves out of the mud and began sprinting toward a brighter future.

RECOUP

When facing decisions that involve shaking things up, you need to recognize that being avoidant, stuck, resistant, or delaying is sometimes simply due to mental exhaustion or burnout. Despite the tremendous resilience of the human brain and body, sometimes we need to give them a rest so they can recoup their full abilities. It's easier said than done when we find ourselves up to our eyebrows in quicksand.

One of the most costly examples of failing to recoup before suffering a huge loss occurred in November 2011, when António Horta-Osório, CEO of Britain's Lloyd's Banking Group, was forced to take an extended enforced break due to stress and overwork. Horta-Osório had joined the group earlier that year and had become CEO in March. By the fall he was suffering from such acute insomnia that he remained awake for five straight days. With no rest and increasing stress and mental exhaustion, he was forced to seek medical help. The results were dramatic; shares in Lloyd's fell 4.4 percent, a whopping $1.5 billion reduction in market capitalization. Horta-Osório eventually returned to the bank in late December, but he forfeited his bonus and was forced to radically alter both his work and personal habits.

A savvy leader learns to recognize the telltale signs of mental exhaustion:

- *Physical Symptoms.* Feeling tired most of the time but finding it difficult to sleep; suffering more illnesses, such as colds and bouts of the flu; losing or gaining appetite and not eating well; gastrointestinal problems; experiencing more headaches and muscle pains than usual.

- *Emotional Symptoms.* Feelings of helplessness; depression; anxiety; irritability; self-doubt; reduced life satisfaction; decreased sex drive.

- *Behavioral Symptoms.* Declining ability to concentrate and focus; impaired decision making; social withdrawal; self-medicating with drugs or alcohol; unusual procrastination; decreased attention to physical health/wellness/hobbies.

Like Horta-Osório, we sometimes ignore these symptoms until mental exhaustion strikes. In times like these, we need to slow down and give ourselves sufficient rest and recovery time. Be assured, it will all be there when you get back. Get away from it all, both physically and mentally. Reach out to your social support network and consider seeking professional help.

Once you come back to work refreshed and raring to go, apply some preventative measures to keep from crashing again. As always, the simplest advice applies; eat well, get enough sleep, exercise, engage in play and social activities with friends, read a book or go to the movies or theater, spend time enjoying your hobbies (or find a new one), meditate or do anything else that lets off steam. One of my clients keeps a daily journal in which she writes down all the good and bad events of the day. Just committing it all to paper puts everything in perspective and calms her down. Know when to say no to that invitation to add one more straw to your weary camel's back. Last but not least, turn off the cellphone and ignore your computer, at least once a day.

As we've discussed, developing habits take time. However, our brains love to form new ones, especially healthy, positive ones that will prevent exhaustion, help you switch gears, and give you the break you need to re-energize and make clear-headed decisions.

WRAP UP

Like every other human being on the planet, leaders are only human, albeit humans with a lot of responsibility for people, processes, and important decisions that can make or break a company. And nothing will make or break a company more surely than the way a leader handles change. Will you remain mired in the mud and perish? Or welcome change and thrive? To thrive you need to become more aware of the psychology behind your own and your people's responses to change. That awareness in and of itself will help guide better decisions about the future.

Why Do Good Teams
Go Bad?

AS AN EXPERIENCED human resources director, Lily thought she had seen it all. She was preparing to investigate a sexual harassment complaint against a vice-president at a large pharmaceutical company. A cashier, Rosa, claimed she had received unwanted attention from Scott, a popular, attractive, and influential executive with an impeccable twenty-five-year record at the company.

During the initial meeting with Scott's boss, Roger, and other senior executives, Lily realized she was being stonewalled. "Scott is a saint," insisted Roger. "He would *never* do such a thing, especially to someone like *her*." An eyewitness, Lily pointed out, had confirmed the complaint. "Give me a break," Roger laughed. "You'd take the word of some minimum-wage floozy, a disgruntled employee, over a church-going, happily married man like Scott?" When Lily reported this conversation, her own boss suggested she close the case.

Desperately wanting to do the right thing, she went back to Rosa, hoping the young woman could provide more evidence to support her claim. Rosa, with great reluctance, took a photo from her purse, handing it to Lily. It was shocking. There was Scott completely naked and fully aroused.

On a return visit to meet with the executives, Lily, without a word, dropped the photograph on the table. Hostility quickly turned to embarrassment. A negotiated settlement allowed Scott to resign, Rosa to withdraw her complaint, and Lily to file the offending photo in a confidential file.

How do intelligent, ethical, and otherwise good individuals, like the pharmaceutical executive team members, make such a stupid, ethically questionable group business decision? Why did they do something on a team they would never dream of doing on their own? Well, as you can probably guess, it's in our nature, or as a neuroscientist might say, "It's in our brains." Group dynamics exert an incredibly powerful force on our individual behaviors, thinking, and emotions.

If you thought individual psychology could get messy, wait until we delve into the unbelievably complicated and confusing world of group psychology. To help make sense of it all, we will explore six factors that govern group dynamics and can take you into a whole world of hurt if you do not manage them effectively:

- The inevitability of groups

- The "us" vs. "them" mentality

- Group conformity

- Social loafing

- Emotional contagion

- Smart people, dumb group decisions

Few other aspects of organizational life pose greater challenges to a leader than the behavior of people in groups.

THE INEVITABILITY OF GROUPS

Humans have always affiliated with groups and teams in order to survive and thrive. Groups influence almost everything we do, from families, friends, and colleagues to religious organizations, social clubs, networks, work teams, and professional associations. Group dynamics affect collections of people who come together for every activity from a wedding ceremony to a funeral.

In one interesting study, Henri Tajfel and his colleagues showed participants slides of paintings by Klee and Kandinsky. The researchers told the participants that their preference for one painting over another would determine which of two groups they would join—a research design tactic aimed at creating an "us" versus "them" mentality. After each participant stated a preference, the researchers would escort that person to a cubicle and invited him or her to distribute virtual money to members of both groups. The subjects never met one another, did not know any other individuals personally, and could only be identified by a number that indicated a preference for Klee or Kandinsky.

The participants systematically favored their own group based on the choice of one painting over another. How could these *minimal* groups inspire systematic bias?

According to *social identity theory* (SIT), a term coined by Henri Tajfel and John Turner in the 1970s, people derive a sense of their self not only from their personal identity (unique personal characteristics) but also from their association and identification with one or more social groups (male, female, black, white, brunette, blonde, workgroup A, workgroup B, etc.). Social identity allows us to identify with each other and act together by reaching consensus on what matters, on what rules/norms will govern behavior, and on how to define and work toward shared goals. Group membership provides people with a sense of belonging, a basic and universal human need to know who we are and how we fit into the world. No wonder we gravitate toward groups of all kinds. Once we join a group, however, some truly fascinating dynamics kick in.

US vs. THEM

From May 2006 to October 2009, Apple aired 66 "Get a Mac" television commercials featuring a plump, bumbling PC user and a hip, cool Mac user. They made us laugh. But they also illustrated an important group dynamic:

the "us" versus "them" mentality. Did viewers want to join the once dominant, now moribund PC user group or the once outsider, now sexy Mac
user group?

In a world of constant choice, our selections, from friends and lovers to
computers and cars, define who we are and separate us from other groups.
Once you ally yourself with a group, you begin to enjoy wonderful benefits,
such as cooperation and cohesiveness, but you also begin to fall prey to some
disturbing liabilities, such as prejudice and corruption. "We" can accomplish
anything; "we" are good. "They" are incompetent; "they" are bad.

Our minds naturally exaggerate the differences between our group and
their group. This "us" and "them" distinction fosters intra-group cooperation, inter-group competition, both productive and unproductive behavior,
and a range of work environments, from the nurturing to the toxic workplaces. Three mental processes come into play:

- *Social Categorization.* The classification of people and qualities allows us to identify and relate to them (black/white, male/female,
  blonde/brunette, marketing/manufacturing). These categories help
  us make sense of our world, provide us with information about
  people, and give us a way to define ourselves and our place in the
  world. Categorizing also helps define appropriate behavior dictated
  by our group's norms.

- *Social Identification.* The adoption of the beliefs and behaviors of
  the group sets us apart from others. "I am a Catholic; I believe in
  the Virgin Mary; I go to mass; I honor the Pope." Through social
  identification our membership in the group becomes emotionally
  significant because our adoption of the group's norms becomes integrated with our sense of self-identity and esteem.

- *Social Comparison.* The comparison behavior all humans display
  allows us to maintain our personal and group-based self-esteem
  and see our group as better than other groups (think of this as

downward comparison on a group level). Sometimes we make small distinctions and comfortably co-exist with other groups (the various departments in a company); sometimes we draw big distinctions and treat other groups as rivals (Red Sox fans versus Yankees fans).

Study after study has shown that humans favor and strive to enhance the status of the groups to which they belong. This means conferring superiority on our group and inferiority on all others. The gap between "us" and "them" widens.

One of the most famous psychological demonstrations of this phenomenon occurred in 1954, when social psychologist Muzafer Sherif and colleagues conducted the "Robbers Cave Experiment." The researchers took a group of typical young boys to a summer camp at Robbers Cave State Park in Oklahoma and randomly assigned them to two separate groups whom they kept isolated from one another. The groups adopted names, The Rattlers and The Eagles. After an initial period of bonding, they told each group of boys about the other group. Now the games began. As the two groups engaged in head-on competition, they began behaving badly, resorting to name-calling, self-segregation, raids, and singing derogatory songs about the rival group. For the final phase of the study, the researchers created a situation that required the two groups to work together cooperatively on a problem, the solution of which would allow both groups to prosper. Sherif and his colleagues found that over time, the tensions between the groups declined as they gradually viewed the opposition more favorably.

Most groups, teams, and organizational cultures adopt certain formal or informal initiation rites. At "Alpha Beta" fraternity, upperclassmen may subject pledges to all sorts of humiliating tasks and group problem solving that forge strong bonds among the recruits. These can run from innocuous games to abusive hazing. These initiation practices can also include bullying or ostracizing, both those in the "other" group and/or members of the "in" group who have transgressed in some way. In the professional world, fledgling doctors and attorneys sacrifice sleep and any semblance of a personal life to prove their dedication to the profession or law firm. Navy Seals do it. Girl and Boy Scouts do it. Recall what we learned about sunk costs bias in Chapter 6. Once we have invested blood, sweat, and tears in becoming a member of the group, we will think twice before quitting.

This "us" versus "them" mentality can also stimulate healthy workplace competition. However, problems inevitably arise when the competition starts crossing the line from nurturing to toxic or the cohesiveness becomes so strong that you can't unglue it. When healthy rivalry becomes bullying or people remain with the group because they fear reprisals, a leader should ease up on the "us" versus "them" mentality. This might involve slightly re-arranging competitive groups by switching a few people from one group to another or setting up a task that requires inter-group cooperation, as Sherif and his colleagues did with the boys at Robbers Cave.

GROUP CONFORMITY

Remember your parents telling you when you did something stupid or dangerous with your friends, "If your friends jumped off the Brooklyn Bridge, would you?" Conformity tends to rule group behavior, whether it's a gang of teenagers smoking cigarettes or a workgroup skipping out on a conference in Las Vegas to play the slots. We all feel the impulse to conform because we fear the consequences of social rejection.

Enron offers a particularly painful example of conformity gone wrong. Although several factors lead to the decline and fall of the energy giant, including corruption and greed, the basic corporate culture fostered conformity and penalized dissent. One tool Enron management used to enforce conformity was the organization's performance-review system, jokingly nicknamed the "rank-and-yank" process. Twice a year, an internal Performance Review Committee (PRC) graded employees on a scale of 1 to 5 on ten separate criteria. An employee's ratings determined whether the employee was grouped with the top performers who received big rewards, among the middle performers who were given six months to make huge improvements in their performance, or among the lowest performers who got the axe. Peter Fusaro and Ross Miller summed it up in their book *What Went Wrong at Enron*: "Enron created an environment where employees were afraid to express their opinions or to question unethical and potentially illegal business practices. Because the rank-and-yank system was both arbitrary and subjective, it was easily used by managers to reward blind loyalty and quash brewing dissent."

Conformity can cause people to justify bad behavior. Psychologist Solomon Asch conducted a famous study about conformity using a line judgment task. He asked 123 participants to look at lines drawn on a page and identify which line best matched a base line. The answer seemed perfectly clear.

Asch placed each participant in a group of fellow experimental subjects who, in fact, had received instructions to choose a particular match, even if it did not match at all. One by one, the confederates gave their predetermined answers before the uninitiated subject stated a choice. Astonishingly,

- 50 percent of participants gave the same wrong answer as the others on more than half of the trials.

- 25 percent of participants refused to be swayed by the majority's false judgment.

- 5 percent of participants always conformed to the majority's incorrect opinion.

- 33 percent was the average conformity rate across all trials.

When Asch later asked the participants to explain their behavior, he found that the majority felt anxious and self-conscious during the trial. They feared earning the majority's disapproval. Despite having initially formed the correct answer, many came to question their own good judgment as others expressed false opinions. Others simply did not want to stand out from the crowd. A small number even refused to accept the truth after they learned of the hoax.

Over the years, research has shown that several factors influence conformity in groups, including (Figure 7-1):

FIGURE 7-1   Factors That Influence Group Conformity

Group Size	Maximum conformity occurs in groups of 3 to 5 people. More makes no difference; less can reduce the tendency to conform.
In/Out Groups	People conform to the "in" group, especially if they find the other people attractive and feel emotionally attached to them. Like attracts like. Unlike stimulates dislike and nonconformity.
Dissent	If someone perceived as competent disagrees or can't decide, the tendency to conform declines.
Mood	Good moods promote conformity and agreeableness.
Task Quality	Important tasks or ones about which people feel ambiguous will more likely inspire conformity.
Fear	Crises that make us fearful and cause feelings of relief when they pass promote conformity.
Personality	People with a greater need for social approval and structure and/or lower self-esteem more easily succumb to the influences of conformity.
Culture	Individualistic cultures (typically Western ones) produce less conformity than collectivist cultures (often East Asian ones). However, both types of cultures will band together against outsiders.

Social/Group Norms	Group norms and codes of behavior strongly influence conformity.
Authority/Leadership	Some leaders create conditions that favor conformity or obedience.
Gender	Men and women conform in similar ways; however, women are more likely to conform in public, group-pressure situations. Same-sex groups will more likely conform than mixed-sex groups.

Social conformity can produce both good and bad effects in business situations. While cohesive groups can accomplish amazing results, extreme group conformity can stifle creativity, innovation, critical thinking, decision making, and problem solving. On a large scale, social conformity can breed a productive and supportive culture, but taken to the extreme, it can cause people to turn a blind eye to wrongdoing, the equivalent of jumping off the Brooklyn Bridge with your friends.

To avoid the possibility of good teams going bad, leaders should exercise care when setting up teams. A leader can establish a "rule of alternatives" that encourages people to come up with more than one viable option when making a decision or embarking on a task. Furthermore, the leader can make sure people know they can and should challenge conforming behaviors that may lead to breaches of ethics, the law, or bad business decisions. Self-awareness can also provide potent medicine. Learning the basics of group dynamics will help people understand and deal with the good and bad effects of conformity. Leaders who see a good team going bad must intervene immediately. Quite often a leader can't see it happening because he or she has also conformed to the group. In that case, a trusted adviser or a coach can provide objective advice on getting the team back on track.

SOCIAL LOAFING

In George Orwell's 1946 classic novel *Animal Farm*, a group of farm animals set up a commune, ensuring equality among all animals. Nice idea. But here's what really happened: Most animals ended up working their tails off for the benefit of a few lazy animals, the head pig exhorting, "All pigs are equal; but some pigs are more equal than others." Psychologists refer to this phenomenon as *social loafing*, and one of my clients, Elaine, knows it all too well.

Elaine worked as one of six human resources directors for a large investment bank. In addition to managing their own geographical areas, the directors occasionally came together to work on projects as a team. One director, Tony, had worked for the company for thirty years, investing a lot of time and energy winning the respect of senior leadership. But as Elaine saw it, Tony only cared about those above him, paying little attention to his peers and caring little about the HR department's welfare as a team. Spitting mad, Elaine says, "He hasn't done a thing on the Rewards and Recognition Program we've been developing for eight months!"

Tony only attended meetings when upper management appeared; he would then dominate the meeting and take credit for his teammates' work. This infuriated Elaine because Tony did almost nothing on the components of the program for which he was responsible, which left other group members picking up the slack. They felt they had no choice but to do his work because they took pride in the project and wanted it to succeed.

Elaine and the other directors complained about Tony's behavior to their boss. But their boss, Frank, couldn't see the real dynamic because at meetings he saw the "good" Tony. Tony never took seriously the comments his teammates made about good-for-nothing freeloaders. Despite Tony, the project ended beautifully and the team won awards for their excellent work. Still, Elaine confessed, "It irritated everyone on the team to see Tony's name on the plaque. He took some of the shine off."

People who worked for Tony took his behavior as a benchmark: Come and go as you please, let others do the real work, schmooze the boss to shine in the eyes of those above you. It also demoralized people who worked for difficult directors. Over time, the whole human resources department earned the disdain of the other departments throughout the company.

That's when Frank was replaced. The new vice president, Lydia, saw right through the smoke and mirrors. When the recession caused a company downsizing, Tony got the very first pink slip.

Psychologists have known about social loafing ever since 1913, when Max Ringelmann, a French professor of agricultural engineering, attempted to measure the efficiency of machine versus manual methods on farms. As Ringelmann measured the pulling strength of men tugging ropes, either separately or in groups of various sizes, he made a very interesting observation. On the face of it, all men appeared to be pulling equally. Here's what was really going on: The more men there were pulling the rope, the less each man pulled. Each man worked almost half as hard in a group as he did when he worked alone.

Recent scientific studies have shown the same effect. In 1979, Bibb Latané, Kipling Williams, and Stephen Harkins asked subjects to shout and clap as loud as they could, first individually, then in a group. If one casually listened to the collective noise, it sounded as though each individual were contributing equally. Here's what was really happening: Each individual shouted and clapped less loudly in a group. The researchers coined the term *social loafing* to describe the reduced effort individuals will put into a task when working with a group. Latane and his colleagues went so far as to call this a type of social disease, with "negative consequences for individuals, social institutions, and societies." Common sense suggests that a team will accomplish more than an individual. Surely, six people will gather more berries than a single gatherer; a group of hunters will more quickly slay the saber-toothed tiger than a single hunter. Maybe not!

In 1993, Steven Karau and Kipling Williams reviewed seventy-eight studies of social loafing to identify the root causes. Their review created the *collective effort model* (CEM). The salient point was how we see the connection between our individual effort and the expected outcomes. If you believe all your hard work will result in a valued outcome (bonus, recognition, or pride) to you and the group, you will do all you can to achieve your goal. If, on the other hand, you think your work will only add to one-sixth of a desired result, go unnoticed, or contribute to a seemingly senseless group goal, you will not work so hard and may be on your way to being a social loafer. Karau and Williams found some common themes in all the research:

1. Social loafers cross gender, culture, and task; but women and people from Asia seem less likely to loaf.

2. Social loafers may or may not realize they are loafing.

3. Social loafers do not loaf as much with close friends and valued teammates.

4. Social loafers are more likely to loaf when they:

   - Think their work gets lost in the collective.

   - See a task as meaningless to themselves and the group.

   - Cannot compare their group's work to the work of other groups.

   - Lack understanding of the expectations for outcomes.

   - Join a group composed of strangers.

   - Expect their co-workers to perform well.

   - Repeat the work of other group members.

Anyone can do a little social loafing from time to time, but when it seriously hampers a team's productivity, a leader must take steps to remedy the situation. To ease the infection (or to prevent it in the first place), I recommend using the STOP LOAFS method (Figure 7-2):

FIGURE 7-2   STOP LOAFS Method

S	Set Small Groups	Social loafers are deterred when they work in smaller groups.
T	Tie Tasks to Vision	Social loafers are deterred when they see the task as crucial to the organization's well-being.
O	Observe Need for Buy-In	Social loafers are deterred by specific, measurable objectives that promote buy-in.
P	Provide Peer Evaluation	Social loafers are deterred by feedback from one's peers.
L	List and Enforce Ground Rules	Social loafers are deterred by rules of accountability for results and how the team leader or group members deal with loafing.
O	Open Minds to Group Dynamics	Social loafers are deterred by an educated team that understands group dynamics and will call each other out on loafing behaviors.
A	Act All-for-One and One-for-All	Social loafers are deterred when there is a sense of personal responsibility for each other's behavior.
F	Foster Group Bonding	Social loafers are deterred by strong interpersonal bonds, group morale, and mutual respect.
S	Salute Success	Social loafers are deterred when rewards reinforce the individual and group contributions.

Whatever steps you take to ward off social loafing, you will still need to consider the ways individuals influence the way others behave.

EMOTIONAL CONTAGION

In 2004, football player Terrell Owens ("T.O.") signed with the Philadelphia Eagles. At that time, knowledgeable fans considered Owens one of the best wide receivers in the sport. Prior to his arrival, the Eagles had performed well, but not well enough to make it to the Super Bowl. However, in 2004, with Owens's help, the team won thirteen of sixteen games, the best record in the NFL, and finally made it to the big game. Owens, despite a severely injured leg that kept him out of the last four games of the season, rushed back against doctor's orders to join his team at the Super Bowl. Though the Eagles lost, they turned in an extraordinary performance, and Philadelphia went wild.

In the off-season after the Super Bowl, Owens demanded he be rewarded for his performance with an enhanced contract, even though he knew that the Eagles' policy prohibited such renegotiations. After management turned down Owens's demand, the once cohesive team began to fall apart. At the start of the 2005 training camp, the unhappy and bitter Owens became such a destructive and distracting force in the locker room that management sent him home. They could not tolerate his constant criticism of Donovan McNabb, the team's starting quarterback. Owens's behavior created division among the team, with some players siding with him and others with McNabb. Owens's individual rancor eroded team cohesiveness, drew team focus away from the goal of getting to another Super Bowl, and began to hamper performance on the field. Mid-season, the Eagles decided to cut their losses and send the toxic Owens packing—too late, unfortunately, for the team to get back on track. In one short year, the Eagles went from the strongest winning record in the NFL to one of the worst, going 0–6 in the NFC East in the 2005 season.

Emotions can spread like wildfire in the workplace. One angry, critical, and nasty personality can bring down the whole team. By the same token, one joyful, supportive, and lovable team member can lift the whole team up. Psychologists call this *emotional contagion*.

Decades of research have shown that emotions strongly influence our memory, our emotions, our perception of events, our thought processes, and ultimately, our behavior. In the workplace, people's moods tremendously impact decision making, problem solving, attention/focus, interpersonal interactions, performance, productivity, and the whole organizational culture.

Sigal Barsade, currently a professor of management at The Wharton School, conducted seminal work in 2002 into the positive and negative effects of the emotional dance that takes place in every group. For the study, she assigned ninety-four business school undergraduates to twenty-nine different groups ranging in size from two to four participants, including one ringer (otherwise known as a confederate), an actor from the drama department. Each group would decide how to allocate money from a bonus pool. Unbeknownst to the rest of the group, the ringer was instructed by Barsade to act out different mood and energy levels, such as cheerful enthusiasm, serene warmth, hostile irritability, and depressed sluggishness.

Barsarde found that the participants acted differently depending on the actor's performance. The actor's cheerfulness made the group more cheerful; the actor's anger made the group angrier. Positive emotions created more cooperation; negative emotions increased conflict and decreased cooperative decision making.

Barsade observed, "People are walking mood inductors, continuously influencing the moods and then the judgments and behaviors of others." The effect occurs in every type of organization, in every industry, and in every large and small workgroup.

Emotional contagion involves both subtle and not-so-subtle psychological and physiological processes. It begins with our human tendency, starting in infancy, to mimic the nonverbal behaviors, facial expressions, body language, speech patterns, and vocal tones of others. Mommy smiles down on you, you smile back. Daddy frowns, you cannot help frowning, too. This automatic mimicry triggers a physiological feedback loop where the muscular and glandular responses from mimicking trigger an emotion. Mommy smiles, you feel happy; Daddy frowns, you feel sad.

That explains face-to-face contagion. But what about teams with members working in different locations, who phone, email, instant message, and text each other? One fascinating study conducted in 2011 by Arik Chesin, Anat Rafaeli, and Nathan Bos examined the effect of texting on emotions. Not surprisingly, the researchers found that both happiness and anger can spread easily via text. Josephine's sad emoticon causes Bob and Sarah to share her unhappiness. Everyday people compose a hasty email or type a quick reply to an IM, hitting "send" before they contemplate how certain words and tones and emphases might affect the recipient. Note the difference between "Please bring me the Doolittle contract" and "PLEASE BRING ME THE DOOLITTLE CONTRACT!" Even a missing comma can send the wrong cue. "Let's eat, Bob," means something entirely different from "Let's eat Bob." Most of us have also replied to something we meant to forward. A literary agent, responding to an editor's rejection, emailed the message "What a moron!" to the editor when he meant to forward it to the author. He wished he'd thought twice before sending. Not noticing you hit the wrong letter on the keypad or not observing your smartphone's unfortunate autocorrect can also get you in hot water: "Very sorry I kissed our boss at the conference!" You meant, "Missed our boss."

Researchers have been looking into the underlying processes that account for remote emotional contagion, but some preliminary findings support the idea that in the absence of conventional nonverbal cues, we look for other sorts of cues (the emphases conveyed by **boldface**, *italics*, and CAPS, smiley faces, and punctuation marks!). Such cues can ignite emotional contagion just as surely as face-to-face human emotion can. That's why we call those little smiley faces "emoticons."

A leader's contributions to emotional contagion greatly influence a team's results. In 2005, researchers Thomas Sy, Stéphane Côté, and Richard Saavedra examined the effects of a leader's mood on groups. Using 189 undergraduate volunteers, divided into 63 groups of three, "leaders" chosen from each group viewed either a humorous video clip of David Letterman (to evoke a positive mood) or one depicting social injustice and aggression (to evoke a negative mood) before the leaders interacted with their respective teams to work on an assigned task. Measurements of each team member's moods before and after the task proved that the leader's mood infected the group's mood. The teams in good moods worked together smoothly and performed better on an assigned task than those in bad moods.

Beyond its impact on group dynamics, emotional contagion can impose serious consequences on the culture of an entire organization, which can and will affect customers, clients, and others who intersect with the organization. Zappos, a retailer renowned for its superior customer service, has co-created with their employees and instilled throughout the organization ten core values, known as their ten commandments, that have an uplifting, positive, and enthusiastic tone. People at Zappos do not pay mere lip service to them; they live and breathe them every minute of every day. The company's leaders stress them so heavily when they hire, train, promote, and reward their people that the values come to govern everyone's daily behavior. They're contagious. They affect face-to-face encounters, emails, phone calls, and IMs.

Keeping emotional contagion on a positive track requires conscientious effort. In your own organization, use these tips to instill and maintain the right mood:

- *Check yourself.* As with most everything a leader does, maintaining accurate self-awareness of your own mood and your nonverbal behaviors goes a long way toward fostering positive emotional contagion. Don't think you can successfully mask your emotions and moods. They invariably seep into our tone, facial expressions, posture, and the like. Sometimes you should walk away and repair your mood before it takes a toll on those around you. When you can't take a break, just admit you woke up on the wrong side of the bed and tell people to ignore you until you get your head screwed on straight.

- *Apply empathy.* The best teams follow the basic rule that members can point out a teammate's bad mood, without fear of retribution, provided they do it in a helpful, empathetic way. This, of course, is probably best done in private, as it can be embarrassing for some to be called out or corrected in a group setting. Just as we may have trouble recognizing our own mood states and the impact on others, the same is true for the people with whom we work closely. Ask what you can do to help. Listen to their stories. But whatever you do, withhold judgment or criticism. This helps a team member recognize and adjust his or her own mood and establishes the foundation for a collectively empathetic and caring team.

- *Use humor.* Not every situation lends itself to a good laugh, but nothing diffuses unhappiness more quickly than something funny that instantly lightens the mood. Sometimes just a smile and a pat on the back will do the trick. Mary Helen Immordino-Yang, a cognitive neuroscientist and educational psychologist, suggests that if you feel gloomy, hold a pen or pencil crosswise in your mouth to simulate a smile. Yes, it sounds silly, but it works because doing so activates your smile muscles. Remember Mommy smiling down on you? A simple expression can alter a mood.

- *Employ positive e-communication.* Every email, IM, or text you send can either irritate or please the recipient. Never forget the little courtesies and pleasantries, such as "please" and "thank you." Does a smiley face or silly emoticon make you smile? They put a little positive emotion into the message and just might boost the mood of someone who could use a good smile. If emoticons aren't your thing, try ending with "Have a great day" or "Enjoy your weekend." Such statements create a positive, empathetic experience for the reader.

- *Monitor team culture.* As my mother used to say, "You're an intelligent young woman, but if you know you should make some changes and don't, then we may need to rethink the intelligent part." As a group leader, you must obtain the information you need to effect changes in team mood. Ignoring emotional contagion will only make it worse. In some cases, you may need to extract a bad apple from the barrel because you decide to rethink "the intelli-gence part" and replace the bad apple with a good one. That may also apply to you as the leader. Some people are not team players and should find a work environment more suited to them, perhaps dropping out of the orchestra to start a one-man band.

SMART INDIVIDUALS, DUMB GROUP DECISIONS

In Great Britain they don't vacuum the carpet, they Hoover it. That's how established Hoover brand vacuum cleaners have become in their culture. However, when the competition starts to eat into market share, especially during an economic recession, even the most stable of products can find it-self in trouble.

In order to combat several quarters of declining sales in the UK in the early 1990s, Hoover unveiled a major new promotion for their English and Irish customers: Buy any Hoover Vacuum over £100 and get two free round-trip airline tickets to a major European or American city.

The promotion worked beautifully. Sales soared. Appliance stores began running out of machines. Hoover factories went all-out with seven-day pro-duction schedules. In the end, 200,000 to 300,000 customers had qualified for the airline fares.

That's when some genius at Hoover finally did the math. For the price of a vacuum cleaner, Hoover had promised two airline tickets that cost a lot more than even a top-of-the-line new vacuum cleaner, especially the ones to the United States. Hoover had not done the math, but Hoover's cus-tomers had.

When the company reneged on its offer, Hoover's customers saw red. The company's up-selling and confusing phone support further fueled the public outrage. Soon the press and the courts got involved. When the dust finally settled, Hoover suffered a £48 million loss, fired the top three members of the European division, and closed all of Hoover's English factories. The once happy Hoover customers still "Hoovered" their carpets, but more and more often with a Dyson or a Vax.

Smart individuals can and do make dumb group decisions, like the one dreamed up by Hoover management. Why does that happen? Psychologists attribute it to some basic causes: *group overconfidence, group polarization,* the *common information bias,* and in some cases, simply *groupthink.*

OVERCONFIDENCE

Individuals, in general, tend to feel overconfident in their own knowledge, skills, abilities, and predictions. For instance, 81 percent of individuals rate themselves in the top 30 percent of safe drivers. Enamored of our own skills, we can discredit good information or evidence that would help us reach a better decision or see ourselves in a more realistic light. Research bears it out in the corporate ranks as well, showing that CEOs consistently overvalue and overestimate their ability to generate returns, often resulting in poor merger and acquisition decisions. Traders and investors notoriously overestimate their prediction skills, often with disastrous results.

There's nothing wrong with a high degree of confidence. It helps us get the job done and done well. But when we cross the line to overconfidence, things begin to spin out of control. It occurs most often when we possess a tremendous amount of information about a task or issue, when we have gotten knee-deep in the task, and surprisingly, when the task poses a huge challenge. Overconfidence stems from our natural tendency to turn a blind eye to all the myriad ways a situation or problem can unfold (*availability bias*), from our propensity to seek out and weigh only the information that supports our beliefs or decisions (*confirmation bias*), and from our inclination to stick to and overvalue only one value or idea (*anchoring bias*). Finally, because we often gain insight from hindsight, we frequently assume that we can predict the future when, in fact, we really can't see around the corner (*hindsight bias*).

If those biases run rampant in the minds of individuals, just guess what they do to groups. Overconfident individuals tend to grow even more overconfident in groups. Our biases may lead us to make a poor decision, but in a group that shares our biases, we can make a lollapalooza of a bad decision. Even more than usual, we ignore outside advice. A catastrophic example occurred at NASA in 1986, when a team of brilliant scientists and engineers ignored outside advice about the danger of the *Challenger* launch, which resulted in an explosion seen live on millions of television sets around the world. Research has shown that both individual and group overconfidence worsens in situations without verifiably right or wrong answers, exactly in that gray area where almost all business takes place. The larger the group, the more likely it will develop overconfidence.

The composition of a group also influences its degree of confidence. In a 2002 study, Stefen Schulz-Hardt, Marc Jochims, and Dieter Frey asked participants to assess the validity of a hypothesis about the financial wisdom of a new corporate opportunity. The researchers found that groups that shared the same initial perceptions of the alternatives felt more confident than those who held a variety of views. Interestingly, the researchers found a high level of confirmation bias in homogenous groups, which led them to prefer information that supported their preconceptions. Voilà! When others agree with us, there's nothing we can't do!

Increasing commitment to an idea, like the sunk-cost bias we discussed in Chapter 6, also heightens group overconfidence. The tendency to persist in a course of action, despite evidence that argues against it, can lead to poor group performance. The social bonds among group members can escalate commitment, especially in highly cohesive groups where strong bonds stimulate the desire to gain social approval through conformity. *Semper Fi!* can generate spectacular results, but taken to an extreme ("Right or wrong, I will follow you into hell") can lead to just the opposite.

COMMON KNOWLEDGE

People in workgroups/teams tend to overemphasize, discussing ad nauseum, information held by the majority at the expense of information held by the minority. This is known as the *common information bias* or *common information effect*, and problems arise when the "minority report" would have led to better results. Yet research has shown that even when the group does accept the minority report, the group usually ends up dismissing it because it does not support common group knowledge. Paradoxically, organizations assemble teams to come up with innovative ideas, only to find them preoccupied with old, shopworn ideas. This particularly afflicts groups operating on a tight schedule, because weighing new options takes more time than sticking with old ones.

Daniel Gigone and Reid Hastie introduced the common knowledge effect in their 1993 study, which involved 120 college students from the University of Colorado. The researchers randomly assigned students to three member groups and instructed each individual in the group to read short descriptions of several target students and to make individual and then group consensus judgments about those students' grades in the course. Some of the information possessed by the individual group members was shared across the group and some of the information was not. However, everyone received some combination of the target students' high school grade point averages, Scholastic Achievement Test or American College Test percentile scores, self-reported percentage of lectures and recitations attended for the course, self-rated enjoyment of the class, self-rated academic anxiety, and/or self-rated workload in other courses.

They found that information held by all group members before the group discussion more strongly influenced the groups' judgment about the target students' grade in the course than information held by only one group member. In other words, groups weigh shared information more heavily than unshared information.

This common knowledge effect is not a problem when a group possesses 100 percent accurate information. But when does that ever happen?

The business world usually operates in the gray areas between black and white. Several reasons explain our preference for commonly held information. First, we easily access common knowledge. It's the path of least resistance. Group members prefer to exchange information held in common because they receive more favorable reactions.

Individual biases also come into play as group members often enter a discussion with preferences aligned with the shared information. "It has worked for us in the past; it will work for us in the future." New information, ideas, and facts suggest a need for change, and as we saw in Chapter 6, people resist change. Staying in the comfort zone of common knowledge can hold change and the discomfort it causes at bay.

POLARIZATION

You might think moderate opinions will eventually tone down extreme views, but that seldom happens. People in groups come to "polarize" their views toward more extreme positions. Hundreds of studies have shown that after a group discussion, people who supported a war beforehand become more supportive, and people who support a political position become more supportive of that position. Group discussion strengthens, rather than tones down, a group's strong inclinations.

To examine the impact of groups on decision making, a study conducted by Thomas Walker and Eleanor Main in 1973 analyzed decisions of federal district court judges sitting alone or in groups of three. Walker and Main found that when judges sat alone, they took an extreme course of action 30 percent of the time. When sitting in a group of three, they took an extreme course of action 65 percent of the time. The study shows that joining a similarly inclined group makes decision makers more willing to accept, rationalize, and embrace extreme views.

Psychologists have postulated three main theories to explain why people participating in group decision making increasingly polarize and strengthen their initial preferences, and why those people who hold dissimilar preferences at the outset often end up changing their minds and accepting the majority opinion:

1. *Persuasion.* People change their minds when they pay attention to what they deem rational arguments offered by other group members.

2. *Comparison.* People change their minds to conform to the group, especially when they accept those norms as socially desirable.

3. *Differentiation.* People change their minds to accommodate a decision they think the group should make.

Not all groups polarize. The more well established the group, the more comfortable the members feel with one another, the more they trust one another, and the more they know about the issue at hand, the less they will become polarized. In fact, in well-established groups like these, especially under time pressure, people will more likely compromise and reach a middle ground in their decision making. New groups taking on new tasks stand a much higher chance of becoming polarized in order to thwart the insecurity caused by anything new.

GROUPTHINK

Last but not least, we come to groupthink, perhaps the most well-known negative effect that takes place when people congregate in groups. First researched by Irving Janis in 1972, groupthink refers to a way of thinking that can occur when pressure to agree leads people in the group to a biased appraisal of options and, ultimately, to poor and even calamitous decisions. Janis proposed that certain characteristics of groups tend to encourage groupthink, including strong group cohesion, high levels of stress, a strong and directive group leader, high insulation from valuable outside opinions, isolation from other groups, a lack of norms for evaluating information, and low member self-esteem and confidence.

You can recognize groupthink by its typical symptoms: close-mindedness, lock-step conformity, self-censorship, overestimation or stereotyping of outsiders, and a sense of invulnerability and moral superiority. When members feel compelled to agree with the leader and with one another, they do not express reservations openly and offer little criticism. This self-censorship bolsters the fictional belief that everyone wholeheartedly backs what the group thinks, says, and does.

Groupthink undermines the long-term viability of the team as bad decisions pile up. Ultimately, the team can be rendered ineffective because it has denied too much useful information and has failed to make contingency plans. Well-known examples discussed by Janis include the United States' failure to anticipate the attack on Pearl Harbor and the escalation of the Vietnam War, where contradictory views against the war were reportedly prohibited in the decision-making rooms. It also made headlines when it helped demolish Enron and Lehman Brothers.

Ironically, groupthink itself may well be an example of groupthink. The term has migrated into everyday parlance, becoming an unquestioningly accepted concept. However, the scientific community has begun doubting its validity owing to a lack of supporting empirical evidence. Although many of the group dynamics, such as confirmation bias and pressure toward conformity, described by Janis are correlated with poor group decision-making processes, these dynamics or group tendencies often occur (and occur together) when groups are not engaged in groupthink. In addition, some of the conditions that purportedly give rise to groupthink, such as group cohesiveness, do not necessarily lead to poor group decision making. Nevertheless, the symptoms used to describe groupthink do exist, no matter what label you put on them.

COUNTERACTING THE TRAPS

Setting up and managing good groups requires careful thinking about the team's composition, size, objectives, and protocols. To counteract some of the common problems that can make a good team go bad:

Establish Group Diversity. Although a leader might feel tempted to assemble five like-minded people on a team, uniformity can stifle creativity and breed lackluster results. Consider selecting a diverse group of people who represent, as much as possible, different genders, ages, ethnicities, functional skills, and experiences. Make it clear to the team why you did so. "You'll see some unfamiliar faces here because I want to make sure we get a wide range of input as we try to invent a new toothpaste container."

Define Expectations. If leaders clearly state the results they expect from a group, whether in an ad hoc meeting or an ongoing work team, they can more easily keep everyone's effort on track toward the desired goal. That also helps ensure accountability for results. After all, it's not easy holding people accountable for results if you have never told them exactly what you expect them to do. "We will create specifications for a new type of toothpaste tube by close of business on Friday."

Emphasize Collective Awareness. If team members understand common group biases, they will more easily spot and correct their biases. "Look, we all prefer to squeeze the toothpaste tube rather than roll it up. Let's keep that in mind when someone suggests a new type of tube that might require rolling it up."

Provide the Right Training. Although leaders commonly hire people who will make good team players, they do not necessarily train people to work well in teams. Unless every member of your team has actively played team sports throughout his or her life, some individuals may find it unfamiliar territory. Yes, everyone may naturally gravitate toward groups, but effective group behavior requires certain skills, such as performing a specific role despite the fact that you could perform other roles just as well. Tackle teamwork training as thoughtfully as you do technical or on-the job training. Developing a set of teamwork skills among your people not only enhances their self and social awareness, it also provides them with the tools they need to operate successfully in a group.

Team skill training can come from an outside consultant or your organizational development department. Get your team thinking about the nature of group dynamics and the collective strengths and weaknesses of a group by actively discussing such questions as:

1. What are the strengths of our team?

2. What are the weaknesses of our team?

3. What are the roadblocks we seem to face when it comes to:
   - Communication?
   - Decision making/problem solving?
   - Managing project, time, and delivery?

4. What conditions do we need to thrive?

5. What conditions cause us to suffer?

Such discussions heighten everyone's awareness of what it takes to function productively in a group. "Let's review our last major breakthrough, when we invented the tuna fish can style key for rolling up a toothpaste tube."

Stress Freedom of Thought. A leader can prepare the team for an important meeting by urging them to do their homework individually and bring to the meeting information and ideas free from team influence. Stress that no bit of data and no possible alternative is too silly or dumb to present to the meeting. "Before we get together for our first team session on Wednesday, I want you to research and think deeply about the history of the toothpaste tube. Jot down facts and ideas that pop into your head as you do your homework."

Insist on Information Sharing. A leader must insist on information sharing. When people can freely access all information during a discussion, they feel less inclined to leave out material that might lead to a better decision or solution. Recommend that everyone list all of the information in their possession that relates to an issue. "Who wants to talk about the invention of the first toothpaste tube? Let's examine every little wrinkle our competitors have added over the years."

Promote Innovation. A good leader stimulates people to climb over the mental fence that can keep a group from devising, openly discussing, and adopting new ideas and solutions. Priming a group to think critically and creatively, versus just reaching a consensus, helps a team share more information, challenge each other without rancor or judgment, and get better results. "We all know the two classic ways to get toothpaste out of the tube, but can we dream up a way that does not involve squeezing or rolling up the tube? And, by the way, why does toothpaste even need to come in a tube? I'll take the person who comes up with the most outrageous idea to lunch."

WRAP UP

From the first primates to climb down from the trees, to our cave-dwelling ancestors, to modern-day *Homo sapiens*, and from little Mom-and-Pop bodegas, to sprawling multinational conglomerates, folks always have and always will feel impelled to form and join groups. Every group, from a mixed-doubles tennis team to a 250-person sales force, comes under the influence of group dynamics. Understanding those dynamics helps leaders create and manage teams more effectively and to keep them from falling prey to negative group behaviors that can make a good team go bad.

CHAPTER

8

What Causes a Star to Fade?

A NEW CLIENT RECENTLY ASKED me for consultation about a career-threatening problem. Almost ten months earlier, Dan had joined a software development company as a product engineer. His new job, helping a team develop an innovative product called Widget, completely energized him. He saw unlimited career possibilities ahead, and the new salary and bonus structure completely blew away what he'd earned at his last job. He would be working from home, something that made him a little nervous until his new boss promised that they bring all of their telecommuters to the home office every quarter to connect with their teammates.

Dan hit the ground running and enjoyed smooth sailing at first. Widget was coming along nicely, he thought. Working smoothly across different departments, he built many strong relationships inside the company. He went above and beyond his job description, developing leads for the sales team and cultivating good relationships with potential clients. So why was he sitting in my office with the look of a man about to jump out of a plane without a parachute? To paraphrase the classic line in the movie *Cool Hand Luke*, "What we got here is failure to engage."

Sitting in my office with his head down and his shoulders slumped, Dan told me that he could not wait to get out of the company and into a job, "where people are not such a bunch of backstabbing liars." Gradually, he revealed the reasons he had gone from excited, committed, and hardworking to depressed, frustrated, and looking for a new job.

As we'll soon see, Dan had fallen victim to a classic organizational problem: the failure to engage people. The Gallup Organization spent thirty years interviewing close to 17 million employees to come up with one undeniable conclusion, published in the *Journal of Applied Psychology*: Employee disengagement can hurt productivity, performance, discretionary effort, workplace safety, loyalty, morale, and ultimately, the bottom line. Like a lot of current business clichés, we all know about engagement. But do we really know what it means?

ELUSIVE ENGAGEMENT

Many leaders can't define it but know it when they see it. Top research and consulting firms, such as Gallup and Blessing White, have studied the concept using large databases of employees and employers in every imaginable industry around the world. Each has based its measurements on different definitions and drivers, even though they have been searching for common threads. The Conference Board penned one simple, clean definition: "A heightened emotional connection that an employee feels for his or her organization, that influences him or her to exert greater discretionary effort to his or her work." In psychological terms, engagement is a state of mind driven by behavioral, cognitive, and emotional factors.

Numerous tangible and intangible aspects of how people interact within an organization influence engagement, including, but not limited to:

- *Work.* The components that dictate how a company functions, its structure, its reputation, its culture, its practice of social and global responsibility, the tasks its people perform, the nature of the work, and available resources.

- *Processes.* The policies and procedures that govern company operations, including performance reviews, information management and communication, general and human resource management practices.

- *People.* The quality and effectiveness of a company's leaders, managers, employees, and customers, and the strength of their inter- and intra-relationships.

- *Benefits.* The tangible and intangible rewards people receive including pay, bonuses, health care, recognition, awards, job security/stability, and sense of community from the company.

- *Opportunities.* The methods used to gain advancement and opportunity, including career-development programs, training and learning initiatives, exposure across different levels and functions, and standards for promotion.

- *Investment.* The investment, financial and emotional, a company makes in its people through respect for work/life integration, the physical work environment, alignment between the work people do and the overarching goals of the organization.

These various factors do not influence every individual's engagement the same way. A young recruit may long for advancement while an experienced manager may appreciate job security and company benefits. In most cases, however, engagement arises from the fabric woven from all of these threads.

Regardless of why and how engagement occurs, research and surveys have consistently shown that engagement applies to every type of work environment and figures prominently in business outcomes. Rodd Wagner and James Harter, as part of their work for the Gallup Organization, found clear connections between employees who feel fully engaged in their work and higher rates of retention, lower rates of turnover, reduced absenteeism, greater productivity, enhanced profitability, fewer workplace accidents, and more intense customer satisfaction and loyalty.

The Gallup research also showed that:

- Publicly traded organizations with highly engaged people reported 3.9 times the earnings-per-share growth as those in the same industry with less fully engaged people.

- Organizations with the highest engagement scores enjoyed an 83 percent chance of achieving above-average business performance levels. Those with the lowest levels of engagement could expect no more than a 17 percent chance.

Although engagement researchers employ different methodologies, they agree that this elusive concept plays a vital role in an individual's contribution to desired business outcomes. You can't do it superficially by merely taking your team out for a casual dinner and hoping that a few slices of pizza will magically inspire them to greatness. You must build engagement into the very fabric of the organization. You must work on it just as diligently as you work on improving the bottom line. It's not easy, because almost every day we find ourselves up to our eyebrows in all the daily crises, big and small, that make us too busy to win, too proud to see, and too afraid to lose (see Chapter 1). Busy with the business of busyness, we lose sight of what really matters to our people and unintentionally disengage the very people on whom the success of our organization depends.

Remember Dan and his eleven-month plunge from engagement to disengagement? His star faded for two essential reasons:

1. His employer motivated him but failed to engage him. Motivating and engaging people are not the same thing.

2. His employer breached a psychological contract, an unspoken understanding between them. Breaching the contract poisons engagement.

MISUNDERSTOOD MOTIVATION

Motivation makes us do what we do. Beginning in infancy, our biological hardwiring causes us to react in certain ways to all types and intensities of motivation throughout our lives. But how does motivation differ from engagement? Engagement encapsulates the "what" of motivation. *What* makes us do what we do? It also includes the "how" and "why" behind what we do. It incorporates our motivational drives, our social connections, and our sense of personal meaning.

What went wrong at Dan's company? Dan's work team included nine other people: the product director (Michael); a project manager (Laura): two other product engineers (Nick and Taylor), two programmers (Gary and Derrick), the sales director (Deborah), and her sales managers (Rick and Christine). Dan, Taylor, Derrick, and Laura began working for the company at around the same time, when Widget was moving from beta testing to market. Soon after Dan started his job, he introduced Deborah to one of the decision makers he knew at a large New York banking group, because he felt confident Deborah could clinch the deal. If the team could make this sale, it would change the game for the company, as in the past they had sold most of its products to smaller financial institutions. Leadership was so excited about this potential sale that they promised a big bonus for each team member if they closed the deal.

For six months the team feverishly wooed the decision makers at the banking group and eventually won the sale. However, when the team popped the champagne cork and ripped open the envelopes containing their bonuses, their smiles turned to frowns. The leadership team preempted any questions about the paltry bonuses with the argument that the company needed to keep investing in new products and that the team would eventually receive the promised reward. The team was not happy. They had heard that song before.

In one short month, complaints from their new customer started rolling in. Widget was not doing what the sales team had promised. Dan, Derrick, Taylor, and Laura began working around the clock to fix the bugs, which turned out to be bigger and nastier than anyone imagined. It turned out that Deborah, the project director Michael, and the other veterans on the team knew about the flaws but had kept them from the leadership team. They hoped the new kids would fix the glitches before Widget hit the market.

Eventually the team patched up Widget, not only debugging it but also adding some new components that made it even more useful in large applications. Deborah and Michael took full credit for the accomplishment and received the kudos. Dan and his counterparts got scolded for the time they spent fixing something that never should have broken in the first place. That's when Dan's star imploded.

Simply put, the leaders made a promise they failed to keep. They failed to engage. In 2011, the international giant Blessing White issued a global employee engagement report reflecting information gathered during interviews with HR departments and line leaders, as well as online survey responses of 10,914 individuals from North America, India, Europe, Southeast Asia, Australia/New Zealand, and China. The study found that engaged employees remain with their employer because of what the employees *give*: the enjoyment of their work and the satisfaction of making a contribution. Motivated but not fully engaged employees stay with their employer for what they *get*: a good salary, bonuses, career advancement, a secure job, and/or pleasant job conditions.

Over the years, several theories have emerged to explain motivation. In this chapter we will explore the one that uses the idea of extrinsic (external) and intrinsic (internal) factors to explain the forces that motivate us.

- *Extrinsic Motivation.* The old-fashioned carrot-and-stick approach encourages someone to perform a task to gain recognition and rewards or to avoid punishment and other negative consequences. External motivators, as a means to an end, include winning or losing compensation, raises, bonuses, recognition, awards, praise, or a promotion. "I am working hard because I want the bonus to buy a new car" or "I am working hard because my boss threatened me with a demotion." Dan's company used external motivators of a promised big bonus and recognition to spur Dan's team to close the big sale.

External motivators promise satisfaction that the task itself might not deliver. Writing a user manual for Widget may be as exciting as watching paint dry, but the promised bonus or carrot keeps Dan hard at work.

- *Intrinsic Motivation.* The heart and soul of deep commitment, intrinsic motivation compels people to perform a task because "It's the right thing to do." They also enjoy doing it because it bestows fulfillment, empowerment, and excitement. While people appreciate external rewards, those rewards are not the primary reason they engage.

  Writing the user's manual for Widget is something Dan finds fun and fulfilling. Dan, Taylor, Derrick, and Laura also felt intrinsically motivated to fix Widget. They had invested a lot of time and energy winning the contract. They took pride and ownership in its successful implementation. Fixing its problems gave them that same sense of pride and professionalism.

Intrinsic and extrinsic motivation affects each of us in uniquely personal ways. Extrinsically motivated people go through the motions to get the carrot or avoid the stick. Intrinsically motivated people who feel deeply committed consider the complexities and possibilities of performing a task, methodically gathering and processing information and creatively integrating it into their work. Which is the best way to get stellar results? It's a no-brainer. Intrinsic motivation fires people up from deep inside their heart and soul. It engages them.

But this may surprise you. In some cases, working for the extrinsic reward (the carrot) can reduce the intrinsic motivation (the heart and soul). Extrinsic rewards for performance, specifically tasks that require creative, out-of-the-box thinking, can create a conflict between the joy of doing a good job and doing it for the reward. When Edward Deci studied this theory in 1971, he found a trend toward a decrease in intrinsic motivation when students received money as an external reward for completing a task. Positive feedback, reinforcement, and support, on the other hand, increased intrinsic motivation.

Teresa Amabile, a leading researcher on creativity, tested this notion in the workplace. She argues that promising only extrinsic rewards, raises or bonuses, deters individuals from applying creativity to a task. This happens when people perceive that every move they make will affect—improve or harm—their financial livelihood. We are not talking about fair compensation for work but, rather, a preoccupation with compensation that makes people cautious. That caution inhibits them from expansive thinking. Amabile found that leaders who reward employees with bonuses or rewards for meeting or exceeding expectations should also respect the power of intrinsic motivation. Leaders who emphasize, support, and reward creativity, and who foster workplaces that provide an opportunity to learn and grow, generate inspired solutions. Leaders who fail to cultivate intrinsic motivation (the heart and soul) generate uninspired solutions.

In his book *Carrots and Sticks Don't Work*, author Paul Marciano stresses the important relationship between motivation and engagement. High levels of engagement cushion the effects of a poor work environment, and that can influence people's motivation to cope with challenging deadlines, limited resources, or even nasty bosses. When times get tough and rewards grow scarce, the intrinsically motivated tough of heart keep harvesting results and truly shine. The extrinsically motivated "carrot munchers" eventually fall behind when rewards diminish and fail to get terrific results.

There is a biological and psychological interplay between motivation and engagement. High engagement and intrinsic motivation add tremendously to the reasons people work hard. Each side of the equation progressively influences the other side to create and enhance the working environment. In a positive culture of engagement, people naturally go the extra mile for your team, for your customers, and for your company. That's why you need to watch for organizational decisions, environments, attitudes, and behaviors that interfere with engagement. Interference can lead to a breach in the psychological contract.

THE PSYCHOLOGICAL CONTRACT

After Dan's team solved the product emergency problem, Dan found himself growing more and more disillusioned. What he saw as manipulative and self-serving management had driven half the team to other projects during the most critical period of the product's lifecycle. The project's leaders hid information from the team, then took credit for the creative results the team produced. Adding insult to injury, there was the incredible shrinking bonus. All of this had shattered Dan's dream of building a super product.

Widget was not doing what the company promised it would do. Even though Dan and his team fixed the problems and created some satisfying additional features, he knew the product could not meet long-term expectations. That ultimate failure challenged his personal integrity.

Every company and every boss enters into a *psychological contract* with their employees. Denise Rousseau, professor at Carnegie Mellon University, defines the psychological contract as an individual's beliefs about the mutual obligations that exist between the employee and the employer. It's a two-way street: "You can expect this from me. In return, I will give this to you." These obligations involve both stated and unstated promises the parties make to one another. In past decades, the obligations included such rewards as a pension (a term that rarely appears anywhere but on Wikipedia) and almost guaranteed job security. The employer's stated obligations (the tangibles) include pay, reward systems, benefits, and resources to do the job. An employee agrees to arrive on time and work to fulfill the employer's expectations. An employer's unstated commitments (the intangibles), including respect, fairness, meaningful work, and other workplace conditions you can't easily quantify, far outnumber the stated ones.

A psychological contract, whether between you and your best friend or between you and your immediate superior, revolves around two behavioral concepts: *social exchange theory* and the *norm of reciprocity*. Social exchange theory says that social behavior results from an exchange in which we weigh a relationship in terms of a cost-benefit analysis. Naturally, we strive to maximize benefits while minimizing costs or just to keep the scales balanced. If the scale begins to tilt to disfavor us, we will begin to suffer behavioral, emotional, and attitudinal consequences. "You promised me a promotion if I succeeded with this project. I did, but you passed me over. Now I'm livid." The norm of reciprocity defines what you will do for someone if he or she does something for you. "If you let me take the lead on this project, I will exceed your revenue expectations."

The psychological contract incorporates tangibles and intangibles from both parties, as depicted in Figure 8-1. Although they appear in nice, neat boxes in this chart, the elements evolve over time and often cross the boundaries between tangible and intangible.

These obligations arise from written documents, verbal promises, interactions with hiring teams, recruiters, and other employees, experiences working in the organizational culture, and even an employee's past work experiences. In essence, this contract adds unspoken and unwritten elements to the formal employee/employer contract. Although it is a dynamic contract that evolves over time, initial experiences shape many of the expectations associated with the contract. In turn, the contract influences and shapes the behavior, attitudes, and expectations of both parties.

To complicate matters, no two people comprehend the elements of the contract exactly the same way. As we have learned throughout this book, a host of psychological biases can distort our perceptions. These distortions, coupled with all the usual miscommunications that occur between people, can wreak havoc on the psychological contract. Tangibles, such as position, pay, and benefits, often bring people into an organization. Intangibles, such

FIGURE 8-1 Psychological Contract Tangibles and Intangibles

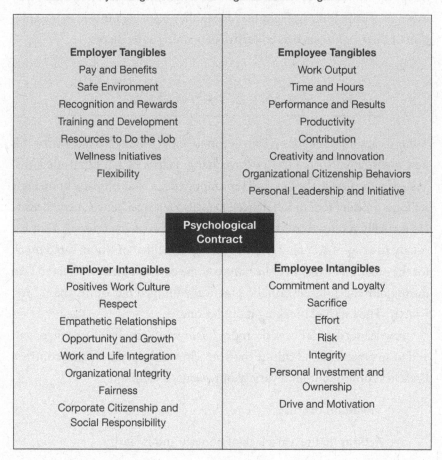

Employer Tangibles	Employee Tangibles
Pay and Benefits	Work Output
Safe Environment	Time and Hours
Recognition and Rewards	Performance and Results
Training and Development	Productivity
Resources to Do the Job	Contribution
Wellness Initiatives	Creativity and Innovation
Flexibility	Organizational Citizenship Behaviors
	Personal Leadership and Initiative

Psychological Contract

Employer Intangibles	Employee Intangibles
Positives Work Culture	Commitment and Loyalty
Respect	Sacrifice
Empathetic Relationships	Effort
Opportunity and Growth	Risk
Work and Life Integration	Integrity
Organizational Integrity	Personal Investment and Ownership
Fairness	Drive and Motivation
Corporate Citizenship and Social Responsibility	

as corrosive corporate culture, lack of appreciation, myopic leadership, or a tarnished organizational reputation, often drive them away.

As in romantic relationships, both parties to the contract usually enjoy a honeymoon period. Rousseau describes new employees who feel optimistic about the relationship, expressing high initial expectations of the job. When reality sets in, expectations shift. Expectations can decline a few percentage points and not severely damage the relationship, or they can enter free-fall, sending the relationship into an abyss of disappointment. This is what happened to Dan and his team. When these intangibles diminish or disappear, individuals can feel forced into a fight/flight response. Flight may mean they leave bitterly. Fight may mean they resort to outside representation of their rights, such as collective bargaining agreements.

BROKEN PROMISES

As his disappointment grew, Dan began to regret leaving his old job for this new nightmare. Normally a positive, hardy fellow, he felt blindsided, disgusted by the deceit, the lies, and the crappy ethics of a company knowingly selling a product that didn't deliver. Dan also felt torn between two bosses. He formally reported to Michael, but Deborah kept intervening. Dan felt caught in a tug-of-war between two managers, neither of whom cared much for the other. As I explained the nature of the psychological contract to Dan during our coaching session, he practically jumped out of his chair. "Yes! Exactly! They started breaking it on day one."

Few leadership failures do more harm to an employee's engagement and to an organization's culture than breaches of the psychological contract. Breaches come about for a variety of reasons, including:

- Violations of trust

- Actions that reveal a lack of honesty and integrity

- Behaviors that violate ethics or the law

- Promises that get broken

- Assignments that intrude on personal time

- Job descriptions and expectations that are ill-defined

- Environments that are difficult and depressing

- Leaders who drastically alter the deal

Dan was experiencing the perfect storm of every possible breach of contract. His behavior and attitude at the company were changing. As the breaches accumulated, he went from excited, motivated, and productive to disengaged and disinterested. Dan's behavioral and attitudinal change is not surprising. A 2007 study of more than 100 prior research studies undertaken by Hao Zhao and colleagues found that breaches of the psychological contract resulted in a number of changes in the minds of employees. They experienced sharp declines in:

- Job satisfaction

- Performance

- Loyalty and trust

- Interest in working beyond a job description

- Cooperation and sharing with peers

At least one attitude did increase, however: interest in seeking better opportunities elsewhere. File all of these attitudes under "W" for "Withdrawal." Withdrawal can run the gamut from wordless rebellion to outright violence. Another study, conducted by P. Matthijs Bal and colleagues, found that contractual breaches influence different age groups differently. Younger employees lose their sense of trust and commitment; older ones lose their sense of job satisfaction.

This fact should greatly concern current leaders, particularly as they contemplate and prepare for the Millennials who will increasingly assume leadership positions in the coming years. Numerous studies and engagement surveys have shown that the next generation of young leaders already feels less positive and engaged in their jobs. A major gap has opened up between what they expected and what they have received from their employment, having entered the workforce during a massive recession, with high unemployment and low career mobility. Their idealism clashes with what they see as outdated corporate values and rampant corporate corruption.

Starting a career with an already broken psychological contract creates significant behavioral, emotional, and attitudinal consequences. How do you engage young people whose high, and perhaps unrealistic, expectations have been dashed by the reality of going to work in a bad economy? What kind of leaders will they become? Can you help them become great leaders?

You start with understanding the effects of perceived breaches in the psychological contract. Originally discussed by Albert Hirschman in 1970, then expanded upon by later investigators, the effects fall into four broad categories:

1. *Exit:* Leaving or planning to leave the organization.

2. *Voice:* Speaking up to address the breach with superiors, co-workers, family, and friends.

3. *Loyalty:* Suffering in silence and hoping the problem will solve itself.

4. *Neglect:* Making a half-hearted effort to do the work.

If playing the waiting game or speaking up does not remedy the situation, an unhappy employee will likely progress from neglecting his or her work to eventually getting fired or leaving to find another job.

According to the principle of emotional contagion, which we discussed in Chapter 7, all four behaviors can adversely affect others in the organization. If my teammate Raji suffers, I suffer; if he speaks up, I take his feelings to heart; if he neglects his work, so do I (or I have to cover for him); if he leaves, I consider following in his footsteps. It can affect me even more when the emotions flow from my boss.

A 2010 study by Prashant Bordia and colleagues found that a breach of the psychological contract between the organization and a supervisor trickles down to employees who work for the supervisor, ultimately breaching the supervisor/employee contract and, in the long run, the company/customer contract. Customer care declines, customers feel dissatisfied, and the company loses business.

In this way, engagement poison can seep into an organization's culture, and once it does, it takes a powerful antidote to neutralize it. Two symptoms—cynicism and burnout—can prove especially virulent.

CYNICISM AND BURNOUT

Dan's loyalty to the organization gradually diminished. He finally talked to Michael about his situation, but true to form, Michael brushed off Dan's complaints. As he continued to suffer, he felt burned out, began to neglect his work, complained about his situation, and, predictably, contemplated quitting. The once optimistic Dan had become a cynic.

Dan is not alone in the contemporary workplace. A sour economy, headlines blaring a continuous stream of corporate malfeasance, longer work hours, fear of joining the unemployment line, and a precipitous decline in the reciprocal loyalty between employers and their employees that once characterized American corporate life have contributed to a veritable plague of employee cynicism. In 1998, James Dean and colleagues defined employee cynicism as "a negative attitude toward one's employing organization," and proposed that cynicism begins with a belief that the organization's management and leadership lack integrity. It's a belief that results in disparaging remarks, sharp criticism, and a host of negative behaviors toward the organization.

In 2003, Jonathan Johnson and Anne O'Leary-Kelly studied the relationship between a psychological contract breach and cynicism. Relying on information gathered from bank employees, their supervisors, and organizational records, the researchers discovered that employee cynicism derives not from bad attitudes people bring to the workplace but from their experiences on the job. Cynicism can also lead to emotional exhaustion and burnout. Some people seem more susceptible to developing a bad attitude, feeling pessimistic, and badmouthing their bosses and peers. They earn a reputation as bad apples that spoil the whole barrel, but even those rotten apples become that way through experience.

Experience shapes our core beliefs and sense of self. Water that flows off one duck's back may make another duck feel like it's being waterboarded. "I can use a good shower," says the resilient duck that draws on reserves of psychological capital (a mix of self-efficacy, resilience, hope, and optimism) and mental hardiness to buffer the effects of a bad experience. The cynical duck lacks those reserves. It thinks poorly of itself and believes it can't survive the bad experience. It employs cynicism as a sort of shield against overpowering emotions that can lead to burnout.

It's always tempting to dismiss the cynics and embrace the believers. Our human nature urges us to blame the negative attitudes and behaviors of others on their negative personalities. Psychologists call it the *fundamental attribution bias*. This bias causes us to overvalue personality-based explanations for the behaviors of others and to undervalue environmental factors. The paradox of the fundamental attribution bias, however, is that the rules change if it applies to us. If we feel undervalued by the organization, it must be that the organization is at fault. If Dan complains about his situation, Michael and Deborah just chalk it up to his whining nature, ignoring the managerial missteps that have turned him into a whiner. But, if either Michael or Deborah started to feel the way Dan felt, he or she would quickly blame the organization as well.

Here's where a leader can learn from the situation and avoid making a huge mistake. Far from being rotten apples, cynical employees possess valuable information that can keep the whole barrel from getting spoiled. If bosses could look past what they see as whining and ask employees, and themselves, what causes these complaints, they might be able to come up with a cure for the ailment. That would require knowledge of the nature of engagement, a suspension of judgment, an open mind, a good deal of self-awareness, and a willingness to make some changes in their own approach to management.

Engagement is not a luxury these days; it's a necessity. Companies that have begun to believe in this concept have gained a competitive advantage. What, exactly, can you do to engage your people and keep them engaged?

THE SLAM MODEL

The good news: There is an engagement elixir. The not-so-good news: It varies from organization to organization. That's why I have developed a way of thinking about engagement that will help you tailor an engagement strategy to the unique nature and needs of your organization.

SLAM	
S	Social Connection
L	Leadership Excellence
A	Aligned Culture
M	Meaningful Work and Life

I've developed this model as I've worked with individuals and organizations over the years to come to grips with motivational and engagement problems in the workplace. It incorporates all of my experience and the latest research in the field into an easy-to-remember and useful tool for creating and maintaining engagement in the workplace. Its holistic point of view respects all of the important aspects of human nature: psychology, physiology, emotions, attitudes, and behaviors.

SOCIAL CONNECTION

Think about the last time you left a group of people you really cared about, left home to go off to college, left college to take your first important job, or left one job for another one. If you have formed strong social connections with your classmates and colleagues, you found it a rather wrenching experience. It's hard to leave friends behind. The research by the Gallup Organization that we discussed earlier in this chapter cited two especially critical elements related to workplace engagement: "I have a best friend at work" and "My supervisor and other people care about me as a person." These social connections mean a lot to people.

Our basic and powerful need for social connection figures prominently in our work lives. Engagement, retention, performance, productivity, cultural commitment, wellness, and stress reduction depend on it. That's why a leader must concentrate on fostering relationships. A smart leader:

- Encourages and supports social events, sometimes including family and friends. Attending a company picnic and playing in the annual softball game enhance the ties that bind people together.

- Holds regular staff meetings with some open-ended items on the agenda. Putting the hectic workday on hold and discussing important issues draws people into a circle of mutual caring and respect.

- Emphasizes the value of team-based volunteering, which not only enhances peoples' sense of purpose and meaning but also strengthens organizational values. Working to renovate a community playground unites the team behind a project that carries meaning far beyond the office.

- Convenes company-wide celebrations to honor achievements. Receiving public recognition and watching colleagues accept awards strengthen social bonds.

- Fosters team-based wellness competitions. Joining in a fitness campaign can unite people in a cause that delivers tangible benefits.

- Allows for occasional extended lunches or end-of-day get-togethers. Spending a little company time on something enjoyable makes people feel closer to one another.

- Designs off-site overnight retreats. Engaging in a late-night bull session gives people a chance to develop their relationships outside the work environment.

- Includes qualitative as well as quantitative measures in performance appraisals. Knowing the organization values the intangibles, such as supporting colleagues in distress and helping people feel good about themselves as whole persons, not just automatons cranking our widgets and contributing to the bottom line, goes a long way.

You can undoubtedly add to this start list, but you get the point. Stronger social connections lead to higher levels of engagement.

LEADERSHIP EXCELLENCE

Janine told me a story about her path to entrepreneurship. Back in her late twenties she had worked for an accounting firm. Her boss, Todd, ran his department by the book. When Janine's veterinarian called, telling her that her gravely ill seventeen-year-old spaniel would need to be put down, Janine tearfully asked Todd for the day off. Hunched over his keyboard, Todd muttered, "No. The policy says you must give me forty-eight hours notice for a vacation day." As he kept typing, she asked if she could come to work two hours late the next day. He said nothing.

The next day, still mourning the loss of a pet she had loved for more than half her life, she walked into the office at 10 A.M. Todd met her at the door, turned on his heel, and said, "Follow me." Seated in Todd's office, she watched as he filled out a form to report her insubordination. Not once did he make eye contact or express concern for her loss. "That's the very moment I began plotting my departure. It felt terrible, but it was, in a way, the best thing that ever happened to me. It pushed me to start my own company. Todd taught me everything I needed to be a success: Just do the opposite of what he did."

I wish I could say that excellent leaders outnumber all the insensitive and emotionally clueless Todds in this world, but that's sadly not true. Remember Julius and Augustus Caesar from Chapter 5? Chances are you've worked for more than your fair share of the ego-driven Julius Caesars of the business world. Engagement depends more than anything else on the sort of panoramic leadership Augustus practiced throughout his tenure as Rome's leader. The mindset of an excellent leader spreads throughout the organization and to all stakeholders. So does the attitude and behavior of a myopic one. When it reaches customers, the organization's reputation and bottom line suffer.

In 2009, Deloitte research proposed that key retention strategies during tough economic times include excellent leadership, transparency, and work environments where honesty and integrity rule. By contrast, weak, self-serving leadership consistently results in stress, poor mental health, inhibited performance, and high levels of turnover. Excellent leaders:

- Think and behave panoramically.

- Eliminate myopic attitudes and behavior.

- Close their mouths and open their ears to learn what their people feel and need.

- Create safe cultures where people freely ask for help and never fear making a mistake.

- Develop emotional intelligence, self- and social awareness, and relationship skills.

- Encourage others to do the same.

- Remain visible, present, and open to all feedback.

- Model the attitudes and behaviors they expect of others.

- Create and maintain a culture of pure transparency.

- Align people with the organization's values.

- Stress how every job fits into the organization's strategy and goals.

- Follow through on promises and commitments and all psychological contracts.

- Restore broken contracts.

- Practice the highest levels of ethics and integrity.

- Welcome and share input, feedback, and ideas from all levels.

- Establish and manage expectations.

Leaders like Todd who fail to practice those principles end up losing their peoples' trust and respect. Their people include not only every employee from the C-suite to the mailroom but also shareholders, customers, suppliers, government watchdogs, and everyone else who comes into contact with the organization. Janine swore she would never treat her people the way Todd treated her, and on that promise she has built a wildly successful company of her own.

One final note: Never delegate engagement to the human resources department. When it comes to engaging and keeping people engaged, the buck both starts and stops on the leader's desk.

ALIGNED CULTURE

The Methodist Hospital System in Texas consistently wins awards for employee and customer satisfaction and enjoys enviable retention rates. They do it not just with comprehensive management and development initiatives but also with a steady emphasis on aligning everyone with the company's purpose and values. Alignment, they know, will help create engagement at all levels. Every person in the hospital system, whether they serve as vice-president of marketing or cafeteria cashier, understands how his or her role fits into the bigger picture of the hospital's mission. Every action an employee performs and every word he or she speaks either supports or undermines the company's overarching values. This deep psychological and behavioral buy-in has propelled Methodist Hospital System to excellence, year after year.

Sadly, too many organizations post their values, vision, and mission on their website and include material about them in packets they give new employees, but they do not weave them into the fabric of the organization. They pay only lip service to them, failing to live and breathe them. Ask their people to state the organization's values and mission, and you'll hear them stammer and stutter before they say, "Um, to sell a lot of widgets?" That's a sure sign the organization has paid scant attention to alignment.

When leaders don't hold true to their corporate values or make exceptions when the going gets tough, they not only violate the psychological contract but they also fail to fulfill our basic human need to understand the context in which we work. Do we just sell widgets, or do we improve our customers' lives by helping them solve their problems? Ignoring alignment is like disregarding a child's basic needs. Do it often enough, and you'll wake up one day with a juvenile delinquent on your hands. What do you think of the following code of ethics?

Respect. We treat others as we would like to be treated ourselves. We do not tolerate abusive or disrespectful treatment. Ruthlessness, callousness, and arrogance don't belong here.

Integrity. We work with customers and prospects openly, honestly, and sincerely. When we say we will do something, we will do it; when we say we cannot or will not do something, then we won't do it.

Communication. We have an obligation to communicate. Here, we take the time to talk with one another and to listen. We believe that information is meant to move and that information moves people.

Excellence. We are satisfied with nothing less than the very best in everything we do. We will continue to raise the bar for everyone. The great fun here will be for all of us to discover just how good we can really be.

Sounds good, right? It may surprise you to learn that this code comes from Enron, the failed energy giant that once proclaimed itself a "global corporate citizen." Clearly the words did not translate into action. The way a company presents itself, both inwardly and outwardly, influences an employee's personal self-esteem, personal value, and personal pride. If a company not only talks a good game but also walks a good game, it engages its stakeholders.

To make sure you walk a good game, you can begin by:

- Defining and redefining your vision, mission, values, and purpose concretely. This does not just involve senior leadership; it should also include input from all other levels, because all levels must put the mission and values into practice. Creating a cross-functional, cross-layer group to evaluate and re-evaluate will get the most meaningful results.

- Replacing the concept of "hiring warm bodies" with a philosophy of comprehensive organizational fit with respect to personality, relationship style, work style, team consciousness, and so on.

- Presenting prospective employees with the good, the bad, and the ugly about the company so they truly know what to expect.

- Adopting management and leadership principles that support the culture.

- Developing people to fit the culture.

- Shifting from the traditional one-day to two-week orientation process to one designed to promote on-boarding with the company's mission and values.

In my consulting practice I talk about getting everyone on board with the organization's values and mission. An organization should develop on-boarding strategies for employees at every level, as well as for all shareholders, customers, suppliers, the media, governmental and regulating agencies, and anyone else who comes into contact with the organization.

Ongoing efforts to synchronize an organization's values and mission with its hiring practices, retention strategies, management and leadership principles, business models, human resources practices, corporate citizenship behaviors, and corporate image fuel engagement.

MEANINGFUL WORK AND LIFE

For the sake of argument, let's make some very general assumptions about the average worker during the five-day workweek. Accounting for a forty-six-week year (allowing for a two-week vacation, ten sick days, and ten public or floating holidays), he or she:

- Works for approximately forty-seven years.

- Works forty hours a week, or 1,840 hours a year.

- Sleeps forty hours (eight hours a night) during the workweek, or 1,840 hours a year.

This means a worker spends about a third of his or her time sleeping and a third of the time working. That doesn't leave much time to shower, eat, take care of one's family, decompress, spend time with friends, run errands, exercise, walk the dog, feed the cat, and goof off. Furthermore, in the days of social media, emails, and smartphones, the nine to five, Monday to Friday workweek has overflowed into most people's personal lives. And how many people do you know who actually work only eight hours or sleep a full eight hours?

Do you want to spend one-third of your life at a brain-numbing, soul-sucking job that will turn you into a cross-eyed zombie? Or do you want to pursue a great career that will satisfy your desire for meaning and achievement? Psychology and personal experience teach us that when we don't feel fulfilled, or can't find meaning in what we spend one-third of our life doing, our feelings of despondency and disappointment poison every other part of our lives, including a good night's sleep.

More and more these days, people demand fulfilling work and a balance between that work and the rest of their lives. If you find it, you benefit from more than a paycheck; you enhance your pride, your self-esteem, and your sense that what you do makes a real difference in the world, all important aspects that contribute to physical and emotional well-being.

In the old manufacturing-based world of work, people changed to fit the work. An assembly-line worker at Ford's Model T factory changed from working as a farmhand who could hear birds sing as he worked outdoors, to working as a pair of hands screwing wing nut A onto bolt B as he listened to the clang of metal striking metal. In the new information-based work world, people expect the reverse. They expect the organization to adapt to their human needs. They want to smell the roses and hear the birds sing. They demand workplace flexibility, benefits that enhance their health and well-being, respect for their humanity and their need for a harmonious home life, and corporate behavior that reflects a higher degree of ethics and responsibility. They will work from home and anywhere else via technology, but they also occasionally need to go home during regular work hours to attend to personal duties. They want to offer their talent in exchange for meaningful work and a meaningful life. Organizations that strive to fulfill that desire automatically generate engagement.

I abhor the phrase "work/life balance," which suggests that one's work and one's life sit at opposite ends of a teeter-totter. It's not a matter of getting the two on a horizontal plane; it's a matter of *integrating* them into a smooth and seamless whole with the ability to unplug and disconnect to refuel.

We're also not talking about humoring and coddling a new generation of workers who bring a sense of entitlement to the workplace. Yes, many members of this generation have enjoyed a lot of spoon feeding and hand holding and pampering, but even more will willingly work their tails to the bone for the rewards of a great career. (I cover this extensively in my book *Y in the Workplace*.) Some of the productive and profitable work/life accommodations an organization can add to its standard benefits package include:

- Flexible hours that still add up to a full workweek. A night owl might get more done from 9 P.M. to 5 A.M. than the morning lark who prefers a traditional 9 A.M. to 5 P.M. day.

- Telecommuting that lets individuals and teams work at a distance from the conventional office. A programmer in Austin, Texas, can be just as effective working from home and developing close working relations with his colleagues as two teammates who sit side by side in a cubicle in Silicon Valley.

- On-site childcare that lets fathers and mothers interact with their children during lunch hours and breaks. A new mom will feel better at her desk when she knows she will be able to check in on her two-year-old throughout the day.

- Fitness rooms, gyms, running tracks, stress management classes, and playrooms that help people cope with the pressures of today's high-pressured work environments. A desk jockey will return to work refreshed and energized after a good workout.

- Creatively designed workspaces—environments that feel more like places where people will love to work than like little boxlike prisons that give them claustrophobia. Lots of fresh air, natural light, and bright colors energize people, while stale, air-conditioned, gray-walled, fluorescently lit barns make them feel like cattle waiting for slaughter.

- Opportunities for people to spend part of their time working on projects outside the scope of their jobs that engage their wide-ranging interests and provide cross-training, exposure to an outside perspective, and often transferable skills.

- Individual or organization-wide volunteer projects, or in the case of larger organizations, paid sabbaticals where leaders and managers can spend a few months teaching or working for not-for-profit organizations.

Such gestures mean the world to people because they show respect for the whole person and the whole person's life outside of work. Employees will often brag more about these sorts of meaningful benefits than the formal package of pay, bonuses, and health care. If your company loves you, you love your company. And you'll lay down your life for what you love.

SLAM IN ACTION

Located in a refurbished church, SEER Interactive impressed me more than any company I visited this year. A SEO and SEM consulting firm based in Philadelphia, SEER operates with a work environment reminiscent of what I have read about Google, which has done so much to create a place where people love to work. SEER Interactive has racked up an amazing number of accomplishments, such as inclusion in Philly's 100 Fastest Growing Companies (2011, 2010, 2009, 2008) and Best Places to Work (2011). It happened because its founder and leader Wil Reynolds made it happen.

Wil started SEER in his house in 2002, but didn't hire his first employee until 2005. As so often happens, he struck out on his own because a short-sighted boss said no to Wil's request to come in early and work through lunch in order to leave an hour early for his volunteer work at a local children's hospital. Four days after that fateful no, Wil quit and started SEER. As he recalls, "When you look at the impact you want to have in the world, no other company allowed me to do what I wanted, so I built my own, based on what I believe in." He believed in some principles not common among SEO/SEM companies, such as integrity, doing what you say you are going to do, and putting clients first.

He describes SEER's mission this way: "We do the right thing. If you expect that karma will come back to you, then you put less bad out there." This philosophy inspires the culture he has built at SEER, the firm's leadership and management philosophy, its hiring and firing practices, the way its people manage client relationships, and everything else the company does to engage its stakeholders. You can see it and feel it. SEER's people:

- Logged 1,600 volunteer hours in 2011 alone. Wil expects this number to increase every year as more and more people join the company.

- Share many attributes; they enjoy hanging out with each other both at work and outside the office. Wil believes that a company that celebrates together stays together.

- Feel free to express an opinion, no matter how seemingly dumb, outrageous, or contrary to current thinking. Wil knows that creativity can come from going over the edge.

- Work in a people-friendly open environment with plenty of nooks and crannies where they can go to meditate or chat with colleagues and visitors.

- Enjoy, as Wil puts it, "a conduit to get people to their next level in their life." Wil accepts the fact that advancement may involve a move up the ladder at SEER or a move to another job, or even a move to a person's own start-up venture. They believe in the importance of developing people, regardless of where they eventually go. They may come back, and, if not, they may send business your way.

- Bring their talent to the job because their ideals fit with the company's values and mission. Wil insists that motivation comes from within, not from an inspiring leader or guru.

- Encounter few roadblocks that can get in the way of smart, creative people eager to solve problems. Wil makes sure that procedures and protocols do not become so firmly entrenched that they hamstring his people from doing what they need to do to get the best results.

- Know their voices will be heard and that they will be respected and rewarded and managed in a personal way. Wil listens to people all the time, whether on the job or at happy hour. What he learns enables him to tailor his management, recognition, and rewards to individual preferences and approaches.

- React to the company as they would to a graduate school rather than a factory. Wil encourages continuous learning throughout the company.

It all adds up to full-blown engagement. It includes well-understood values and mission, but more than that, it represents an integrated way of thinking about and doing good work.

WRAP UP

Engagement is not a checklist: Throw a pizza party (check), offer a bonus (check), say "You did a great job" (check). Nor is it a feel-good fad: Make 'em feel pampered (check), get on the bandwagon (check). People instinctively recognize true engagement when they see it, and true engagement provides the key to productivity and profitability. It defines the company's character and the values it respects through thick and thin. It develops and nurtures a positive and robust culture. It stresses leadership excellence. It honors the subtleties and realities of the psychological contract.

Engagement is about hiring for cultural fit. It's about recognizing how much meaning work can and should provide to our individual and collective identities. Most important, it's about treating people as people, not "human capital" or a "human resource" or some other cold business term.

Smart leaders must constantly monitor the four essential elements of engagement: Social connection, Leadership excellence, Aligned culture, and Meaningful work and life. When your organization gets this right, you will find it much easier to keep a firmer grip on all those quirky, messy, psychological, emotional, behavioral, cognitive, and physiological subtleties of human nature that everyone brings to the job.

The Aha Moment

I recently delivered the keynote address to the women car dealers at the National Automobile Dealers Association's annual conference. I talked about leadership and psychology, making my case about the powerful impact human psychology has on day-to-day leadership and the contagions we can cause and spread. At one point in the speech—I still don't know why—this popped out of my mouth: "When people suck, we just kind of suck back." The women's reaction went from quiet shock to murmurs of amusement to, finally, big smiles and enthusiastic nods.

That phrase was a defining moment for me because it put into perspective what had kept me up all those nights, as I tried to figure out what to do about my underperforming office manager Hope. It reminded me of how much I had I learned from the experience.

I had let my young employee, my colleagues, our clients, and myself down. I had been unable to see myself the way I would have seen someone else doing the same thing. I had let all my knowledge and skill as a leader fly out of my head while I wallowed in self-doubt. I worried that I had made an irreparable mistake and I would never find a way to recover my company's once bright and vibrant culture. I sucked. Everyone around me kind of sucked right back.

Preoccupied with my own screw-up, I couldn't see a way out of the mess. I resisted change and, as the leader, dragged everyone around me down into the same muck. At the time my schedule looked like the Invasion of Normandy, with all my boats in the water and all my planes in the air: back-to-back consulting engagements, endless emotion-fraught coaching sessions, major public speaking commitments—on top of trying to serve my organization as a great leader and contemplating the upheaval that firing Hope and training a replacement would surely cause. I was a basket case of frayed nerves, a sleep-deprived, brain-frazzled doctor who could not heal herself. Good grief! What was I thinking?

Well, I did finally get my head screwed back onto my shoulders—by applying all of the concepts we've explored in this book. I stopped sucking as a boss, and my company regained its former culture of service and accountability. I love working there, the clinicians love working there, and our clients get the help and support they need in a safe and comfortable environment. Our new office manager, Jennifer, is warm, intelligent, and charming, and she does a great job at work. We still hit the occasional roadblock or pothole, but our strong team quickly navigates around every obstacle. What turned it around? After a lot of reflection, I boiled it all down to three basic rules and one simple formula that help me get back on track when I start to suck as a leader.

Three Simple Rules

1. Seek self-awareness.

2. Help others gain self-awareness.

3. Remember we're only human after all.

The Formula

- Admit the problem.

- Recognize that my thoughts and actions contributed to the problem.

- Identify the causes of those thoughts and actions.

- Detect the cognitive biases involved.

- Think up new ways to manage the causes and biases.

- Adjust my leadership approach accordingly.

- Make amends with the people I hurt.

- Expect to make more mistakes but strive to deal with them differently.

Despite my handful of gray hairs from the experience, which I have fondly nicknamed Hope, I'm glad I made the mistakes because I learned so much. I'm glad I live in a world full of unpredictable, messy, complicated, illogical, and fallible human beings who make life and work so fascinating. I'm glad I can be so unpredictable, messy, complicated, illogical, and fallible myself. Those facts of human nature will never go away, but through a commitment to self-awareness we can all become more highly attuned to the subtle and not-so-subtle red flags that sometimes pull us off course.

Each of us can strive every day to be a better person and a more effective leader. We can take responsibility for being the best leaders we can be for all of those who rely on us. Whatever the nature of your business, you are in the people business. You are a people person. One of the best leaders of people in history, Field Marshall Lord Slim, said it best: "Leadership is just plain you."

References

CHAPTER ONE

Adkin, Mark. *Goose Green: A Battle Is Fought to Be Won.* London: Orion Publishing Group, 2007.

Adler, Rachel F., and Raquel Benbunan-Fich. "Juggling on a High Wire: Multitasking Effects on Performance." *International Journal of Human-Computer Studies* 70, no. 2 (2012): 156–168.

Bandura, Albert. *Social Learning Theory.* Englewood Cliffs, N.J.: Prentice-Hall, 1977.

———. "Self-Efficacy Mechanism in Human Agency." *American Psychologist* 37 (1982): 122–147.

———. *Social Foundations of Thought and Action: A Social Cognitive Theory.* Englewood Cliffs, N.J.: Prentice-Hall, 1986.

———. *Self-Efficacy in Changing Societies.* Cambridge, UK: Cambridge University Press, 1997.

Doll, Bradley, B., Kent E. Hutchison, and Michael J. Frank. "Dopaminergic Genes Predict Individual Differences in Susceptibility to Confirmation Bias." *Journal of Neuroscience* 31, no. 16 (2011): 6188–6198.

Hsee, Christopher K., Adelle X. Yang, and Liangyan Wang. "Idleness Aversion and the Need for Justifiable Busyness." *Psychological Science*, June 2010, 926–930.

Iyer, Pico. "The Joy of Quiet." *New York Times*, December 29, 2011. http://www. nytimes. com/2012/01/01/opinion/sunday/the-joy-of quiet.html?_r=2&page wanted= 1&ref = opinion.

LaMarre, Heather L., Kristen D. Landreville, and Michael A. Beam. "The Irony of Satire Political Ideology and the Motivation to See What You Want to See in *The Colbert Report*." *International Journal of Press/Politics* 14, no. 2 (2009): 212–231.

Lord, Charles G., Lee Ross, and Mark R. Lepper. "Biased Assimilation and Attitude Polarization: The Effects of Prior Theories on Subsequently Considered Evidence." *Journal of Personality and Social Psychology* 37, no. 11 (1979): 2098–2109.

Pashler, Harold. "Dual-Task Interference in Simple Tasks: Data and Theory." *Psychological Bulletin* 116, no. 2 (1994): 220–244.

Snyder, Mark. "Seek and Ye Shall Find: Testing Hypotheses About Other People." In *Social Cognition: The Ontario Symposium on Personality and Social Psychology*, edited by Edward T. Higgins, C. Peter Heiman, and Mark P. Zanna, 277–303. Hillsdale, N.J.: Erlbaum, 1981.

Wardrop, Murray. "Swan Hunter Cranes Leave the Tyne, Ending 145 Years of Shipbuilding." *The Telegraph*, April 6, 2009. http://www.telegraph.co.uk/ news/uknews/ 5112148/Swan-Hunter-cranes-leave-the-Tyne-ending-145-years-of-ship building.html.

Westen, Drew, Pavel S. Blagov, Keith Harenski, Clint Kilts, and Stephan Hamann. "Neural Bases of Motivated Reasoning: An fMRI Study of Emotional Constraints on Partisan Political Judgment in the 2004 U.S. Presidential Election." *Journal of Cognitive Neuroscience* 18, no.11 (2006): 1947–1958.

CHAPTER TWO

Centers for Disease Control and Prevention. "Zombie Preparedness." Centers for Disease Control and Prevention. http://www.cdc.gov/phpr/zombies.htm.

Davis, Matt. MRC Cognition and Brain Sciences Unit. http://www.mrc-cbu. cam.ac.uk/ people/matt.davis/cmabridge/.

Escalas, Jennifer Edson. "Narrative Versus Analytical Self-Referencing and Persuasion." *Journal of Consumer Research* 34, no. 4 (2007): 421–429.

French, John R. P., and Bertram Raven. "The Bases of Social Power." In *Group Dynamics*, edited by Dorwin Cartwright and Alvin Zander, 259–269. New York: Harper & Row, 1959.

Green, Melanie C., Jennifer Garst, Timothy C. Brock, and Sungeun Chung. "Fact Versus Fiction Labeling: Persuasion Parity Despite Heightened Scrutiny of Fact." *Media Psychology* 8, no. 3 (2006): 267–285.

Heider, Fritz, and Mary Ann Simmel. "An Experimental Study of Apparent Behavior." *American Journal of Psychology* 57 (1944): 243–249.

Hersey, Paul, Ken H. Blanchard, and Dewey E. Johnson. *Management of Organizational Behavior: Leading Human Resources*, 8th ed. Englewood Cliffs, N.J.: Prentice Hall, 2000.

Raven, Bertram H., and Arie W. Kruglanski. "Conflict and Power." In *The Structure of Conflict*, edited by P. G. Swingle, 177–219. New York: Academic Press, 1975.

Stephens, Greg J., Lauren J. Silbert, and Uri Hasson. "Speaker–Listener Neural Coupling Underlies Successful Communication." *Proceedings of the National Academy of Sciences* 107, no. 29 (July 27, 2010). http://www.pnas.org/content/107/32/ 14425. long#aff-1.

Zak, Paul. J. "The Neurobiology of Trust." *Scientific American*, May 19, 2008.

Zak, Paul. J., Robert Kurzban, and William T. Matzner. "The Neurobiology of Trust." *Annals of the New York Academy of Sciences* 1032 (2004): 224–227.

CHAPTER THREE

American Psychological Association. "Stress in America: Our Health at Risk." January 11, 2011. http://www.apa.org/news/press/releases/stress/2011/final-2011.pdf.

Beilock, Sian L., and Thomas H. Carr. "When High-Powered People Fail: Working Memory and 'Choking Under Pressure' in Math." *Psychological Science* 16 (2005): 101–105.

Branch, Rhena, and Rob Willson. *Cognitive Behavioral Therapy for Dummies*, 2nd ed. Hoboken, N.J.: John Wiley, 2010.

Cleveland Clinic. "Recognizing Signs and Symptoms of Stress." Cleveland Clinic. http://my.clevelandclinic.org/healthy_living/stress_management/hic_recognizing_signs_and_symptoms_of_stress.aspx.

Kobasa, Susan C. "Stressful Life Events, Personality and Health: An Inquiry into Hardiness." *Journal of Personality and Social Psychology* 37, no. 1 (1979): 1–11.

Lazarus, Richard S., and Susan Folkman. *Stress, Appraisal and Coping.* New York: Springer, 1984.

Seligman, Martin. *Learned Optimism.* New York: Pocket Books, 1998.

CHAPTER FOUR

Anthes, Emily. "Their Pain, Our Gain." *Scientific American Mind*, November/December 2010, 33–35.

Duffy, Michelle K., Kristin L. Scott, Jason D. Shaw, Bennett J. Tepper, and Karl Aquino. "A Social Context Model of Envy and Social Undermining." *Academy of Management Journal* 55, no. 3 (2012): 643–666.

Festinger, Leon. "A Theory of Social Comparison Processes." *Human Relations* 7 (1954): 117–140. http://hum.sagepub.com/content/7/2/117.full.pdf+html.

Garcia, Stephen M., and Avishalom Tor. "Rankings, Standards, and Competition: Task vs. Scale Comparisons." *Organizational Behavior and Human Decision Processes* 102 (2007): 95–108.

Hughes, Marsha, and James B. Terrell. *The Emotionally Intelligent Team: Understanding and Developing the Behaviors of Success*. San Francisco: Jossey-Bass, 2007.

"Jealousy, Envy Common Problems at Workplace." *Windsor Star*, October 2, 2006. http://www.canada.com/windsorstar/news/business/story.html?id= da9df131-959c-4fa7-9bbf-6640a656327f.

Mettee, D. R., and G. Smith. "Social Comparison and Interpersonal Attraction: The Case for Dissimilarity." In *Social Comparison Processes: Theoretical and Empirical Perspectives*, edited by Jerry M. Suls and Richard L. Miller, 69–101. Washington, D.C.: Hemisphere, 1977.

Osborne, Hilary. "Envy in the Workplace: Jealous Guise." *The Guardian*, June 18, 2010. http://www.guardian.co.uk/money/2010/jun/19/envy-workplace-recession.

Parrott, W. G. "The Emotional Experiences of Envy and Jealousy." In *The Psychology of Jealousy and Envy*, edited by Peter Salovey, 3–30. New York: Guilford Press, 1991.

Sabini, John, and Maury Silver. "Why Emotion Names and Experiences Don't Neatly Pair." *Psychological Inquiry* 16 (2005): 1–10.

Schaubroeck, John, and Simon S. K. Lam. "Comparing Lots Before and After: Promotion Rejectees' Invidious Reactions to Promotees." *Organizational Behavior & Human Decision Processes* 94 (2004): 33–47.

Schopenhauer, Arthur. *The Essays of Arthur Schopenhauer: On Human Nature*. Hamburg, Germany: Tredition Classics, 2011.

Smith, Richard. H., ed. *Envy: Theory and Research*. New York: Oxford University Press, 2008.

Smith, Richard. H., W. Gerrod Parrott, Daniel Ozer, and Andrew Moniz. "Subjective Injustice and Inferiority as Predictors of Hostile or Depressive Feelings in Envy." *Personality and Social Psychology Bulletin* 20, no. 6 (1994): 705–711.

Takahashi, Hidehiko, Motoichiro Kato, Masato Matsuura, Dean Mobbs, Tetsuya Suhara, and Yoshiro Okubo. "When Your Gain Is My Pain and Your Pain Is My Gain: Neural Correlates of Envy and Schadenfreude." *Science* 323, no. 5916 (February 13, 2009): 937–939.

van Dijk, Wilco, W., Guido M. van Koningsbruggen, Jaap W. Ouwerkerk, and Yoka M. Wesseling. "Self-Esteem, Self-Affirmation, and Schadenfreude." *Emotion* 11, no. 6 (2011): 1445–1449.

Vecchio, Robert P., and Kim Dogan. "Managing Envy and Jealousy in the Workplace." *Compensation Benefits Review* 33, no. 2 (2001): 57–64.

Wood, Joanne V., Shelley E. Taylor, and Rosemary R. Lichtman. "Social Comparison in Adjustment to Breast Cancer." *Journal of Personality and Social Psychology* 49 (1985): 1169–1183.

CHAPTER FIVE

Anderson, Ray C., and Robin A. White. *Confessions of a Radical Industrialist: Profits, People, Purpose: Doing Business by Respecting the Earth.* New York: St. Martin's, 2009.

Brehm, Jack W. "Post-Decision Changes in Desirability of Alternatives." *Journal of Abnormal and Social Psychology* 52, no. 3 (1956): 384–389.

Cook-Greuter, Susanne. "A Detailed Description of the Development of Nine Action Logics in the Leadership Development Framework: Adapted from Ego Development Theory." Dated 2002, accessed May 2, 2012. www.cook-grueter.com.

Elliot, Andrew J., and Patricia G. Devine. "On the Motivational Nature of Cognitive Dissonance: Dissonance as Psychological Discomfort." *Journal of Personality and Social Psychology* 67, no. 3 (1994): 382–394.

Festinger, Leon. "A Theory of Social Comparison Processes." *Human Relations* 7 (1954): 117–40.

Harung, Harald, Fred Travis, Warren Blank, and Dennis Heaton. "Higher Development, Brain Integration, and Excellence in Leadership." *Management Decision* 47, no. 6 (2009): 872–894.

Hawken, Paul. *The Ecology of Commerce: A Declaration of Sustainability.* New York: HarperCollins, 1994.

Heracleous, Loizos, and Luh L. Lan. "The Myth of Shareholder Capitalism." *Harvard Business Review* 88, no. 4 (2010): 24.

Hernandez, Morela. "Promoting Stewardship Behavior in Organizations: A Leadership Model." *Journal of Business Ethics* 80, no. 1 (2007): 121–128.

Interface. "Values and Mission." Interface, Inc. http://interfaceglobal.com/Company/Mission-Vision.aspx.

Marques, Joan F. "Wakefulness: The Decisive Leadership Skill." *Management Services* 50, no. 3 (2006): 5–6.

Mills, Judson. "Changes in Moral Attitudes Following Temptation." *Journal of Personality* 26 (1958): 517–531.

Ronson, Jon. *"The Psychopath Test: A Journey Through the Madness Industry."* New York: Penguin, 2011.

Rooke, David, and William R. Torbet. "Seven Transformations of Leadership." *Harvard Business Review* 83, no. 4 (April 2005): 66–76. http://hbr.org/2005/04/seven-transformations-of-leadership/ar/1.

Rose, Jacob M. "Corporate Directors and Social Responsibility: Ethics versus Shareholder Value." *Journal of Business Ethics* 73 (2007): 319–331.

CHAPTER SIX

Auletta, Ken. "You've Got News: Can Tim Armstrong save AOL?" *The New Yorker*, January 24, 2011. http://www.newyorker.com/reporting/2011/01/24/110124 fa_fact_auletta.

Baumeister, Roy E., Ellen Bratslavsky, Mark Muraven, and Diane M. Tice. "Ego Depletion: Is the Active Self a Limited Resource?" *Journal of Personality and Social Psychology* 74, no. 5 (1998): 1252–1265.

Bingemann, Mitchell. "Kodak's Demise Is a Warning to Telcos and Media to Adapt." *The Australian*, January 6, 2012. http://www.theaustralian.com.au/ business/companies/kodaks-demise-is-a-warning-to-telecos-and-media-to-adapt/story-fn91v9q3-1226237766519.

Bower, Joseph L., and Clayton M. Christensen. "Disruptive Technologies: Catching the Wave." *Harvard Business Review*, January–February 1995, 43–53.

Burmeister, Katrin, and Christian Schade. "Are Entrepreneurs' Decisions More Biased? An Experimental Investigation of the Susceptibility to Status Quo Bias." *Journal of Business Venturing* 22, no. 3 (2007): 340–362. http://opim.wharton.upenn.edu/risk/library/J2007JBV_KBur,CSchade_ Entrepreneurs.pdf.

Carmon, Ziv, and Dan Ariely. "Focusing on the Forgone: How Value Can Appear So Different to Buyers and Sellers." *Journal of Consumer Research* 27, no. 3 (2000): 360–370.

Christensen, Clayton M. *The Innovator's Dilemma: When New Technologies Cause Great Firms to Fail.* Boston: Harvard Business School Press, 1997.

Dawkins, Richard, and T. R. Carlisle. "Parental Investment, Mate Desertion and a Fallacy." *Nature* 262 (1976): 131–133.

Deutschman, Alan. "Change or Die." *Fast Company Magazine*, May 1, 2005. http://www.fastcompany.com/magazine/94/open_change-or-die.html.

Gilbert, Clark. "Newspapers and the Internet." *Nieman Reports*, Summer 2002. http://www.nieman.harvard.edu/reports/article/101351/Newspapers-and-the-Internet.aspx.

Hummen, Patrick, John Morgan, and Phillip Stocken. "A Model of Flops." Working paper, *RAND Journal of Economics,* Haas School of Business, University of California, Berkeley, 2010. http://faculty.haas.berkeley.edu/rjmorgan/Flops.pdf.

Johnson, Eric, John Hershey, Jacqueline Meszaros, and Howard Kunreuther. "Framing, Probability, Distortions, and Insurance Risks." *Journal of Risk and Uncertainty* 7 (1993): 35–51.

Jost, John T., Mahzarin R. Banaji, and Brian A. Nosek. "A Decade of System Justification Theory: Accumulated Evidence of Conscious and Unconscious Bolstering of the Status Quo." *Political Psychology* 25 (2004): 881–919.

Kahneman, Daniel, Jack L. Knetsch, and Richard H. Thaler. "Experimental Tests of the Endowment Effect and the Coase Theorem." *Journal of Political Economy* 98, no. 6 (1990): 1325–1348.

———. "Anomalies: The Endowment Effect, Loss Aversion, and Status Quo Bias." *Journal of Economic Perspectives* 5, no.1 (Winter 1991): 193–206. http://users.tricity.wsu.edu/~achaudh/kahnemanetal.pdf.

Kahneman, Daniel, and Amos Tversky. "Choices, Values and Frames." *American Psychologist* 39 (April 1984): 341–350. http://web.missouri.edu/~segerti/capstone/choicesvalues.pdf.

Kegan, Robert, and Lisa Lahey. *Immunity to Change: How to Overcome It and Unlock Potential in Yourself and Your Organization.* Cambridge, Mass.: Harvard Business Press, 2009.

Samuelson, William, and Richard J. Zeckhauser. "Status Quo Bias in Decision Making." *Journal of Risk and Uncertainty* 1 (March 1988): 7–59.

Thaler, Richard H. "Toward a Positive Theory of Consumer Choice." *Journal of Economic Behavior and Organization* 1 (1980): 39–60.

"The Last Kodak Moment?" *The Economist*, January 14, 2012. http://www.economist.com/node/21542796.

CHAPTER SEVEN

Allen, Vernon L., and John M. Levine. "Social Support and Conformity: The Role of Independent Assessment of Reality." *Journal of Experimental Social Psychology* 7, no. 1 (1971): 48–58.

Asch, Solomon E. "Effects of Group Pressure upon the Modification and Distortion of Judgment." In *Groups, Leadership and Men*, edited by Harold Guetzkow, 177–190. Pittsburgh: Carnegie Press, 1951.

Baron, Robert S., Joseph A. Vandello, and Bethany Brunsman. "The Forgotten Variable in Conformity Research: Impact of Task Importance on Social Influence." *Journal of Personality and Social Psychology* 71, no. 5 (1996): 915–927.

Barsade, Sigal G. "The Ripple Effect: Emotional Contagion and its Influence on Group Behavior." *Administrative Science Quarterly* 47 (2002): 644–675.

Barsade, Sigal G., and Donald E. Gibson. "Why Does Affect Matter in Organizations?" *Academy of Management Perspectives* 21 (2007): 36–59.

Bazerman, Max H., Toni Giuliano, and Alan Appelman. "Escalation of Commitment in Individual and Group Decision Making." *Organizational Behavior & Human Performance* 33, no. 2 (1984): 141–152.

Berns, Gregory S., Jonathan Chappelow, Caroline F. Zink, Giuseppe Pagnoni, Megan E. Martin-Skurski, and Jim Richards. "Neurobiological Correlates of Social Conformity and Independence during Mental Rotation." *Biological Psychiatry* 58 (2005): 245–253.

Bond, Rod. "Group Size and Conformity." *Group Processes Intergroup Relations* 8, no. 4 (2005): 331–354.

Cheshin, Arik, Anat Rafaeli, and Nathan Bos. "Anger and Happiness in Virtual Teams: Emotional Influences of Text and Behavior on Others' Affect in the Absence of Non-Verbal Cues." *Organizational Behavior and Human Decision Processes* 116, no. 1 (2011): 2–16.

Cialdini, Robert B. *Influence: The Psychology of Persuasion.* New York: Harper-Collins, 2001.

Cialdini, Robert B., and Noah J. Goldstein. "Social Influence: Compliance and Conformity." *Annual Review of Psychology* 55 (2004): 591–621.

David, Barbara, and John C. Turner. "Studies in Self-Categorization and Minority Conversion: Is Being a Member of the Outgroup an Advantage?" *British Journal of Social Psychology* 35 (1996): 179–200.

———. "Studies in Self-Categorization and Minority Conversion: The Ingroup Minority in Intragroup and Inter-Group Contexts." *British Journal of Social Psychology* 38 (1999): 115–134.

Dietz-Uhler, Beth. "The Escalation of Commitment in Political Decision-Making Groups: A Social Identity Approach." *European Journal of Social Psychology* 26, no 4 (1998): 611–629.

Dolinski, Dariusz, and Richard Nawrat. "'Fear-Then-Relief' Procedure for Producing Compliance: Beware When the Danger Is Over." *Journal of Experimental Social Psychology* 34, no. 1 (1998): 27–50.

Eagly, Alice H., and Linda L. Carli. "Sex of Researchers and Sex-Typed Communications as Determinants of Sex Differences in Influenceability: A Meta-Analysis of Social Influence Studies." *Psychological Bulletin* 90, no. 1 (1981): 1–20.

Epstude, Kai, and Thomas Mussweiler. "What You Feel Is How You Compare: How Comparisons Influence the Social Induction of Affect." *Emotion* 9, no. 1 (2009): 1–14.

Fischer, Kurt W., Phillip R. Shaver, and Peter Carnochan. "How Emotions Develop and How They Organize Development." *Cognition and Emotion* 4 (1990): 81–127.

Fusaro, Peter, and Ross Miller. *What Went Wrong at Enron: Everyone's Guide to the Largest Bankruptcy in U.S. History.* Hoboken, N.J.: John Wiley, 2002.

Gigone, Daniel, and Reid Hastie. "The Common Knowledge Effect: Information Sharing and Group Judgment." *Journal of Personality and Social Psychology* 65, no. 5 (1993): 959–974.

Hollingshead, Andrea B. "Information Suppression and Status Persistence in Group Decision Making: The Effects of Communication Media." *Human Communication Research* 23 (1996): 193–219.

Ingham, Alan G., George Levinger, James Graves, and Vaughn Peckham. "The Ringelmann Effect: Studies of Group Size and Group Performance." *Journal of Experimental Social Psychology* 10, no. 4 (1974): 371–384.

Isenberg, Daniel J. "Group Polarization: A Critical Review and Meta-Analysis." *Journal of Personality and Social Psychology* 50, no. 6 (1986): 1141–1151.

Janis, Irving L. *Victims of Groupthink.* Boston: Houghton Mifflin, 1972.

Jugert, Phillip, J. Christopher Cohrs, and John Duckitt. "Inter- and Intrapersonal Processes Underlying Authoritarianism: The Role of Social Conformity and Personal Need for Structure." *European Journal of Personality* 23 (2009): 607–621.

Latané, Bibb, Kipling Williams, and Stephen Harkins. "Many Hands Make Light the Work: The Causes and Consequences of Social Loafing." *Journal of Personality and Social Psychology* 37, no. 6 (1979): 822–832.

Karau, Steven J., and Kipling D. Williams. "Social Loafing: A Meta-Analytic Review and Theoretical Integration." *Journal of Personality and Social Psychology* 65, no. 4 (1993): 681–706.

Kelly, Janice R., and Steven J. Karau (1999). "Group Decision Making: The Effects of Initial Preferences and Time Pressure." *Personality and Social Psychology Bulletin* 25 (1999): 1342–1354.

Kim, Heejung, and Hazel R. Markus. "Deviance or Uniqueness, Harmony or Conformity? A Cultural Analysis." *Journal of Personality and Social Psychology* 77 (1999): 785–800.

Klucharev, Vasily, Kaisa Hytönen, Mark Rijpkema, Ale Smidts, and Guillén Fernández. "Reinforcement Learning Signal Predicts Social Conformity." *Neuron* 61, no. 1 (2008): 140–151.

Malmendier, Ulrike, and Geoffrey Tate. "Who Makes Acquisitions? CEO Overconfidence and the Market's Reaction." *Journal of Financial Economics* 89, no. 1 (2008): 20–43.

Milgram Stanley. *Obedience to Authority*. New York: Harper & Row, 1974.

Odean, Terrance. "Volume, Volatility, Price, and Profit: When All Traders Are Above Average." *Journal of Finance* 53, no. 6 (1998): 1887–1934.

Parkinson, Brian, and Gwenda Simons. "Affecting Others: Social Appraisal and Emotion Contagion in Everyday Decision Making." *Personality and Social Psychology Bulletin* 35 (2009): 1071–1084.

Postmes, Tom, Russell Spears, Khaled Sakhel, and Daphne de Groot. "Social Influence in Computer-Mediated Communication: The Effects of Anonymity on Group Behavior." *Personality and Social Psychology Bulletin* 27 (2001): 1243–1254.

Reitan, Harold T., and Marvin E. Shaw. "Group Membership, Sex-Composition of the Group, and Conformity Behavior." *Journal of Social Psychology* 64 (1964): 45–51.

Ringelmann, Max. "Recherches sur les moteurs animés: Travail de l'homme." *Annales de l'Institut National Argonomique* 2e, tom 12 (1913): 1–40.

Schoenewolf, Gerald. "Emotional Contagion: Behavioral Induction in Individuals and Groups." *Modern Psychoanalysis* 15 (1990): 49–61.

Schulz-Hardt, Stefan., Marc Jochims, and Dieter Frey. "Productive Conflict in Group Decision Making: Genuine and Contrived Dissent as Strategies to Counteract Biased Information Seeking." *Organizational Behavior and Human Decision Processes* 88 (2002): 563–586.

Sherif, Muzafer, O. J. Harvey, B. Jack White, William R. Hood, and Carolyn W. Sherif (1961). *The Robbers Cave Experiment: Intergroup Conflict and Cooperation.* (Orig. pub. as *Intergroup Conflict and Group Relations*). Middletown, Conn.: Wesleyan University Press, 1988.

Smith, Fiona. "Innoculate Against Emotional Contagion." *Financial Review,* November 22, 2011. Retrieved August 2, 2012. http://tools.afr.com/viewer.aspx?URL=EDP://c192e8a4-0ff9-11e1-ba88-8609d6e54817.

Sniezek, Janet A., and Rebecca A. Henry. "Accuracy and Confidence in Group Judgment." *Organizational Behavior & Human Decision Processes* 43 (1989): 1–28.

Svenson, Ola. "Are We All Less Risky and More Skillful Than Our Fellow Drivers?" *Acta Psychologica* 47, no. 2 (1981): 143–148.

Sy, Thomas, Stéphane Côté, and Richard Saavedra. "The Contagious Leader: Impact of the Leader's Mood on the Mood of Group Members, Group Affective Tone, and Group Processes." *Journal of Applied Psychology* 90, no. 2 (2005): 295–305.

Tajfel, Henri. "Experiments in Intergroup Discrimination." *Scientific American* 223 (1970): 96–102.

Tajfel, Henri, and John C. Turner. "The Social Identity Theory of Inter-Group Behavior." In *Psychology of Intergroup Relations,* edited by Stephen Worchel and William G. Austin, 7–24. Chicago: Nelson-Hall, 1986.

Tajfel, Henri, M. G. Billing, R. P. Bundy, and Claude Flament. "Social Categorization and Intergroup Behaviour." *European Journal of Social Psychology* 1, no. 2 (1971): 149–178.

Tong, Eddie M. W., Cindy R. M. Tan, Nareeman A. Latheef, Mohammad F. B. Selamat, and Dennis K. B. Tan. "Conformity: Moods Matter." *European Journal of Social Psychology* 38, no. 4 (2008): 601–611.

Turner, Marlene E., and Anthony R. Pratkanis. "Twenty-Five Years of Group-think Theory and Research: Lessons from the Evaluation of a Theory." *Organizational Behavior and Human Decision Processes* 73, no. 2–3 (February 1998): 105–115.

Walker, Thomas G., and Eleanor C. Main. "Choice Shifts and Extreme Behavior: Judicial Review in the Federal Courts." *Journal of Social Psychology* 291, no. 2 (1973): 215–221.

Yates, J. Frank. *Judgment and Decision Making.* Englewood Cliffs, N.J.: Prentice-Hall, 1990.

Zappos.com, Incorporated. "Zappos.com, Inc. Code of Business Conduct and Ethics." http://www.zappos.com/c/code-of-conduct.

Zarnoth, Paul, and Janet A. Sniezek. "The Social Influence of Confidence in Group Decision Making." *Journal of Experimental Social Psychology,* 33 (1997): 345–366.

CHAPTER EIGHT

Abraham, Rebecca. "Organizational Cynicism: Bases and Consequences." *Genetic, Social, and General Psychology Monographs* 126, no. 3 (2000): 269–292.

Amabile, Teresa M., and Steven J. Kramer. "The Power of Small Wins." *Harvard Business Review* 89, no. 5 (2011): 70–80.

———. *The Progress Principle: Using Small Wins to Ignite Joy, Engagement, and Creativity at Work.* Cambridge, Mass.: Harvard Business Press, 2011.

Avey, James B., Fred Luthans, and Carolyn M. Youssef. "The Additive Value of Positive Psychological Capital in Predicting Work Attitudes and Behaviors." *Journal of Management* 36, no. 2 (2010): 430–452.

Bal, P. Matthijs, Annet H. D. Lange, Paul G. W. Jansen, and Mandy E. G. Van Der Velde. "Psychological Contract Breach and Job Attitudes: A Meta-Analysis of Age as a Moderator." *Journal of Vocational Behavior* 72, no 1 (2008): 143–158.

Blessing White, Inc. "Employee Engagement Report: Beyond the Numbers: A Practical Approach for Individuals, Managers, and Executives." December 2011. http://www. blessingwhite.com/content/reports/blessingwhite_2011 _ee_report.pdf.

Bordia, Prashant, Simon Lloyd D. Restubog, Sarbari Bordia, and Robert L. Tang. "Breach Begets Breach: Trickle-Down Effects of Psychological Contract Breach on Customer Service." *Journal of Management* 36, no. 6 (2010): 1578–1607.

Bordia, Prashant, Simon Lloyd D. Restubog, and Robert L. Tang. "When Employees Strike Back: Investigating Mediating Mechanisms Between Psychological Contract Breach and Workplace Deviance." *Journal of Applied Psychology* 93, no. 5 (2008): 1104–1117.

Conference Board. "Employee Engagement." http://www.conference-board.org/ topics/subtopics.cfm?topicid=40&subtopicid=250.

Conway, Neil, and Rob B. Briner. *Understanding Psychological Contracts at Work: A Critical Evaluation of Theory and Research.* Oxford, UK: Oxford University Press, 2005.

Dean, James W., Pamela Brandes, and Ravi Dharwadkar. "Organizational Cynicism." *Academy of Management Review* 23 (1998): 341–353.

REFERENCES

Deci, Edward, L. "Effects of Externally Mediated Rewards on Intrinsic Motivation." *Journal of Personality and Social Psychology* 18, no. 1 (1971): 105–115.

Deci, Edward L., Richard Koestner, and Richard M. Ryan. "A Meta Analytic Review of Experiments Examining the Effects of Extrinsic Rewards on Intrinsic Motivation." *Psychological Bulletin* 125, no. 6 (1999): 692–700.

Deery, Stephen J., Roderick D. Iverson, and Janet T. Walsh. "Toward a Better Understanding of Psychological Contract Breach: A Study of Customer Service Employees." *Journal of Applied Psychology* 91, no. 1 (2006): 166–175.

Deloitte. "Managing Talent in a Turbulent Economy: Keeping Your Team Intact. A Special Report on Talent Retention." September 2009. http://www.deloitte. com/view/ en_ GB/uk/services/consulting/human-capital/bc8d8c7837cd 3210Vgn VCM 100000 ba42f00aRCRD.htm.

Harter, James K., Frank L. Schmidt, and Theodore L. Hayes. "Business-Unit-Level Relationship Between Employee Satisfaction, Employee Engagement, and Business Outcomes: A Meta-Analysis." *Journal of Applied Psychology* 87, no. 2 (2002): 268–279.

Harter, James K., Frank L. Schmidt, and Emily A. Killham. "Employee Engagement, Satisfaction, and Business-Unit-Level Outcomes: A Meta-Analysis." Technical paper, Gallup Organization, July 2003.

Hirschman, Albert O. *Exit, Voice, and Loyalty: Responses to Decline in Firms, Organizations, and States.* Cambridge, Mass.: Harvard University Press, 1970.

Johnson, Jonathan L., and Anne M. O'Leary-Kelly. "The Effects of Psychological Contract Breach and Organizational Cynicism: Not All Social Exchange Violations are Created Equal." *Journal of Organizational Behavior* 24, no. 5 (2003): 627–647.

Kalimo, Raija, Toon W. Taris, and Wilmar B. Schaufeli. "The Effects of Past and Anticipated Future Downsizing on Survivor Well-Being: An Equity Perspective." *Journal of Occupational Health Psychology* 8, no. 2 (2003): 91–109.

Kelloway, Kevin E., Niro Sivanathan, Lori Francis, and Julian Barling. "Poor Leadership." In *Handbook of Work Stress*, edited by Julian Barling, E. Kevin Kelloway, and Michael R. Frone, 89–112. Thousand Oaks, Calif.: Sage, 2005.

Lawrence, Paul R., and Nitin Nohria. *Driven: How Human Nature Shapes Our Choices*. San Francisco: Jossey-Bass, 2002.

Lipkin, Nicole A., and April J. Perrymore. *Y in the Workplace: Managing the Me First Generation*. Pompton Plains, N.J.: Career Press, 2009.

Marciano, Paul L. *Carrots and Sticks Don't Work: Build a Culture of Employee Engagement with the Principles of RESPECT*. New York: McGraw-Hill, 2010.

Maslach, Christina, and Michael P. Leiter. "Stress and Burnout: The Critical Research." In *Handbook of Stress Medicine and Health*, edited by Cary L. Cooper, 155–172. London: CRC Press, 2005.

Rousseau, Denise, M. "Psychological and Implied Contracts in Organizations." *Employee Responsibilities and Rights Journal* 2 (1989): 121–139.

———. *Psychological Contracts in Organizations: Understanding Written and Unwritten Agreements*. Thousand Oaks, Calif.: Sage, 1995.

———. "Schema, Promise and Mutuality: The Building Blocks of the Psychological Contracts." *Journal of Occupational and Organizational Psychology* 74 (2001): 511–541.

Rusbult, Caryl E., Dan Farrell, Glen Rogers, and Arch G. Mainus. "Impact of Exchange Variables on Exit, Voice, Loyalty, and Neglect: An Integrative Model of Responses to Declining Job Satisfaction." *Academy of Management Journal* 31(1998): 599–627.

Smoking Gun.com. "Enron's 'Code of Ethics.'" Retrieved May 19, 2012. http://www.thesmokinggun.com/documents/crime/enrons-code-ethics.

Turnley, William H., and Daniel C. Feldman. "The Impact of Breaches of Psychological Contracts on Exit, Voice, Loyality, and Neglect." *Human Relations* 52, no. 7 (1999): 895–922.

Wagner, Rodd, and James K. Harter. 12: *The Elements of Great Managing*. Omaha: Gallup Press, 2006.

Wanous, John P., Arnon E. Reichers, and James T. Austin. "Cynicism About Organizational Change: Measurement, Antecedents, and Correlates." *Group and Organization Management* 25, no. 2 (2000): 132–153.

———. "Cynicism About Organizational Change: An Attribution Process Perspective." *Psychological Reports* 94 (2004): 1421–1434.

Warr, Peter B. Work, *Unemployment and Mental Health*. Oxford, UK: Clarendon Press, 1987.

Withey, Michael J., and William H. Cooper. "Predicting Exit, Voice, Loyalty, and Neglect." *Administrative Science Quarterly* 34 (1989): 521–539.

Zhao, Hao, Sandy J. Wayne, Brian C. Glibkowski, and Jesus Bravo. "The Impact of Psychological Contract Breach on Work-Related Outcomes: A Meta-Analysis." *Personnel Psychology* 60, no. 3 (2007): 647–680.

Index

"Disruptive Technologies" (Joseph Bower and Clayton Christensen), 164
dissent, in groups, 182
distress, 62–64
diversity, in groups, 200
Doll, Bradley, 19
dopamine, 19, 107, 157–158
downward social comparisons, 98
Duffy, Michelle, 110–111
Dunlap, Al, 128–129, 135

earnings, employee engagement and, 208
Eastman Kodak, 149–152
The Ecology of Commerce (Paul Hawken), 137
effort, in groups, 184–187
egocentric thinking, 83
ego depletion, 156
ego development, 135–136
Einstein, Albert, 157, 158
electronic communication
    and emotional contagion, 192
    and paraverbal communication/
        body language, 56, 57
emergency response, to stress, 61–62
emoticons, 190, 192
emotional contagion
    and breach of psychological
        contract, 218–219
    in groups, 188–193
    and stress, 76–77
The Emotionally Intelligent Team
    (Marcia Hughes and James Terrell), 117
emotional maturity, evaluating, 117
emotional reasoning, 81
emotional state, self-efficacy and, 25, 26
emotional symptoms
    of mental exhaustion, 171
    of stress, 68
emotions
    and *Cain and Abel* effect, 97
    change and, 154

corrosive competition and, 101–102
    envy, 106–112
    reasoning and, 18–19
    related to competition, 112–114
    schadenfreude, 103–107
    storytelling to evoke, 47–49
empathy, 54, 191–192
Emperor's New Clothes syndrome, 91
employees, obligations of, 213–215
employers, obligations of, 213–215
endowment effect, 161–162
endurance, in stress management, 89–90
energy
    recouping mental, 170–171
    for worrying, 74
engagement, 205–233
    and business outcomes, 207–208
    and cynicism, 219–220
    definition of, 206
    and disengaged employees, 205–206
    influencing factors in, 206–207
    and motivation, 209–213
    and psychological contracts, 213–220
    and rapport, 40
    at SEER Interactive, 231–233
    SLAM model for improving, 221–233
Enron, 180–181, 199, 226
envy
    and *Cain and Abel* effect, 97
    and competition, 107–112
    and emotional maturity, 117
    jealousy vs., 107
    as motivation, 109–110
    and schadenfreude, 106, 107
    self-relevant, 110
    in workplace, 109–111
Escalas, Jennifer Edson, 46
eustress, 62, 63
exhaustion, 156–158, 170–171

Pompey the Great, 121
postconventional stage (of ego
    development), 135, 136
power, 34–43
    coercive, 35, 37
    connection, 36, 37
    expert, 35
    formal vs. informal, 37
    informational, 35, 37
    legitimate, 35, 37
    in relationships, 34–35
    reward, 36, 37
    see also referent power
predictions, 75
prefrontal cortex, 19, 45, 152–154
processes, engagement of employees and,
    206–207
Prodigy, 154
productivity, 11–14
proxy comparisons, 98
psychological capital, 220
psychological contracts, 213–220
    breaches of, 216–220
    and cynicism, 219–220
    definition of, 213
    and disengagement, 208
    tangibles and intangibles in,
        214–216
Purgatorio (Dante Alighieri), 104, 108

quantitative performance measures, 223

Rafaeli, Anat, 190
rapport, 39–41
rationalization, 131, 133–134
Raven, Bertram, 35–36
reality checks, of stress management
    capability, 90–92
reasoning, emotion and, 18–19
reciprocity, norm of, 214
referent power, 36–43
    definition of, 36, 37
    influence and, 38–39

and rapport, 39–41
and trust building, 41–43
reframing, of change, 167–170
relational philosophy, 51–58
    and body language, 55–58
    and listening, 53–55
relationships
    and envy, 111
    fostering of, 222–223
    power in, 34–35
remote emotional contagion, 190
Rescorla, Rick, 61, 62
resilience, 77–78, 220
resistance to change, 151–152
    at Eastman Kodak, 149–150
    exhaustion associated with,
        156–158
    and sunk costs, 158–159
respect, referent power and, 38–39
responsibility, 137–140
retention, employee, 224–225
retreats, off-site, 222
reward power, 36, 37
rewards, dreaming of future, 83
Reynolds, Wil, 231–233
right
    insisting you are, 83
    need to be, 17
Ringlemann, Max, 185
risks, fear of taking, 21–26
"Robbers Cave Experiment," 179, 180
Roman Empire, leaders of, 121–122
Rooke, David, 136
Roosevelt, Theodore, on responsibility,
    137
Ross, Lee, 15–16
Rousseau, Denise, 213, 215
Royal Fleet Auxiliary, 3
"rule of alternatives," 183

Saavedra, Richard, 190
Sabini, John, 110
sabotage, 11, 111